Parenting
by
Heart

How to Stay Connected
to Your Child
in a Disconnected World

by
Dr. Ron Taffel
with Melinda Blau

PERSEUS PUBLISHING
Cambridge, Massachusetts

Many of the designations used by manufacturers and sellers to distinguish their products are claimed as trademarks. Where those designations appear in this book and Perseus Publishing was aware of a trademark claim, the designations have been printed in initial capital letters. (e.g., Froot Loops)

Cataloging-in-Publication Data available from the Library of Congress

ISBN 0-7382-0599-0

Perseus Publishing is a member of the Perseus Books Group

Find us on the World Wide Web at http://www.perseuspublishing.com

Perseus Publishing books are available at special discounts for bulk purchases in the U.S. by corporations, institutions, and other organizations. For more information, please contact the Special Markets Department at the Perseus Books Group, 11 Cambridge Center, Cambridge, MA 02142, or call (800) 255-1514 or (617) 252-5298, or email j.mccrary@perseusbooks.com

First paperback printing, December 2001
1 2 3 4 5 6 7 8 9 10—05 04 03 02 01

To my mother and father
R. T.

In loving memory of my mother
M. B.

Contents

Ⅱ
Everyday Myths and Everyday Skills

Preface to the Second Edition

A decade has passed since *Parenting by Heart* was first published. My wife, Stacey, and I were relatively new parents; our oldest child, Leah, was only four when it was written. Yet by that time I had already become so deeply involved with families from all walks of life and all regions of the country, that I'd gotten an unusual glimpse into contemporary family life. The unique message of *Parenting by Heart*—that modern parents and kids need to connect more than ever before, and that the pop culture we live in makes connecting even more difficult–touched a nerve. Within a couple of months of publication, several national magazines offered me the chance to become their parenting columnist. For six years I wrote a monthly feature for McCall's magazine entitled "The Confident Parent," and then, after our second child, Sam, was born, I moved on to *Parents* magazine where an every-other-month column better matched the increasing demands of our growing family. During this time I saw *Parenting by Heart*'s "creating connection" theme become part of the national childrearing agenda.

Looking back it probably shouldn't have been a surprise that this book touched a nerve. *Parenting by Heart* grew out of my experience working with an unusual combination of people. By 1989 I'd done over three hundred talks in schools, religious and community centers with parents of "normal" children, run a large not-for-profit mental health clinic for kids and parents in trouble, as well as tended to my own child and family private practice. Dealing with such a variety of settings gave me an inside view of everyday interactions between parents and children, interactions that felt new and a bit alarming: somehow the quality of connection between parents and kids was being threatened. I heard loud and clear that even good children (and young children, to boot), were over-powering their harried parents with endless negotiating, backtalk, and an astonishingly effective pop-culture driven, kiddie network that fueled "the gimmees" as early as pre-school.

Just as worrisome, parents were baffled by all the contradictory advice being offered by the childrearing establishment: psychologically derived ideas such as quality time, positive discipline, active listening, while wonderful contributions seemed to work for awhile and then lose power with sophisticated kids. Just as parental powerlessness bred a feeling of disconnection within homes, across backyard fences families were also feeling increasingly isolated from each other. In a time of urban and suburban sprawl, the fabric of neighborhood life seemed to vanishing. Malls became the anonymous hub of daily activity. Overscheduled families waved to each other as they frantically ferried themselves between longer commuting destinations and endlessly proliferating after- school programs. PTA involvement had been declining for several decades making it common for stretched-to-the-limit mothers and fathers to have little contact with the parents of their child's classmates. And while 12-step "support groups" of all kinds were helpful at recreating a sense of community, they arose mostly in response to life-threatening crises. Rarely did they address the everyday support-connection that parents needed *before* kids found themselves to be in trouble.

In this context, *Parenting by Heart* spoke directly to the disconnection modern families were just beginning to describe. While psychological theory had traditionally emphasized the importance of kids *separating* from their parents *Parenting by Heart* redefined the major challenge of contemporary family life as one of *connecting*–a need that is even more apparent today. In a culture that becomes increasingly chaotic and disorganized by the moment, *Parenting by Heart* offers ways to create greater connection with kids even as our time together is ever more harried and precious. In this sense, the "heart" of this book is learning how to change destructive dances with children, so that the valuable moments we *do* have together are not lost to our own ineffectiveness. Dances are those repetitive interactions we are all vulnerable to, but can't seem to stop—that end up in our yelling, nagging, threatening, spanking, feeling bullied, resentful and so on. Once destructive dances are addressed then it's possible to implement the various strategies offered here, techniques that are designed to increase healthy connection with our kids and between families.

Each strategy has been thoroughly tested in the real world. By now hundreds of thousands of parents have tried these techniques, many of which seemed downright unconventional a decade ago: How to create consequences that bring kids closer to us, promote a sense of healthy guilt and responsibility, praise kids without spoiling them, help kids to open up without turning oneself into a pseudo-therapist, and so on. Since my experience is steeped in real-life family interactions, techniques are offered with a child's typical response, so that parents can be prepared to meet the savvy resistance of today's precocious kids. In addition, there are guidelines for spending family time together that may not sound much like "quality" time, but are practical *and* enhance the ability to promote *your* beliefs and values in the face of a 24/7 pop culture.

Lastly, as connection is increased at home, I outline how to create greater connection between isolated families through what I call "peer groups for parents." The idea that adults need to be at least as connected as the kids' peer network was one of the most widely acclaimed contributions of *Parenting by Heart* and is still just as essential—perhaps more so—today. This concept has been embraced nationally by parents, experts and school administrators and continues to be one of the major reasons I am invited to address community organizations around the country. In fact, a decade and over one thousand talks later (post-Columbine and after the validation of Hillary Clintons's, *It Takes A Village to Raise a Child* and Mary Pipher's, *The Shelter of Each Other,* among many others), it is clear that the need for everyday parent peer groups is finally taking hold.

The widespread acceptance of ideas that were once thought to be somewhat unconventional is satisfying to me. In fact, when *Parenting by Heart* was first published, I'm not sure that I, or the editors, knew exactly how relevant the issues were that were being raised. So, *Parenting by Heart* is being reissued to reflect its serious, yet practical content. To break old, ineffective dances and to create greater connection through a balance of consequences and compassion (what I called a decade ago, the "empathic envelope.") is a serious message indeed. This is the deeply hopeful theme of *Parenting by Heart*. Kids, despite their precocious, often unruly ways, still need to feel "held" by strong and confident parents. They yearn for this security and connection as much as we parents do. What's more, parents isolated within their own homes, cannot do an effective job at guiding children. We need to become more connected to each other in ways that prevent, rather than react to crises.

Ultimately, children of all ages need to feel a community of adults around them, adults who can change worn-out, destructive dances that get in the way of love and connection. The more we can connect with our children when they are young, the less we will have to worry about them when they enter the dangerous passage of adolescence. I hope this book is as helpful to you as it has been to hundreds of thousands of others over the years. As a parent myself, I know how much it matters that the love we feel for our kids is effectively communicated and felt by them—every day of our lives.

— Ron Taffel, Ph.D.
　September 2001

Preface

This book is about challenging the myths of modern parenting so that you can learn to connect with your kids in ways that help them grow into healthy adults.

The first part deals with the five most prevalent myths that I hear in my work with families, myths that make our role as parents much more difficult. Without examining these cliches of modern child rearing, parents will keep falling into the same traps again and again.

When the myths are uncovered for what they are, however, a logical framework for child rearing begins to emerge. I call this framework the *empathic envelope*. The first part will describe in clear terms what the empathic envelope is and how you can use it as a companion and guide in everyday life with children. This will give you a foundation for the skills section in part two.

In the second part of the book, I've distilled the child rearing techniques that parents *and* children have reported to me as being the most effective for connecting to our kids. These also are organized around the myths and cliches of parenting that continually sabotage even the most expertly applied techniques. Since I work with families as a whole, I hear both sides. I see parents and children trying to wrangle it out together in front of me. I see how different techniques actually play themselves out in day-to-day life. Because of this, every suggestion I make will be presented with step-by-step guidelines. These will prepare you for how your child and family will react to new techniques, how to persevere in the face of their reactions, where you're likely to run into trouble in terms of your own attitudes and beliefs, and how long you can expect any technique to be effective.

Throughout, I've tried to keep the dual focus of the work I

do with families, challenging parenting myths we take for granted and offering specific suggestions for specific situations. In the end you should walk away from this book a little more realistic about what you can expect of yourself and your child, a little less self-conscious about every move you make as a parent, and a little more confident about how to connect with your children in ways that will help them grow.

The emphasis here is on straight talk and realistic goals, and I will say at the outset what I say at every parenting seminar I give: Carefully evaluate the suggestions in these pages—after all, you know your children and yourself better than I do. Do only what feels right for you—or it will be unauthentic and doomed to fail. Being a parent is too complicated and emotional a task for magical techniques and miracle cures. When it comes to the long haul of raising a child, the tortoise always wins.

Please write. Let me know how things go. I will pass along what you tell me to other mothers and fathers. Parents everywhere, trying to bring up kids in a plugged-in, supercharged, high-tech world, need all the information and support we can give each other.

Write to:

Ronald Taffel
Institute for Contemporary Psychotherapy
1 West 91st Street
New York, New York 10024

Acknowledgments

My mother and father provided the soul for *Parenting by Heart*, and my pediatrician, Dr. Volmer, gave it the spirit. He died when I was thirteen, but by then he had already inspired me to become some kind of doctor when I grew up. I will never forget Dr. Volmer's housecalls. He used to come into the room, feel my feverish and morose little head, and exclaim, "You call this sick? You got it easy, lying around all day. I wish I could do that! So why not?" And before I knew it, he had clambered onto the bed with me, pretending to take a snooze until I "woke" him up with my laughter. Ten minutes after this bit of zaniness, he would be dispensing wisdom, easing worries, and calming fears. Dr. Volmer's willingness to break the rules and be a human being—his ability to be a reasonable soothing voice—made a lifetime impact on me and on the spirit of this book. Even so serious a subject as child rearing doesn't have to be without some laughs.

Unfortunately, much of my early psychology training was the antithesis of Dr. Volmer's easy-going style. Though I met many wonderful and wise people along the way, I found too much of an ivory tower, almost cultist atmosphere in the mental health field. I was also surprised to find that formal psychology was extremely critical of the parents who raised our patients. Clinicians rarely thought of mother or father in sympathetic terms. Having been raised by parents who, of course, made mistakes but were truly well meaning, I felt deeply offended by this practice. As a student, however, I could do nothing about it.

Fortunately, along the way, I also met and was influenced by numbers of humane and generous people: Dr. Bernard Kalinkowitz was an inspiration to me in my clinical psychology training; Dr. Aryeh Anavi "stretched" my thinking during my internship at Einstein Medical Center; Dr. Dorothy Gartner provided an excellent foundation in child therapy when I was director of Child and Adolescent Treatment, Downstate Medical Center; the Institute for Contemporary Psychotherapy gave me the opportunity to develop a family treatment center; and finally, Elizabeth Carter, my supervisor and colleague in family therapy, shared her vast stores of common sense and wisdom as we worked together with dozens of families.

For ten years, I did therapy with children alone, with parents in guidance sessions, and with children and parents together in family therapy. I never realized how helpful this multifaceted perspective would be until one evening when I was asked to fill in at a local school's PTA workshop. Having by then sat with hundreds of families trying to wrangle things out, I recognized how difficult it is for all of us actually to apply child-rearing techniques to real-life situations. Because of this, I took a very cautious approach, encouraging parents to *think small*. And I emphasized that the last thing parents needed to become were therapists or child-rearing technicians.

Within a couple of years, I was doing about forty workshops a year and, though both my parents had since passed away, I found myself back "home" again. There was something very familiar in the worried, exasperated, and well-meaning expressions I would see in parents' faces as they poured out their concerns. What also struck me were the impossible myths that today's parents carry around: family harmony is a realistic goal; you've got to be consistent; quality time is really what matters; you should never punish, bribe, or ever make your kids feel guilty; and so on. The amount of self-consciousness and turning oneself inside-out was like a collective straitjacket—binding, inhibiting, and, ultimately, reducing creative options. All this in the face of modern kids, who grow up too fast, are exposed to too much, and demand independance far too soon.

When one night, an eleven-year-old boy in a workshop said, "I just wish my mother and father had more self-confidence as parents," I realized he had hit on something very significant. Kids are still kids, but the world has changed very dramatically since we grew up. And, in many ways, parents don't have the support that existed for previous generations—extended family, close-knit neighborhoods, happily-ever-after marriages, the luxury of just one job per family. Between parenting without a safety net and the child-rearing myths that a "therapized" culture has encouraged, it's no wonder that mothers and fathers lack self-confidence, are constantly afraid of doing irrevocable harm to their children's development, and don't trust their own instincts as parents.

So, with the encouragement of Jim Levine, who heard me speak at his son's school, I started to put together a written version of the talks I'd been giving for the last decade. Without Jim there would have been no book, and through the years, he encouraged and pushed me, becoming an esteemed colleague and trusted buddy. Melinda Blau, my co-author, entered the picture when the serious writing began. I could not have made a better choice. Our professional and personal relationship was without a single note of discord during a process that is usually filled with anxiety for everyone involved.

Finally, I am grateful that my wife Stacey and daughter Leah are here to share this with me (and if all goes well, our second child will have been born by the time of publication). Stacey, more than anyone, knows what an act of love *Parenting by Heart* has been—how the soul of my parents and the voices of thousands of families I have worked with find expression in these pages.

R.T.

I

Basic Myths
and a New Framework

1

The Myth of the Overinvolved Mother and the Underinvolved Father

If you were a kid raised on "Father Knows Best" or "The Brady Bunch," you may have had a startling realization when you became a parent yourself—the realization that real life bears no resemblance whatsoever to life in those sweet and placid situation comedies. If there are any shows on TV that reflect the real life I see these days as a family and child psychologist, they're more likely to be "The Simpsons," or "Married . . . with Children" than "The Donna Reed Show."

Hollywood's mythmakers from the '50s and '60s never could have prepared us for the modern six-year-old who understands the concept of "merchandizing," for eight-year-olds who can argue like L.A. lawyers, or for ten-year-olds who have seen more explicit sex and graphic violence than the average thirty-five-year-old mom or dad.

And today's scriptwriters might learn a thing or two from this real life account from the mother of a seven-year-old:

> *I was five minutes late picking up Elizabeth from school. Instead of simply crying or being upset, she*

> *kept demanding where I'd been. I said to her, "I'm*
> *sorry, I was late. I was wrong. The bus got stuck."*
> *Elizabeth said to me, "That's absolutely no excuse.*
> *Don't you realize the kind of PSYCHOLOGICAL*
> *DAMAGE this can cause me? I saw a show on "Don-*
> *ahue" about parents like you. It was called MIDDLE*
> *CLASS PARENTS WHO NEGLECT THEIR*
> *CHILDREN!"*

No wonder some of us feel overwhelmed, or like we just fell off the pumpkin truck, when confronted with the demands of modern parenthood. And it's not only that today's kids are often frighteningly sophisticated. The strength of the family to "hold" these high-tech, supercharged children has diminished at the same time that kids' power has increased. Divorce, two-income families, job mobility, anonymous neighborhoods and bedroom communities, long commutes, few extended family members around to pitch in —these have all strained parents' capacity to feel powerful and effective.

Even the boundaries of home and family in the 1990s have fundamentally changed since the days of Ozzie and Harriet or Desi and Lucy. With the boss able to fax, modem, and messenger tasks in at any time, the division between the workplace and the living room (or bedroom) is becoming a quaint memory of a bygone era.

When you put it all together, the modern family has a kind of upside down feeling, with parents feeling alone, up against a powerful kids' subculture that begins in early grade school and gathers momentum as the years go by. The container around the family begins to feel more like a sieve rather than a firm boundary made up of your values, your ideas, and your beliefs.

Yet despite all the forces impinging on home and hearth, most parents still manage to stay in charge just enough to provide a container that works tolerably well. We may not be the perfect parents we think we should be, but a major point in this book will be—*who is?*

Regardless of your self-doubts and regardless of how ragged the process seems, the majority of kids actually *turn out okay.* But how can you make sure it happens that way in *your* family? How can you ensure that *your* kids stay on the safe side of trouble and avoid the kinds of serious emotional difficulties that persist into adulthood?

Fortunately, the answers are not as complex as we sometimes believe. In over twenty years of experience working with children and their families, I have become convinced that child rearing is essentially figuring out how to handle that classic moment of truth—"Look Ma, no hands!"—and the million and one variations on the theme that happen at every age.

Think about it for a minute. Do you really know what this expression—"Look Ma, no hands!"—means? It can be taken in two ways. You can put the emphasis on the "no hands" part, which focuses on the independence of the action, on doing it alone; or you can notice that what the child actually says is, "Look Ma!" Even in this gesture of autonomy, she is still trying to connect in some way with you. And you have to figure out how to respond.

Should you leave your child alone knowing there's a possibility that he'll fall flat on his face?

Should you hover around and risk being "overinvolved," perhaps getting in the way of her developing greater self-confidence?

Do you pay attention to that look of glee in his eye as he sees the fear in your face?

Do you clap with delight or do you ignore her showing off?

The questions are endless. And as your child matures, the risks involved when she says, "Look Ma, no hands!" become more frightening, happen too quickly, and come in more unexpected ways than most parents are comfortable with.

Deciding whether to hold on or whether to let go is the ongoing dilemma of parenting. It comes with the territory. And we're always asking ourselves: Which part matters the most in raising healthy children?

As a parent you probably realize that both do. Yet for almost a hundred years the mental health establishment has put the emphasis on the "no hands" rather than on the "Look Ma!" The emphasis on separation that underlies all psychological theory and almost all child-rearing advice has been a major source of confusion. Regardless of the advice about letting go and the warnings about being overinvolved, parents constantly feel that children (including the most rebellious adolescents) pull for *connection* even while they try to separate.

Most of us think that we have done our job successfully as parents when our children are autonomous and independent. We believe that the job of a parent is essentially to "let go." Few of us would disagree with this definition of maturity, but the mental health profession has taken this bias toward letting go one step further. It has equated childhood dependence with neurosis, lack of separation with pathology.

After listening to families from all walks of life, I have become concerned that the "hurried child" now has a "self-conscious Parent"—parents who constantly second-guess their natural instincts about what makes for healthy connections with kids. We worry endlessly about being overprotective, overinvolved, overstimulating, suffocating. At the other end of the continuum, we wonder whether we're being understimulating, depriving, self-absorbed, unavailable, or narcissistic. From having parents who may have rarely reflected on their child rearing, we have in one generation become parents who question ourselves endlessly.

Often our first thoughts are, "How am I damaging my child?" "What irreparable harm have I caused by this action?" "What's the *one* right thing to do?" We picture our child in twenty years on a therapist's couch or in a support group complaining bitterly about us or—with a little imagination—exposing to millions our toxic parenting on some "Donahue" of the future. With all these concerns, parents are in danger of becoming parent-therapists, not parent-people; child-bearing technicians, not human beings. And the absolutely central fact that parenting is learning how to connect with kids is being lost.

Fortunately, when you get past all the "shoulds" and "should nots" in child rearing, connecting is not such a mysterious and complex business. I think the same dynamic exists in all families where parents stay connected with their children, and where children grow into healthy adults. Regardless of age, economic group, or whether the family is intact, the most successful parents I have met over the years have one thing in common: they attempt to provide for their children what I call an empathic envelope.

The empathic envelope is like a container around your kids and your family, a boundary between your family and the outside culture. Theoretically, as the parent, you are in charge of this container. It is made up of *your* values, *your* expectations, and *your* ways of being with your children. It is the feeling you get visiting someone else's house and immediately experiencing the difference between your family and theirs: the values, the kind of language that is allowed, the habits and the rituals that they have. Forget for a moment whether you agree or not—every family just *feels* different. And this differentness is a crucial fact of life for your children. It gives them a sense that they *belong* somewhere, that they are *held* by their parents in a safe and secure place: "This is my house, I know what to expect. I belong."

In more successful families the empathic envelope is

almost palpable. One can feel it expanding and contracting depending on how old the child is, what his or her basic temperament is like, the emotional environment of the household, and finally, a factor that is rarely mentioned in the literature, how exhausted parents may be from having to deal with all of the above.

In successful families the empathic envelope derives from three basic qualities: 1) compassion, 2) consequences, and 3) communication.

The first, compassion, is the ability to understand your child's experience as he or she goes through different ages. By understanding her experience I mean that you *try* to figure out what she needs, you try to "get" what she is saying, even if she can't say it directly.

The second characteristic is struggling to provide consequences for your child's behavior. In other words, to attempt to stay in charge by translating beliefs and values into clear expectations.

The third characteristic is communication between yourself and your child. This includes time together with your child—both so-called "quality" and everyday time.

The combination of these three simple qualities creates an environment in which children end up feeling *held* and *guided*. They know that you will try to be compassionate. They know where your limits are on most issues. And they can count on spending time together.

Obviously, maintaining a good empathic envelope is an astonishingly difficult task. As soon as mom and dad find just the right combination of compassion and limit setting, something in the child or the family suddenly changes and a whole new equation is necessary. As one articulate sixth grader recently told me:

> *I seem to be changing a lot these days. Sometimes my parents treat me like I was still a fifth grader and it*

makes me incredibly mad. By the time they see that I'm older and more mature, I change again. What it all adds up to is that they're constantly one or two steps behind me.

(As any parent knows, of course, ten minutes after such rational talk, this same child could easily throw a tantrum befitting a two and a half year old.)

The confusing but inevitable push of children to grow up, and the parental responsibility to caretake *bump up against each other* every day. Children and parents continuously struggle at the edge of the envelope. Far from being a problem, however, this natural friction is an essential part of successful parenting.

Why? Because children need to *feel* the envelope—they need to rub up against the force of our values, our expectations, our emotions, and our fumbling attempts to understand them. If the envelope expands too quickly (too much freedom too soon), children experience a lack of connection. They will then act up until they feel the envelope snugly around them once again. This is why children often provoke us until we react. One father described this phenomenon to a group of parents who were nodding their heads in recognition:

Every time my eight-year-old girl provokes us and we finally stand up to her, not only doesn't she get mad, she actually looks **relieved.** *It may not happen right away, but maybe fifteen minutes later she'll come out of her room as if nothing happened.*

Contrary to popular belief, children (even adolescents) are not only pushing for independence, they are pushing for contact and connection. It is a major error to think independence is all they are after. They need an empathic envelope around them, and they *will do whatever they must* to feel its presence.

How can I be so sure that knowing how to connect lies at the heart of child rearing? How can it be true when half the time you approach your kid she says, "Leave me alone," or if you try to help him he says (since the age of two and a half) "I want to do it myself!" or if you ask her what happened in school today the most likely answer is, "Nothing!" How do you spend time together when, by a certain age, your kids don't want to be seen in the same time zone with you? How are you connected if you spend much of the day bickering over all those little things that need to get taken care of?

I am sure that connection is the key because after working with thousands of parents and children I have seen the consequences of *disconnection* all too often. If you loosen the envelope and simply let go too quickly, your kids will drift out of the container to a place where they can once again feel *contained*. On the other hand, if the container is so tight that your kids can't breathe, they will run from you to find a place where they can be held more comfortably.

Where do kids go when the empathic envelope is too tight or too loose? To that other readily available envelope—the peer group. If you think about it, a peer group is nothing but an empathic envelope without adults around. It has the same three characteristics of a family. It has its own type of empathy ("We understand you, even if no one else does."); it has clear expectations ("Break the rules and you're out!"); and it offers kids a chance to spend time with one another.

The truth is that most children will stop at nothing to feel contained. They will make friends who are abusive to them; they will try to get into cliques that have strict, even harsh, rules and regulations. And eventually, if things are bad enough, they may even be drawn to gangs that put them at risk with the law.

The need to be held and contained becomes very clear

when a crisis develops. Organizations such as Phoenix House, Daytop Village, Mothers Against Drunk Driving, The Stepparent Foundation, and eating disorder support groups are *all* empathic envelopes for kids and families in crisis.

People don't outgrow their need to be held, either. Adults in trouble seek out the same kind of experience. Fifteen million Americans attend Alcoholics Anonymous, Overeaters Anonymous, Narcotics Anonymous, Adult Children of Alcoholics, Incest Survivors Groups, and so on. All of these are empathic envelopes for people with serious problems.

The truth is that from the day we're born until the day we die we need to feel held and contained somewhere. We can let go and become independent only when we feel sufficiently connected to other people.

Every Parent's Dilemma

Connecting is difficult, especially between parent and child. There is a built-in developmental push that makes harmony only a temporary state. In fact, even when things are going well you probably don't feel 100 percent at ease. More likely you feel that you are loosening the envelope a little *more* than you feel comfortable with—and your child probably says that it's a little *less* than what he wants.

This friction begins when your child takes his first steps. He wants to run across the floor; you're hovering nearby, just hoping he doesn't fall down and bang his head on the coffee table. And it continues straight through adolescence. She's gotten her driver's license and wants to take the car to the mall; you are paralyzed with fear or follow her in your neighbor's car.

This is how it is. There is a natural friction at the heart of the parent-child connection. And this friction cannot be erased, nor *should* it be entirely. Your child grows from rubbing up against you, rubbing up against the envelope of *your* beliefs, *your* values, *your* emotions, and *your* concern. If you don't give them something firm to hold onto and to be held by, they will have to look for it somewhere else. Children need us to be strong and sure. But these days, that is easier said than done.

The Overinvolved Mother

I've found two very basic cultural assumptions that get in the way of effectively connecting with our children. One is a prejudice against mothers; the other a prejudice against fathers.

The prejudice against mothers seems to have been ingrained at the very beginning of Freudian psychology, growing rapidly out of the psychoanalytic belief that the infant was confused where baby ends and Mom begins. Freud and others wrote at length about the intense attachment that is formed shortly after birth and the equally intense struggle to separate that begins in earnest with toddlerhood and the ability to walk. For Freud and his followers, the whole rest of life is essentially a struggle to break out of this early dependence on mother and to establish oneself as a separate person.

Given the fundamental assumptions, it makes sense that most theories of child rearing would emphasis separation from mother as a sign of health and lack of separation as a sign of neurosis. Though there have been moderating voices in twentieth-century psychology, whenever psychological problems arise in adults or children it is a relatively easy step to look at incomplete separation from mother as the cause, and "overinvolved" mothers as the culprits.

Mother-blame as a psychological art-form reached its heyday in the 1950s, '60s and '70s. After World War II mothers were believed to be directly responsible for just about all mental illnesses, even those for which we now recognize at least some biological cause. For example, schizophrenia was thought to be caused by "schizophrenogenic" mothers. Infantile autism, a dread illness of childhood, was supposedly caused by "frigid," "ice-box" mothers. Depression was often understood as a result of "maternal deprivation."

Certainly most garden-variety neurosis was placed at mothers' feet. Over the years terms such as overinvolved, overprotective, guilt-provoking, narcissistic, castrating, manipulative, rejecting, depriving, and seductive were associated with motherhood and became an indelible part of the American psychological landscape. During the same period millions of Americans were on psychoanalysts' couches, blaming their difficulties on their mothers for a full fifty minutes several times a week.

The socioeconomic climate of the post–World War II era, with mothers at home doing the bulk of child rearing, contributed to the image of hovering and overprotective mothers. But interestingly, even though women started to join the work force in droves, the emphasis on the overinvolved mother did not disappear. After reviewing psychological studies during the last decade, one major survey found that mothers were held responsible for their child's problems 83 percent of the time; fathers only 41 percent. Mothers were responsible for seventy-two different kinds of psychological problems in their children. The authors concluded that mothers' relationships with their children were never described as healthy or in only positive terms.

But there is probably another reason why the "overinvolved mother," the mother who is "too emotional" or "overprotective," has gotten a bad rap all these years. Until the early 1980s her moral framework was not at all understood by traditional theorists.

In the early '80s, Dr. Carol Gilligan, a developmental

psychologist at Harvard, made dramatic news by demon-
strating that men's and women's conceptions of morality are
quite different. A girl's natural response seems to be embed-
ded in the idea of a *relationship*; with boys it's the idea of
absolute right or wrong. Unfortunately, in our culture the
male version has been considered the only proper response.

Girls and women who evaluate situations in terms of relationships almost never score as highly on tests of morality as
men do. In other words, from traditional psychology's view-
point, most women are morally inferior to most men. As
shocking as it sounds, this is nothing new in psychology.
Freud himself declared that " . . . for women the level of
what is ethically normal is different from what it is in men.
. . . Women show less sense of justice than men."

As a result of this tradition and other cultural messages,
many mothers carry around the idea that their "female
view" of child rearing is not just different, it's *deficient*. One
woman expressed her conflict about discipline this way:

> *I know that it's important to be tougher with my*
> *son. And I know that I'm supposed to set limits in a*
> *clear and firm manner. Yet I can't stop feeling that*
> *when he hurts, I hurt. It's like cutting off my own*
> *arm. I know it's wrong to feel this way, and I'm*
> *ashamed to admit it. But what am I going to do?*
> *I'm his mother, and that's the way I feel.*

This woman is not alone in her self-doubt and shame, or
in the quickness with which she calls her empathy and emo-
tionality deficiencies in mothering. Yet if she didn't think
that empathy for her son was neurotic and a weakness of
character, it would be easier for her to set workable limits.
The fact that the mental health establishment has equated
separation with health, equated women's morality with soft-

heartedness, and placed mothers on the psychological hot seat has taken a toll on modern mothers.

The recent work of family therapists and developmental researchers will have to go a long way indeed to reverse the basic stereotype of the harmful, toxic, overinvolved mother —to take the self-consciousness out of natural and healthy needs for connection with kids.

The Underinvolved Father

Now it in no way invalidates the anguish of these women for us to realize that there are a great many fathers out there today feeling deficient and uncertain about their own emotional capabilities for precisely the opposite reason. They have been handicapped and made self-conscious by another cultural stereotype. Just as our society for a long time accepted that the proper pattern of moral reasoning was male, we seemed to have universally accepted that the proper pattern for emotion was female.

Until very recently, the traditional psychology that spent so much energy blaming the mother had very little at all to say about the role of the father. In professional circles, as in many households (and in many courts where custody was determined), fathers held the position in the emotional life of the family that seemed slightly marginal. They made money, took out the trash, read their newspapers, and were occasionally brought in for disciplinary purposes.

Men in this era were assumed not to have the desire or the capacity to become truly involved with their young children, assumed to lack the instincts necessary to be warm and nurturing. And a great many men of fathering age today were raised during this time, when, indeed, a man's place was at the office or on a business trip.

Only in the last few years has the unexpected pain of these men become apparent to the culture at large. Jungian psychologists James Hillman and Robert Moore, along with the poet Robert Bly and storyteller Michael Meade, began leading sessions devoted to exploring the male psyche. What they discovered was an incredible upwelling of emotion that had been overlooked during all the discussion of gender in the '70s.

The thousands of men who came to these sessions did not fit the stereotype of *male* that had been rightly targeted for criticism by feminists. Quite the contrary, these men, hurt and confused by their own fathers' emotional distance or limitations, considered all things masculine inherently suspect. Unfortunately, that included themselves.

Like so many men in families, they either gingerly walked on eggs or occasionally smashed them with rage. In part because the positive masculine attributes within them have never been validated by their own fathers, many men lack a certain kind of *confidence* and *calm resolve* which is as useful in raising a family as in anything else. Thus, as the new psychology lifts the veil of the uninvolved father we find a more complicated and sad situation—men who go through life slightly numbed, surprisingly unsure of themselves, and emotionally not quite "there." As fathers, men often feel either like guests in their own homes or clumsy bulls in china shops, deferring to their wives as the "emotional experts" and squelching their own wish to be fully involved.

• • •

In both instances, men's and women's natural emotional instincts to connect, to guide, to express love, are being held hostage to cultural stereotypes. In trying to connect consistently and well with their kids, parents benefit first by getting beyond these barriers and assumptions in trying to understand themselves and each other. Men and women, fathers and mothers may have different parenting instincts, but that does not mean that one or the other is necessarily wrong.

Yet another cultural observer, linguist Deborah Tannen, wrote a recent bestseller called *You Just Don't Understand*, a book about the completely different languages men and women speak, and the very different ways in which men and women make use of the act of talking itself. As parents trying to connect, those equally valid differences in emotional, moral, and linguistic styles are good to keep in mind. Assuming love and goodwill—and cutting out the extremes —women's ways and men's ways each have their own validity.

However it will be accomplished, the new psychology— family therapy, infant research, the women's and men's movements, twelve-step programs—is changing the way we look at children and parenting. A more compassionate, three-dimensional view of human beings has revealed a deep need for connection that begins with birth and never seems to end. The unfulfilled need for connection leaves, as Geneen Roth called it, a "hungry heart." Until we understand how to connect with our children, how to hold them tight, they can never let go and they can never grow up.

2

The Myth of the "In-Charge" Parent
Mutant Ninja Turtles and Other Uninvited Houseguests

In the "ideal" envelope, parents are *supposed* to set the agenda, be in charge, and create the tone.

However, these days things are not so clear-cut. There are constant threats to the integrity of the envelope, constant forces that rupture it. Even the assumption that there is an unbroken container around the family has changed dramatically over the last twenty years. Fifty-one percent of marriages that begin now will end up in divorce, as will 64 percent of second marriages.

Obviously the idea of a neat container around a family with two parents in charge is a bit of an old-fashioned myth. But it's not just the shape of the container around the family that has changed so dramatically over the past several decades. The actual boundary between the family and the surrounding culture has also undergone dramatic pressure. Today's parents have to compete with all sorts of outside forces in relation to their children. Your own values are often drowned out by commercials, by whatever is on cable, and by values portrayed in the movies.

The family, just like the rest of the world, has become

consumerized and commercialized. Any parent can see how early consumerism begins and how much pressure is exerted on parental authority from the get-go. Two-year-olds know the difference between Froot Loops and Krispix. Two-and-a-half-year-olds know the McDonald's jingle by heart. Five-year-olds start pressing for specific designer clothing. Seven-year-olds are knowledgeable about computer gadgetry and video games. Ten-year-olds can tell the difference between a well-prepared meal in a restaurant and one that is poorly done. (I once saw a ten-year-old send back his "Coca-Cola with a little lemon" *three* times before he was satisfied.) Twelve-year-olds can be sophisticated air travelers, and, in some very privileged circles, fifteen-year-olds carry credit cards. How to handle the pressure to supply children with material goods is one of the biggest concerns I hear at my lectures.

Regardless of what kind of strict rules we impose on our children, they just soak up the culture around them. The mother of seven-year-old Jessica refused to let her watch TV (except public TV) or listen to any rock music stations. Mom was amazed when Jessica did a perfect Madonna imitation for her, complete with seductive poses and sexy dance steps. This obviously required a lot of practice and steady viewing. Where did she learn this? When could she practice? None of her friends' parents seemed to know, either.

The more convinced you are that your child is different or that she is too young or that you are too careful, the more surprised you'll be when you find out how much she really knows. Regardless of how you try to keep your children from becoming overly greedy or materialistic, they end up wanting the newest Nintendo games, the latest designer jeans, the most outlandish haircut, and the most expensive sneaker of the month.

This happens no matter what kind of high values you had in mind for your kids.

> *Thirteen-year-old Mark's parents are two deeply committed and ethical people—a minister and his wife. Mark has always been taught that materialism and frivolous spending are unacceptable. This was not done in a heavy-handed way, just as the world perspective the family held. Until he was twelve he never seemed interested in showing off to his friends or bragging about his family's position in the community.*
>
> *One day Mark's mother and father were approached by several shopkeepers in the neighborhood and were told that their boy owed rather substantial sums of money. It turned out that Mark had been borrowing money to pay for video games and CDs.*
>
> *When they discussed it with Mark he finally said, "Dad, Mom, no matter what the two of you believe in, I don't live in a vacuum. I've got to have some of these things like everybody else. I can't stand being so different from anyone else."*

TV, the movies, and Madison Avenue exert their influence on the envelope practically every minute of the day. If this weren't enough to make a parent feel less than in charge, there are other intrusions. For example, your kids are *plugged into each other* by a highly sophisticated web of telephone circuitry. This ability to be involved outside the family is quite different from when we were children. In the old days a kid had to ask Mom or Dad whether he could go over to Johnny's house. Now there are gadgets that can be attached to telephones so that *three-year-olds* are able to direct-dial outside the envelope without having you know. (We won't even mention how an eight-year-old can call a fantasy-sex line from any phone in your house.)

At earlier and earlier ages (girls, in particular, around eight or nine) the phone starts ringing off the hook, not for you, but for your kid. I can call any house and figure out the age of the children by how many times the telephone is allowed to ring before it's picked up:

> *Three rings: children five or under (everyone's too busy or too tired to get to the phone)*
> *Two rings: children six to eight (the length of time it takes your kid to run from the next room)*
> *One ring: children nine to twelve (the length of time it takes your kid to lunge toward the phone and beat you to it)*
> *One-half ring: children twelve to fifteen (the length of time it takes for her to scare everyone off with a piercing, "It's for me!")*

By adolescence, unless you can afford a second line or call-waiting, most parents become more and more isolated. Not so for the kids, who remain firmly in control of the communications lines across the country.

The phone, no less than the TV, takes away from family time of all sorts. When I bring up the "rewards of family mealtime" to many children, they either get annoyed or look at me like they haven't got the foggiest idea what I am talking about. And in fact, when I ask audiences of parents how many of them feel happy with the amount of conversation at the dinner table, *maybe* 5 or 10 percent raise their hands.

By perhaps age ten or eleven some children start calling each other to plan for *dates* outside the envelope.

> *Sara, age eleven and a half, is engaged in a fierce argument with her parents over whether she can go out on a date with a boy in her class. The couple plan to go to an afternoon movie and then for dinner to the local burger joint. She has been on the phone with her friends for the last week working out all the details.*

Although Sara's parents are completely necessary to chauffeur the kids around, they happen to be the last people in the neighborhood to find out. Mom and Dad are shocked about this plan. Sara is becoming hysterical at the thought of not being able to go. She fears being humiliated after all the back and forth the week before.

Kids don't spend time talking to each other outside of the envelope only to discuss exotic events like a first date. They may spend endless time talking without actually having to say anything. A mother says:

I'll walk into my fourteen-year-old's room. I haven't seen her for the entire day, and she's supposed to be doing her homework. Instead, she's sitting on the chair, apparently doing nothing. Except when I look more closely she's got the phone off the receiver and it's on her lap. I ask her what she's doing, and she answers matter of factly, "I'm watching 'Who's the Boss?' with Susan." Susan is on the other end of the phone in her house a mile away.

Today the phone is, much like the schoolyard was, the meeting place for the peer group. Like so much of American society, friendship can now be delivered to your home. This has its positive sides—most peer relationships strengthen and mature children. But it also has its negative aspects—we spend less time together, and there are far more distractions from doing unpleasant activities like homework and chores around the house.

Whether or not TV, the pop culture, or the telephone has any impact on your home, there is no doubt that most parents must face decisions much, much earlier about things they had previously associated only with adolescence. Were you prepared for seven-year-olds who answer back; for eight-year-olds who can argue like Philadelphia lawyers; for ten-year-olds who have seen more explicit sex and graphic violence than you have? Even if you live in a big city and think you've seen everyting, could you possibly be prepared for this following real-life situation?

> *Thirteen-year-old Samantha has been fighting with her parents all week over whether they will let her attend a party without parents on Saturday night. Tickets to the party are being sold by high school students at ten dollars apiece. There will be no adult supervision, and it is expected that hundreds of kids will be there. The party is to begin at midnight and end at 4 A.M. It is located at Times Square in New York City.*

Obviously, with situations like these, frightened parents turn to the child experts for help. The volume of advice emanating from magazines, talk shows, and books can make your head spin. For every problem there are ten different ways of understanding what it really means. And for every problem there are ten different solutions.

Let's look at a relatively easy one. What should you do with an eight-year-old who "won't listen," and won't do chores around the house? Depending on the expert chosen, you will be advised to:

a) listen to your daughter's feelings and understand what is prompting her disobedience of you;
b) negotiate a solution with the girl to create a win-win scenario;
c) place greater responsibility on her by asking her to create appropriate consequences for noncompliance;

d) design a punishment that is a logical consequence of not doing the chores;

e) do something entirely unexpected to throw her off guard and get her attention;

f) don't criticize her disobedience, but praise her actions when she does comply.

Is it any wonder that your head is spinning and you don't always feel in charge of your own family?

All this confusion seeps down to our children inside the empathic envelope. It's not surprising that many sophisticated kids are aware of what easy targets their parents are for blame and guilt. Children are natural experts at these emotions, especially in provoking guilt in modern parents who are obsessed with keeping them happy at all costs.

The "happiness trap," as Nancy Samalin calls it in her wonderful book, *Loving Your Child Is Not Enough,* is a real phenomenon of our time. It occurs when you expect to protect your children from unhappiness and pain at all costs. Being such keen observers, children get the picture that we will go to any lengths to keep them from experiencing disappointment and anger. They watch us on our frantic search to make ourselves superparents. Armed with knowledge from the media and their own networks (kids *do* talk about these things), they zap us with guilt whenever the situation calls for it.

Here's a small sample of accusations that children ages seven to fourteen years old hurled at their parents during everyday disagreements. In the parentheses after each statement I have written the "kernel of truth" that made the parent susceptible to guilt.

> *"You don't want me to be* **happy.** *You* **never** *let me do anything that is* **fun!"** *(to a parent who has been depressed because of several recent deaths in the family)*

"Who cares!" *(to a father who works two jobs to keep the family going)*

"I hate you! I'll never talk to you again!" *(to a parent who actually hated her own mother while growing up and stopped talking to her for two years)*

"You're ruining my life!" *(to a mother who feels guilty for having a full-time career)*

And the most ingenious one I've heard yet, said by an angry thirteen-year-old:

"I'll never let you see your grandchildren when I'm a mother!" *(to a mother who deeply loves little children)*

Are these kids unusually insightful or are they being purposefully cruel? Neither. They are just being children trying to get what they want. However normal it is for children to go for parents' emotional soft spots, the happiness trap allows kids to feel *bigger* than is good for them and causes parents to feel *less in charge.*

What's the result of this? Kids who have trouble coping because they're allowed to be too strong, kids who are not contained by an empathic envelope. As one very honest nine-year-old told me:

My parents don't spoil me in a material way, but they seem to be afraid of making me sad, like I can't handle it or something. By now I think they are right. I can't stand being unhappy or frustrated, even for a minute. By now, anything that makes me nervous or frustrated I'm afraid to do. I know this seems crazy, but I wish they'd just let me stay upset once in a while.

The Myth of Parent-Child Harmony
Why Children Never Let Up on Us and Why They Need Us to Stay Connected

A relationship is like a shark—if it doesn't keep swimming, it dies.
—from Woody Allen's *Annie Hall*

There are many moments in every parent's life when we wonder whether our kids are "out to get us." The points of struggle that erupt during a single day are often endless. They come out of nowhere. We look at our children and the thought crosses our minds: "Who is this person that lives in my house, anyway? I haven't got the foggiest idea of what she really needs."

And the reality is that figuring out what your child needs is often impossible. Even if all the pressures from outside the envelope were to quiet down, it would still be a tremendous challenge to "get it right." The truth is that children, on their path toward adulthood, send out tremendously confusing signals about what they require in order to grow.

Unfortunately, the myth of harmony makes this difficult situation much worse. Despite the fact that we should know better, we cling to the underlying hope that harmony between children and parents is a realistic possibility. This belief has several inhibiting consequences for parents. It makes us think that normal development shouldn't have a roller-coaster feel to it. And it makes us self-conscious in our view of how we should act in order to connect with our kids.

This chapter will show you that between the forces of normal child development and the pressures of everyday life, harmony is an impossible dream and an encumbrance to good parenting.

Normal Development

Picture the empathic envelope. At any moment your child may either be pushing against the envelope trying to get *out* of your control or she may be pulling on you trying to make the envelope *tighter*.

If it were one way or the other all the time you would at least know what to expect. But development is not so straightforward, not so linear. The more likely scenario is that two minutes after pushing against the container for more freedom your child will reverse field and suddenly cling to you for greater connection. It's unpredictable, even maddening. And it's certainly not harmonious. Here are three typical roller-coaster rides from normal everyday life:

The "I Hate You – I Love You" Ride "Our daughter Joan (seven years old) was being particularly insolent. She didn't want to do her chore (setting the table). One thing led to another, and we got into a tremendous fight. She screamed, "You're so unfair!" (for the tenth time that day). And she ran out of the room yelling, "I hate you!" I just accepted it and didn't blow up at her in return.

"Fifteen minutes later she's on my lap kissing and hugging me, telling me she loves me and asking me to braid her hair. I was dizzy from the unexplainable change in the weather."

The *"I'm a Big Shot – Please Don't Leave Me" Ride*   "Our eleven-year-old, Adam, was objecting to the fact that we wouldn't let him go to an athletic event after school because he had to do his homework. A ferocious battle followed in which he tried to negotiate a deal that any of those lawyers on "L.A. Law" would be proud of. We finally let him go. A funny thing happened, though. That night, when *we* had to leave for a dinner appointment, all of a sudden this "big shot" was begging us that we should stay home with him and not leave him alone."

The *"You're Worthless – Can We Talk" Ride*   "Elira (thirteen) has been hanging out at her friend's house one Friday night a month. This particular Friday night the kids were going over later than usual, and we told her she couldn't stay for the whole time. She erupted, calling us old fashioned, and told us we were always against anything that would be fun for her. There was something in her tone this time that truly hurt my feelings. I got tears in my eyes and said to her, 'That's an incredibly cruel thing to say. It hurts my feelings enormously when you say things like that. No matter what you say, you're not staying out till that hour, and we're going to have to figure out a different solution. But I can't even talk to you about it until I feel better about what you just said.' I then left the room. As I walked out, Elira screams one more time, 'I don't care what you feel. What good are you to me anyway!'

"A half hour later I'm sitting in the living room and Elira comes out of her room. She comes over to me and sits on the couch. Without even mentioning what happened before, she starts confiding in me for the first time in months. I was completely stunned at this turnaround. And she never even mentioned the dance again."

Although it first appears that these situations are very different, there is a basic similarity between what these kids did and how their parents responded. All of the parents (either willingly or by chance) figured out the type of connection that would make their child feel *held* and *secure*. The seven-year-old needed her parents to remain calm in the face of her rage. The eleven-year-old negotiator needed to go through intense, serious haggling in order to feel satisfied. The four-teen-year-old needed to know her mother's real feelings and reactions in order for her to settle down.

The Edge of the Envelope

Life around the house is a million and one situations like these. Family life happens at the *edge of the empathic envelope*. This may sound like an unfamiliar and strange concept, but you know exactly what it feels like. It is the continuous hassling, haggling, adjusting, readjusting, negotiating, compromising, problem solving and decision making that go into finding the right kind of connection between you and your child.

Given all the gut-wrenching confrontations parents and children have, it's easy to understand why we lose sight of the fact that connecting goes on in the midst of all this friction. Adolescents are particularly articulate in expressing the relationship between friction and connection. Here's a letter that a thirteen-year-old wrote to me regarding her parents.

> Dear Ron,
> *Adopt my parents* pleeeaaassse*! They are always pushing me and are being nosey. My Mom has to know everything when we snuggle, and at night time I tell her*

everything. She does not want to be seen with me. For example, we are maybe going out to dinner with friends of my parents, and she tells me I can go if I sit at another table. I hate her!

I am annoyed with my Dad for being a jerk and making a spooky voice when I answered the phone this afternoon. I am getting a divorce from them. Take them. They are useless. (I do not mean it seriously.) They do not respect my privacy. Have them please!

Desperately,

Susan

In this one brief note you can see why Susan's mom and dad are pulling their hair out. In order to feel connected, this same girl seems to want opposite things: she wants her *privacy*; she wants to *snuggle* with her mom; she wants to tell her mom everything, *sometimes*; she doesn't want to be excluded, *ever*; and she wants to be able to *hate* and *love* them at the same time.

No wonder her parents are confused and Susan is disgruntled. As soon as they give her what she needs (let's say cuddling), a couple of hours later she'll need to be left alone or she'll pick a fight by being especially provocative.

Here's another dramatic example of a child pushing and pulling on the envelope almost at the same time:

Our thirteen-year-old, Maggie, had been caught drinking several beers at a friend's house. She had never been involved in such a gross violation of rules before. However, she was very belligerent when we confronted her on it. She accused us of not trusting her, of treating her like a baby, of being against her growing up.

That evening, for the first time in maybe eight years, she made us read her the **Berenstain Bears** *at* *bedtime. Not since she was five did we have to sit on the bed with her like this.*

   The next morning she was back to demanding greater freedom and privileges. We thought we were all going crazy.

This back-and-forth behavior does not just hold for adolescents. Connecting at all ages has an element of friction. If two-year-olds could write they would say pretty much the same things teenagers do in two-year-old terms (and so would their parents). Just think back to when your child was an infant. Even breastfeeding, that supposedly most harmonious of times, required continuous adjusting and readjusting until your child felt satisfied and held. Between growth spurts, days off the breast, favoring one breast over the other, long feeds and shorter ones, biting, and finally weaning, mother is constantly having to adjust and readjust in order to connect well enough.

From that point on it never changes. Parents and children forever dance around the edge of the envelope trying to connect in the midst of all this confusing friction. And since children are always rubbing up against us, pushing and pulling at the same time, you can never count on peace and harmony as long as you're a parent.

The Many Faces of Connection

Once you get past the idea that letting go is what makes your child grow or that harmony is a realistic possibility, you have the basic point. Parenting (regardless of confusing signals) is essentially about connecting with your child, even as you let go. In fact, it immediately becomes clear that all child-rearing techniques are simply different ways of helping you and your children connect.

Whatever the latest approach, whether it is Tough Love,

P.E.T., Creative Discipline, Assertive Discipline, Negotiation with Your Child, Siblings Without Rivalry, The Askable Parent—they are all different methods of helping parents and kids connect with each other.

The problem for parents is that between the impossibly harmonious standards of TV shows like "Family Ties" and the fact that we never get a full picture of what *really* goes on in other people's houses, most of us have a very narrow view of healthy parent-child connections.

And the child-rearing myths don't make the job any easier. In any given situation with our children, ten different voices clamor in our minds at once: "I've got to schedule some 'quality time' to connect. . . . Am I sure this is a 'consequence' and not a 'punishment?' . . . I've got to be ready to 'respond' when he brings something up. . . . I don't want him to think I'm not keeping the 'lines of communication open.' . . . I shouldn't 'burden' her with my feelings; after all, 'I'm the parent'. . . . 'Praise the action,' not the child. . . . 'Reflect' back her feelings, 'validate' what she says, show her you're listening. . . . 'Act like a team' with your spouse. . . . 'Never bribe' or threaten. . . . and remember, 'consistency' is crucial."

Now, each of these alone may be good advice. But taken together they create a mythical standard for parents that is impossible to maintain. No wonder parents are becoming more self-conscious and obsessed about whether they're providing their kids with an "optimal growth" experience—while their kids are becoming more and more rebellious and dissatisfied at earlier ages.

The way to get out of this self-consciousness trap is to begin *widening* your view of how successful parents connect with their kids. To do this I have taken a handful of examples of parent-child closeness that, at first glance, fly in the face of parental "shoulds." Each example represents a type of connection that will be expanded in the skills section of the book

(Chapters 6–13). The skills section will offer many options and give step-by-step guidelines about how to institute new techniques. I will go over what to expect from your child and family in response and where you're likely to run into trouble.

But first a little loosening up is in order. Here are a few unlikely faces of healthy connection in successful families. At least one of them has probably happened during the last week in your house. Only you might not have thought of it as healthy. And you may even have looked over your shoulder to make sure no one was watching. Remember, in real life connecting between parents and children

- often temporarily increases tension.
- doesn't always look like "closeness."
- doesn't always look like "sensitive" relating.
- doesn't always happen during "quality" time.
- doesn't always sound "therapeutic."

1) The Family That Goes Berserk Together   Sometimes connecting happens in the middle of a "scene" during which time we can't tell who's who, what's up, or even what it was all about. A father from a decent, usually quiet middle-class family reported the following incident to me:

> *Sunday night Peter (fifteen) turned off a show that Ellen was watching just at the time of the movie's climax. Ellen yelled at him and still was angry the next morning.*
>
> *The next evening, as a punishment, Peter was not allowed to watch TV. A big hockey game was on, and I was watching it in the kitchen as I prepared dinner. Ellen was working at the table on something for her job.*
>
> *Peter came into the kitchen and began to watch the game. We both told him that he had to go out of*

> *the room. Fifteen minutes later he comes running in and says, "There's a penalty shot!" (He'd been listening to the game on the radio.) Then he turned on the TV himself. Ellen quickly ran to the TV and turned it off. Peter started to yell at us and he called me an "asshole." We were all standing there screaming at each other. It was totally chaotic, until I finally threw him out of the room. I can't imagine what the neighbors thought.*
>
> *Thirty minutes later he came out for dinner and we all had a totally pleasant time together, in fact, nicer than usual. I'll never figure it out.*

Am I suggesting that in order to get close to your child you should have an irrational brawl in the living room? Of course not. But if this quiet, upstanding family can "lose it" like this, we all can and, of course, we *do*. Families are irrational. A scene can't always be helped, and most times it passes like a summer storm and everyone feels relieved afterwards. Scenes can serve a function. They break through the fog of everybody's self-absorption and they communicate something that's been put on the shelf. It's only a problem if it becomes repetitive. Then the family gets locked into this one way of connecting, leaving no room for other, less aggressive ways to get close.

2) *Connecting by Becoming a "Less Sensitive Parent"* Sometimes you create more connection by disappearing and blending into the rest of the house. You stop trying to promote "open" communication with your child by being *so responsive*. You stop trying to "relate" and find out what's on his mind. This is especially the case if you tend to pursue a close-mouthed child who makes his presence scarce. Sometimes being in the same house without being so quick to respond creates exactly the right kind of connection for your child.

My thirteen-year-old, Oliver, used to make brief guest appearances and honor us with his presence. I would take advantage of these moments and pounce on him with all the things he wouldn't let me say at any other time and try to create "meaningful" conversation.

I changed that a while ago. Now I alternate between pouncing (which he seems to expect of me) and doing work in the den. Every so often, out of nowhere, he comes by and says, "What's up?" The less I say, and the more I just sort of grunt back at him, the more likely it is that he'll sit down and start telling me things that are on his mind. Then he'll go off, back into his room. If I don't get too "interested" and follow him, he ends up making a pit stop with me in another couple of hours.

With all the emphasis these days on keeping the lines of communication open, it's hard not to be sensitive to a fault. The only problem is that children feel more open with parents who stop trying so hard to relate. As Oliver told me, "When she goes after everything I say and tries to make a conversation out of it, I think she's got nothing else going on in her life—it's up to me to give her something. When I get that feeling I immediately clam up."

So despite your initial concerns that you're shirking your duties as a parent, don't view each possibility to talk as an obligation on your part, or an opportunity lost forever. He'll be back. And you'll feel less rebuked and resentful if you're not always the one who initiates every conversation.

3) Connecting By Going Against Your Child's Wishes   Sometimes going against your child's wishes will lead to a greater connection. No matter how many times you have to make tough decisions for your child's own good, it's hard not to be afraid that taking action will create a permanent wedge between you. And the child's explosive reaction often gets you to back down just to keep the peace. As children get older and more adept at arguing, it becomes even easier to lose sight of how protective action makes kids grateful and relieved, regardless of their initial reaction.

> *Our daughter Erika, who is eight, was being teased a lot in school. We talked with her about how to handle it but nothing was working.*
>
> *At some point, we asked whether it was okay to call the parent of the other child. She went crazy, demanding that we promise never to call. So we listened to her. We gave her more time, but nothing was getting better. Finally, despite her objections, ("I'll die! I'll never be able to go back to school again! I'll never talk to you again!"), we called the other parents and spoke to the school.*
>
> *For one morning the kids gave her a rough time, calling her a tattle-tale. However, everything calmed down immediately afterwards. The taunting stopped. Erika immediately started to feel better. I now realize we did the right thing.*

Because of children's precocious development these days, it's easy to give way to their arguments against intervening, especially when you're not sure of the right thing to do. But in the hundreds of situations I've been through like Erika's, after you've given your child a chance and things don't improve—you must *act*. I have yet to meet a child who did not feel better and more held in the long run. Even if she temporarily gets upset, feeling you as an active presence makes up for the short-term friction you create by going against her wishes.

4) Connecting by "Letting Your Guard Down"   Sometimes, showing how you really feel creates greater connection. Parents often believe that being "in charge" means always being on top—THE PARENT. They think that being securely in charge leads to a more secure child. Every so often the opposite is true. This mother was totally surprised at her son's reaction when she let her guard down one night.

> *Alec, ten, was in a terrible mood. He was haggling over every chore. I was extremely tense because of a job interview the next day.*
>
> *Finally, after he insulted me one more time I broke down. I sat down on the kitchen floor and started to cry. I didn't try to hide how I felt. Alec was stunned and stopped dead in his tracks. He said, "Hey,* **you're** *not supposed to cry!" He came over to me and began to try to make me feel better. I didn't pretend to forgive him right away. Then, without my asking, he boiled water for some tea, saying, "Maybe this will calm you down."*

Even the most hardened child has not forgotten the ability and desire to relate empathically. It's difficult to keep this in mind when there's so much friction in the course of everyday life. Occasionally taking off your "therapist-parent" hat and being an authentic vulnerable human being brings out empathy in children.

Does this lead to a parent losing respect in her child's eye? No, the opposite is true. Alec's mother felt empowered by expressing her real feelings. She became a real person to Alec, a real presence for him. Alec got a chance to feel his impact in a way that was more powerful than a hundred lectures.

5) *Connecting "During the Spin Cycle"*   Sometimes greater connection grows out of the drudgery of everyday life. Modern parents (and our consumer children) tend to think of closeness as requiring special effort or costing a lot of money. Because we're so busy, we place undue emphasis on quality time or on "high-level relating." But in real life you can't always schedule closeness. It most often just happens, without planning, without spending a dime, without any fanfare.

> *I don't understand why, but some of my best conversations with my daughter Kate (eight) start when we're doing the laundry—which she claims to hate doing. Just yesterday we were standing there, not even looking at each other, folding clothes. Out of nowhere she starts talking about our cat Murphy, who died a few years ago. She was very attached to this cat. She started asking me about heaven and hell, and what happens after dying, whether anyone was taking care of Murphy, and how much she misses him.*
>
> *All of a sudden she asks me if **I'm okay**. She tells me she was worried after hearing me say something on the phone about going to the doctor and getting some "tests." I reassured her that I had been talking about a normal exam and that I was totally healthy.*
>
> *She seemed completely relieved. I was amazed at what she had been carrying around for a couple of weeks. When I think about it, we never actually looked at each other during the whole conversation. But I think it was the best talk we've had in a very long time.*

A lot of real connection with children happens *through* other things—when you're playing games or in the middle of mundane activities, not even looking at each other. Unfortunately for us, there's no way to predict when openness will happen next.

Kate's mom needs to keep this in mind so she won't be set up for disappointment. The next laundry-time Kate may do her folding in total silence, throwing the socks around the room or picking a fight with her mom. There's no predictability to "quality time"; there's no scheduling of communication. Grown-ups have a hard enough time talking with each other when there's pressure to open up, and kids are no different.

6) *Connecting by Taking the "Easy Way Out"*   Sometimes a greater connection means temporarily relaxing some rules and beliefs which you hold dear. Parents get caught in a trap by mistaking consistency for rigidity, flexibility for the "easy way out." Occasionally, getting closer means violating special beliefs in a time of real need. Your first reaction will certainly not be one of peace. You will probably feel guilt and self-doubt. You will worry that you're being an irresponsible parent. But, often, greater connection is the unexpected result.

> *Leo (fourteen) had gotten himself into a jam at school. He had procrastinated about a book report that was due the next day.*
>
> *On the last night at around 11:30 he came to me, begging for me to help him. We had always believed that parents should* **never** *do their children's homework. But this night he seemed so panicked that we decided to help him write it anyway.*
>
> *For a couple of hours, until 2:30 in the morning, I stayed up with him helping to compose the report. The room became a madhouse—papers flying everywhere. I even wrote some parts of it myself.*
>
> *He handed the report in and got a B+, which I actually was proud of, though I felt guilty at the same time. We hired a tutor for him the next week.*

Children have a habit of needing us to come through for them in ways that *invariably* run counter to basic values we've tried so hard to teach them—*all* children, not just adolescents. It's precisely at those moments, when you're the most disappointed in their character and like them the least, that you need to reach down inside yourself to be a presence they can feel.

Did Leo's parents create an irreversible precedent by giving in on this one occasion? No, they never did it again. And he, like so many other children, told me several years later that he never forgot how they came through for him.

Did Leo show Mom and Dad his gratitude? You should live so long. But the connection they made with him that evening was appreciated nonetheless.

7) Connecting Through Punishment   Sometimes connecting means coming up with a punishment that makes sense. Your child's first reaction will definitely not be harmonious. He will almost definitely attempt to make you feel like a rotten parent and like you've blown the relationship forever. However, if the punishment is a direct consequence of his behavior and if you follow through with it, invariably your child will end up *closer* to you, not more distant.

> *My son Billy (seven) broke his younger sister's favorite toy. He purposefully smashed it against the wall, into smithereens. When I realized she had done absolutely nothing to provoke him I decided to punish him for it. I yelled at him and took several of his toys away, confiscating them for a week. I said, "You can't destroy her favorite things and not pay a price for it."*
>
> *He was outraged at first, calling me "unfair," and "always favoring her." He screamed and got even more upset as I removed the toys from his room. I was worried about the intensity of his reaction. But*

I stuck to my guns. Later that evening things had quieted down. I found out from his sister that he had apologized to her. For the rest of the week he didn't question the punishment. In fact, when he had a friend over, he brought the incident up himself, almost bragging that I had taken his toys away.

You can read all the books and magazine articles that exist, be bright and accomplished in the outside world, and be a leader of people and organizations. But when your child erupts, you forget everything you've learned. The sheer intensity of it all makes you believe that his hate will last forever and that you have broken the envelope, not strengthened it. It's very difficult to remember that by experiencing your presence he will eventually calm down and be closer to you—let alone brag to a friend about the very thing he so bitterly complained about. Billy felt reassured by his parents' courage. That's why he bragged to his friend—he felt proud of them.

•   •   •

Obviously not everything turns out as well as in these situations. I have chosen them, however, to illustrate how healthy connecting between parent and child has many different faces. It doesn't always happen in typical close ways; it rarely looks therapeutic; and it's never harmonious for any long stretch of time. Yet each of the examples given above has the basic elements of the empathic envelope. I'd like you to start thinking in these terms. First, it's impossible to predict when your child is going to get you to loosen the envelope or make it tighter. All of the parents here felt a little ambushed by their kids and definitely surprised at how things turned out.

Second, and central to each situation, was a basic authenticity—no amateur therapists or two-dimensional parents here. These were real parents and children rubbing up against each other, struggling at the edge of the envelope. In the end the children felt the *presence* of their mothers and fathers. They felt understood and guided by parents who were not twisting themselves out of shape to be people they weren't.

Third, although it's impossible to predict when your kid needs the envelope tighter or looser, *it's a snap to recognize when you've been successful.* Your child will visibly relax, sometime within a few minutes or hours. And despite the degree of natural friction, in many cases she will be more loving than before. Most parents report the aftermath in similar terms—"it was like nothing had ever happened." This is one of the clearest indications that you've established a container that is neither too loose nor too tight. Things don't continue to escalate. They don't stay stuck on the issue—life moves on.

In the process of moving on, the empathic envelope *gradually* becomes wider and more flexible as your child gets older. Regardless of his age, however, and regardless of his protests to the contrary, it should never disappear completely. He needs to feel the empathic envelope around him. He needs to feel the friction of rubbing up against you. He needs to feel held first and *then* he'll be able to let go and become an independent person. It's a long time getting there. And no parents do it the way they think they're supposed to.

Fortunately, creating an appropriate empathic envelope is not so random as it first appears. In fact, after working with families for two decades I've identified three major types of parent-child connection that all kids need during the school years. They are the Parent Protector, the Parent Chum, and the Parent Realist. If you can recognize these three basic ways of connecting and learn how and when to use them, new options will open up. And if you can change along with your child, you and your child will grow together.

4

The Myth of Child Development
Why Parents and Children Need to Connect Differently at Different Ages

In the past, child development experts warned Mom not to hover over her children, to let go. The more independent children became, the healthier they were. It's important to keep in mind that those early child development concepts grew out of the post-World War II psychology movement. The theories were extrapolated from patients in psychotherapy—people who had emotional or adjustment problems and, as adults, were trying to grow up and get away from their parents. Thus, models of child rearing were based on adult patients' memories of what their parents—particularly their mothers—did to them in an extremely overprotective and child-centered society, not on observations of children and parents together.

This post-Freudian approach became extremely popular during The Wonder Years—a time when Mom was in the kitchen when the kids came home from school, and Dad came home for dinner. The empathic envelope was solid and dependable. If a parent couldn't be there to provide guidance at all times, at least grandparents, aunts and uncles, or other members of the extended family were on hand, and so were compassionate neighbors.

Times have changed. Today, the kids let themselves in after school, both parents work, one parent may not even be living at home, the extended family lives in another city, and the neighbors lock their doors. The empathic envelope is constantly straining at the seams, if not rupturing altogether. Those old models of child development, which may have once worked for us, have become outmoded. To be a good parent, separation is only half the picture. In our fragmented, supercharged, fast-paced world, figuring out how to stay connected to our kids is the real challenge—and the other half—of good parenting.

Parent/Child Development

Fortunately, during the last decade a new psychology has been emerging—one that emphasizes the importance of connection rather than separation. We now look at families as "systems," with children connected to their parents and parents connected to their children. The theorists have begun to offer definitive proof of how we affect each other *for the rest of our lives.* Gone is the (pessimistic) idea that all development happens within the first five years of life. Gone is the idea that children are "blank screens" just waiting for us to shape their personalities or, in the view of traditional psychology, for us to "sabotage" their development.

On the contrary, this unbalanced parent-blaming view is giving way to the idea that parents and children progress together, constantly *shaping each other* until the day they die.

This two-way-street approach makes sense. As your child grows and changes, so do you. Just ask yourself: Are you the same person you were before your first child was born? Are you ever the exact same person with each of your children during the course of a single day? Haven't their different personalities, in fact, made you into a different person as you've grown older with them? Does your life with a rough-and-tumble eleven-year-old feel anything like life in the precious little world of an infant? Haven't you become more "street smart," a little more social, even a little (or a lot) moodier as your child enters and leaves adolescence?

Obviously, the answer to all these questions has to be "yes." Forget about the theories—common sense tells us that we're all in it together. That may be part of what's so scary—and humbling—about being a parent today. Once you have a child, you change so much along the way, you don't even recognize yourself by the time they're ready to move out!

What's Happening with Us?

Children don't go through their development alone. Parents go through it *with* them. Ideally, as children get older, parents *and* children learn to do things they couldn't do with each other and act in ways that weren't possible at earlier stages. This is why any effective child-rearing approach might be more accurately called "parent/child development."

It's not just a question of what "stage" the child is in, it's what "stage" are we in *together*? What kind of connection do we need that's going to make the child feel "held" in order to grow up? How do we stay connected—and how do we know what kind of connections are appropriate? These questions are especially important in the context of our supercharged, fast-paced world.

In order to help parents figure out how to answer these questions and stay connected to their children over the course of time, I've divided parent/child development into three easy-to-understand roles: *Parent Protector, Parent Chum,* and *Parent Realist.* These broad categories reflect the three most basic ways of holding our kids so that they feel secure enough to grow.

The Parent Protector (Latency, age five to nine)   In what are sometimes referred to as the "latency" years, between the ages of about five and nine, the world of children expands quickly. They go off to all-day school; they assume greater responsibility and must learn to follow rules; they are faced with painful realities of life outside the home—illness, death, divorce—and they often are but one step removed from early childhood. It's no wonder fear of separation and childhood worries are so intense at this time. Therefore, in order for children of this age to feel secure in the empathic envelope they need us to be Parent Protectors. That is, they need us to soothe their anxieties and fears, to explain what confuses them, and to be their bridge out to the world. The child needs teaching, protection, and continued supervision. In order to stay connected, we must develop our abilities to listen, to play fantasy games, and to create calming rituals. We are the maintainers of their stability. They depend on us to be big, enveloping, bordering—almost—on the magical.

The Parent Chum (Preteen, age nine to twelve)   Around the middle years of school, from age eight or nine, the child's ability to make sense of the world takes a major leap up-ward. As they move out of the family and into the world of school, these children make new friends and, of course, are greatly influenced by the world at large. Whether they're into watching "Married . . . with Children" or "The Simp-sons," or listening to rap, modern preteens are swimming in the values of the pop culture. They're growing up fast and furious, and none of us are ready for this. They're literally Adolescents in Training!

Preteens have it all: moodiness, sloppiness, obstructive-ness, bad taste, clique behavior—traits that have always been associated with adolescents. Their emotional fluidity is incredible. One minute the child is pushing out against the envelope, wanting to be treated as a "grown-up," and the next minute, she's pulling on you, trying to connect like a five-year-old. That means parents have to be flexible as well. We need to be Parent Chums, sharing their interests, doing more with them—*even* as we continue to enforce rules and to provide discipline and guidance. Being a Parent Chum in the face of their outrageous behavior is, indeed, a challenge, but it's a connection that must be made in order to navigate later the stormy waters of adolescence.

The Parent Realist (Early adolescence, age twelve or thirteen to sixteen)   As children enter early adolescence, they spend less and less time home, and definitely less time communi-cating with the family. They start to rebel against parental values; they eschew any semblance of cooperativeness; they'll do just about *anything* to keep you out of their "busi-ness." I'm sure it defies imagination to think of any kind of *connection* that would be welcomed by your teenager. But here's an important point: Rebellion is not the same as total separation. Wanting to develop a unique identity is not the same as wanting to disconnect completely.

Even adolescents need to feel connected to their parents. And in order to help them feel the "safety net" of the em-pathic envelope around them, they need us to be Parent Realists. We have to remain a *presence* in their lives. How do we remain present in the face of their disappearing act? We are Parent Realists—we have to resist the temptation to stick our heads in the sand. We have to be realistic about what they're up to and how much power we have to control to-tally their behavior and to be clear about which issues we want to take stands on. We need to be knowledgeable about what's actually going on in their world. Finally, we need to be realistic about what we have to take care of in our own lives. In other words, we need to be clear about who *we* are —our strengths and the weaknesses we need to work on.

Switching Roles

A great example of all three parental modes in action came from a real-life scene. I was at the dinner table with a long-time friend, his wife, and their three daughters—six, eleven, and fourteen—when I told the father I had brought along the home movies of our old football games in college. The youngest one broke into the conversation with "My Daddy! Boy! He played football? That's great!" She climbed onto his lap and added, "I hope you didn't get hurt." He—as the Parent Protector—responded by saying, "No, don't worry."

Meanwhile, the eleven-year-old piped in: "What? They had football in your day—when dinosaurs roamed the earth? You're kidding!" As the Parent Chum, his quick comeback was, "Yeah, Miss Wisegal. We dinosaurs actually threw the football around. You wanna watch the movie with me?" And she said, "Sure."

Around the same time, the fourteen-year-old said, "Big deal—who cares? Don't bother me. I've got other things to think about. Besides, I don't believe it anyway. Daddy's such a geek—how could he play football?" The Parent Realist father answered, "You mean I'm a bigger geek than Bobby, that kid you have a crush on? Of course, I don't expect that you'd be interested in watching this movie, but if you are we're putting it on in about fifteen minutes."

The father was naturally different with the three girls in ways that allowed him to connect with each one based on her particular needs. He protectively took the little one into his lap; he joked with the middle one, instinctively knowing she would like to be part of the family movie watching; and with the oldest, he knew it would never do to force her into joining the family, so he accepted her need to be different and, at the same time, let her know the family was there for her.

Rolling with the Punches

The Parent Protector role is mostly appropriate with young children, up to around age seven or eight; the Parent Chum is the kind of connection mostly associated with ages nine to twelve; and the Parent Realist deals mainly with kids over twelve. So, you might ask yourself, why would a parent with a teenager care to know about being a Parent Protector? Likewise, if you have a seven-year-old, why bother to read on in this chapter, as I go into greater detail about the Parent Chum and the Parent Realist?

The answer is, these days six- and seven-year-olds are exposed to many of the *same kinds of influences* as fourteen-year-olds—on the street, on the radio (listen to the lyrics of rock songs), and, of course, on TV and in the movies. Just look around. You'll see that the need for being a Parent Realist comes a lot earlier. There's no such thing as waiting for adolescence to hit. Even if your child is only seven, you'd better be aware that she can simply dial a 900 number and tap into a message like this on the local fantasy-sex line: "You're listening to True Confessions. To hear more shocking and explicit confessions call 555-1212. To meet hot singles in your area, call 555-1213"

Parents who have trouble being realistic are usually in for a shock. At one of my lectures, one mother of a seven-year-old stood up and said, "I *know* my child has never seen an R-rated movie," and another mother informed her from across the room, "That's not exactly true. He saw one at my house two weeks ago. I was afraid to mention it before."

Unlike The Fabulous Fifties or other eras when parents could shelter their children from "adult" themes, kids nowadays "fast forward" to other developmental stages. So your young child will invariably need you to be a Parent Realist, as well as a Parent Protector. Likewise, while children grow up so fast in some ways, there's often a leftover "baby" inside that requires you to swing unexpectedly into the Parent Protector role, even when they're preteens and adolescents. (Remember Maggie needing to hear the *Berenstain Bears* at bedtime after her drinking episode?)

In short, because of this "compressed growth," nothing is predictable or orderly in child development. Anyway, kids don't simply pass from one "stage" to another in linear fashion. They make precocious leaps ahead and retrogressive slides backward—sometimes in the course of one day! To be sure, even research confirms the fact that child development isn't as neat and tidy as we once thought. In one significant fifteen-year study, Frank E. Sroufe and June Fleeson, researchers at the University of Minnesota, observed children ranging in age from one year through adolescence. They discovered that kids don't really go through discrete developmental stages. Rather, they "pack" whatever they learn at one stage and carry it into the next. When necessary, children simply dig into their baggage and use whatever they need, even if it's from a so-called "earlier" stage.

This image of a "developmental suitcase" helps us understand some of our children's seeming inconsistencies. For example, when his mother refused to give him permission to go to a party alone, twelve-year-old Isaac screamed, "I hate you. You never let me grow up!" Finally, the mother gave in somewhat, agreeing to let him go if she drove him there (being the Parent Realist, she wanted to be sure the party was chaperoned). But then, out of the blue Isaac asked his mother to make mashed potatoes and fish sticks for dinner, foods he loved as a six-year-old. A few days later, when I asked him about it, he answered, "I just wanted soft food, like when I was a kid." He didn't know why, but Isaac went from being Mr. Mature, pushing against the envelope, to becoming a needy little boy, pulling on the envelope and needing a Parent Protector again.

In the same way, fifteen-year-old Chris, devastated because his girlfriend Jennifer had broken up with him, asked his mother to put on her Parent Protector hat: He asked her to talk to Jennifer's mother. A psychologist who relies on the old, linear model of child development might view Chris's behavior as a sign of immaturity—of regressing to an earlier stage or perhaps being "fixated on Mommy." Rather than being a sign of sickness, however, I see it as a sign of strength —both that he asked Mom and that she responded. Chris got the support he needed and, not so incidentally, he and his mother got just a little closer. (As of this writing, Chris and Jennifer are back together!)

For the rest of this chapter, we'll look at the three types of parent/child connections and examine more closely the anatomy of children in each of the three age categories— always bearing in mind, of course, that there are times when an adolescent needs a Parent Chum or even a Parent Protector, just as there are times when a young child needs a Parent Realist in his corner. So don't focus only on your particular child's age—read about all three ages. In this world we live in, no matter how old your child *really* is, you never know which kid will walk into your house after school today—one who needs a Protector, a Chum, or a Realist.

Latency Age (five to nine): **Help Me!**

Children between the ages of about five and nine need a Parent Protector because they experience a profound expansion in their daily lives. They are exposed to greater demands in school—the beginning of homework, of tackling different subjects. They are expected to think abstractly—deal with reading comprehension, writing, and math concepts, like division and fractions. They are exposed to the ways other families live; and they begin to understand the differences between families—families in crisis, single-parent and stepparent families, poor and wealthy families. They begin to see that theirs aren't the only kinds of parents, or necessarily even the "best" parents. They are also exposed to crime and to tragedies they can begin to grasp, such as the death of a grandparent or a beloved pet, as well as to many new rules that are now enforced *without* the leniency once granted them as younger children.

"Leaving" is a major theme of latency, so separation anxiety is a big factor for these children. However grown up they may seem, kids this age are not that far away from the wild imaginations of preschoolers. Their world is still rich with monsters, goblins, childhood sexuality, worries, superstitions, fears about death. Despite all this, they radiate an "I-can-do-anything" feeling. When these kids who are bursting with life and bubbling over with confidence have to go off to the ordered and more demanding environment of "real" school, imagine how exciting *and* unnerving it must be!

That's where we as Parent Protectors come in, providing routines, rituals, and predictability that will soothe them. For example, bedtime, representing the border between everyday demands and the fantastic images of the dream world, illustrates their need for ritual and routine. Whether you have to put everything away in its proper place, read "just one more" story, bring in yet another drink of water, or lie down and snuggle for a moment, it's all the same. You're being the Parent Protector, soothing them before they go to sleep and let go.

Fears and worries can develop from little pieces of information at this age, again requiring a calming adult presence.

Seven-year-old Regina said to her mother, "I saw a show on TV about this mom being sick and then I heard you talking to Lucy about going to the doctor. I thought something was wrong with you, too." Also, the child's "I'm-the-center-of-the-universe" thinking, left over from preschool, caused her to blame herself: "I thought because I got into trouble at school a couple of times last month that getting upset about me was what was causing you to get sick." Obviously, this mom needed to help soothe and calm Regina down.

With so much going on, don't be surprised if your eight-year-old evidences a sudden interest in religion or pushes you to observe rituals and customs that you haven't observed in years. Again, their love of rules and rituals stems from their desire to make sense of new experiences in an expanding world.

Our kids' need for structure also becomes apparent in their groups and clubs outside the home—and the *structure* is often more important than the activity itself. I once observed a group of eight-year-olds starting a punchball game. Several hours later, I passed the field again, and the kids were still arguing about the rules—*nobody* had even touched the ball yet. They were still screaming and yelling about how the game was supposed to be—and then everyone had to go home!

Later, I asked one of the kids how the game went. "Great!" he said.

"Great?" I responded, a little taken aback. "But you didn't actually *play*."

"So?" he countered. Puzzled by my question, if not a bit disdainful of my ignorance, he walked away.

With such an emphasis on rules, you're likely to hear, "It's not fair," as a response to a multitude of your demands—when you tell them to go to bed or brush their teeth or turn off the TV. These children are obsessed with rules, with what's "fair," and with demands for equal treatment. Try hanging around an eight-year-old for an evening without hearing her yell at Mom or Dad, "You're not my boss!" or "If you don't have to, then why do I?"

Not surprisingly, along with their unceasing emphasis on "fairness," kids this age have a harsh eye-for-an-eye morality. Ask a seven-year-old what should be done regarding some infraction about which he feels strongly, and you'll hear a punishment so severe it has medieval overtones: When Johnny ruined his father's favorite audio tape, the father asked what he thought a "fair punishment" might be. Johnny didn't hesitate: "Don't let me out of my room every night for a month."

Thomas Likona, author of *Raising Good Children*, also illustrates this point when he describes what third-graders considered a fair punishment for a group of teenagers who killed more than a dozen animals in a local zoo: They wanted the older kids *shot* because "the same thing should be done to them that they did to the animals."

This heavy-handed morality has another side, however, which can drive parents crazy. These kids want rules, but they also want to *break* them. Watch out if you're playing a game. They want special consideration, or they just don't want to lose. So they'll try to "bend" the rules—once again, you'll hear, "It's unfair!"

Finally, let's not overlook their budding sexuality, especially in these overtly erotic times. Kids as young as six are exposed to stimulating material—which they don't have to go far to find. Of course, during the preteen and teen years, such interests become more commonplace. For now, however, at one end of the continuum are silly "dirty" jokes and utterly childish titillations: When a mother told her seven-year-old son about one of my lectures and mentioned that I worked at "I-C-P (Institute for Contemporary Psychotherapy)," the boy was in stitches over the initials. "I see pee," he giggled. "Get it?"

At the other extreme are more mature—and troublesome— forays: A suburban mother nearly fainted when her six-year-old daughter came home from school asking what a "oral sex" was. And an entire school was up in arms when a group of eight-year-olds, led by a ten-year-old girl, started making sexually suggestive phone calls to other children's families.

How to Be a Parent Protector

Clearly, it's a tough world for latency-aged children. They have to produce in "real" school, and they're exposed to real life—complete with sex, death, divorce, and illness. And that's just on the outside. Inside, they have to rein in the baby self, deal with a harsh conscience, and come to terms with the fact that the world doesn't revolve around them after all.

What kind of connection do latency-aged children need from the Parent Protector? They need calm, patient, stable parents, and they need rules. They also need "askable" parents—we don't force conversations; we wait until we're asked. *Connecting at this age is most like the therapy model of parenting you'll find in most child-advice books*. In conversations, we reflect back the child's feeling, validate what he or she is saying, and clarify distortions when we hear them. Given the intensity of emotions at this age, all feelings, no matter how wild, need to be taken seriously and responded to in a composed manner.

For example, when seven-year-old Regina revealed she was worried about her mother being sick because of her, the mother, being a Parent Protector, would maintain a connection with her child by responding like this:

> *Mother:* That must have been really scary for
> you . . .
> *Regina:* It was.

> *Mother:*   . . . to think that a little trouble at school could make me sick. *(Mom holds out her arms.)*
>
> *Regina:*   *(Crying a little, she climbs into Mom's lap.)*
>
> *Mother:*   I see how it must have sounded to you, but I was just going to the doctor for my yearly check-up, and you're the last thing in this world that could ever make me sick. In fact, the doctor said I was in perfect health.

The soothing, steady, consoling tone of this conversation has almost a therapy-like feeling to it. Though *not* appropriate with preadolescents and adolescents (in fact, as we'll see later, sounding like a therapist can be deadly with older kids), expressions of validation and calm reassurance are part of the foundation of being the Parent Protector.

As the Parent Protector, you also create a bridge between your child and people in the outside world. Children need our help to create friendships, to find activities and playmates outside the home, to help them make plans. They need our immediate intervention when problems crop up at school, and they need us to speak to other parents when difficulties arise with friends as well.

> *Seven-year-old Andy had been friendly for over a year with Jan, a boy in his class. For several weeks, Andy's mother noticed that her son was coming home from play dates in a sour mood. When she asked Andy if anything was wrong, she got the predictable response of a boy his age: "Nothing." She decided to call Jan's mother, who immediately offered to keep a closer eye on the boys the next time they were at her house. Jan's mother soon realized that her son was teasing Andy and playing more roughly than usual. She intervened by having a talk with her son. Andy's*

mother also talked to him, explaining that she and Jan's mother knew what was happening. Thanks to the mothers' talking, the boys felt "held" in a secure container, and the rough spot in their relationship was soon smoothed over.

Part of being a Parent Protector is making time for certain kinds of activities together. Being first, second, third, and fourth graders, these kids are in love with learning. They especially love learning shared with their parents. They never forget these experiences—school projects, challenging board games, building models together, painting by numbers—you name it. If it has rules, predictability, learning—and a *calm you*—you're creating the empathic envelope they need.

One final and related point: Kids this age are really sensitive to breaks in the empathic envelope. When we scream and when we become irrational, it breaks the connection more profoundly than it would with a preteen or teen. In fact, after asking hundreds of kids this age what they would want to change about their parents, most answer, "When they yell at me." Of course, every parent "loses it," but to be the Parent Protector, it's important to try to *cut down* whenever possible (see Chapter 8 for some strategies that can help).

Obviously, this description of the Parent Protector represents the ideal. None of us is always, or even mostly, patient, reassuring, and unflappable, nor so generous with our time. In the face of a second or third grader's endless need for attention and in the face of the demands of busy, compartmentalized living, we all fall short of this model parent. However, it's also important to remember that for all their spunk and zest for life, these tender-hearted and earnest little souls look to us for reassurance, safety, and predictability in an ever-widening world.

Preadolescence (nine to twelve): **Gross Me Out!**

Nine-and-a-half-year-old Billy has just returned from a month at summer camp. His parents are stunned when their formerly model child turns to them at the dinner table and seemingly without a thought says, "Pass the fucking salt."

Welcome to preadolescence, parents. "What's going on here?" every parent asks. "I thought this wasn't supposed to be happening for another three years?" The truth of the matter is that in preadolescence your child's taste begins to sink to the lowest common denominator of the pop culture. No matter how much time, energy, or money you've devoted to helping your child develop good taste, you'll be sorely disappointed. Preteens these days may not be quite as bad as teenagers, but they're close—and they certainly bear no resemblance to *us* when we were ten years old! And no wonder: We didn't have the benefits of today's popular culture.

Boys seem to relish violence in all forms—slasher movies, gross-out films, action-packed Nintendo games, TV cop shows. Eleven-year-old Lloyd drove this point home when I saw him after a day at the movies. Having crammed his stomach full of Raisinets and Twizzlers and probably suffering from sugar shock, Lloyd confessed what he and his friends really had done that afternoon: sneaked around the neighborhood six-plex, going from one theater into the adjoining one. In several hours, they had seen part or all of *Phantasm II, Dead Calm, A Nightmare on Elm Street, Part V,* and *Blood Beach.* As Lloyd described these movies, I realized that in one afternoon he had seen more murders, dismemberments, and mutilations than I had seen in a lifetime.

Not surprisingly, even Elliott and Nancy, a featured couple on "thirtysomething" have this problem. One of the story lines on the show slated for a pre-Halloween air date revolved around their trying to convince their preteen son, Ethan, *not* to trick-or-treat as Freddy Krueger, the slasher from *A Nightmare on Elm Street*. My heart went out to Elliott as he tried to explain that "scary" need not be quite so blood-curdling.

While girls are not always as spellbound by violence, their cultural values seem no more refined. You may also notice that your daughter's fashion savvy has taken a giant step. She's aware of designer names, labels, and trends. Just like boys', girls' humor can be scatological and downright gross, and they, too, are capable of words once reserved for longshoremen.

The winning combo—bad taste, pop idols, and superficial values—wreaks havoc in our homes. Understandably, parents feel that the invasion of the mass culture is a noxious pollutant—like smog from industrial factories, and that it's poisoning our kids.

While we're on the subject of toxic waste, consider your preadolescent's room: decay, destruction, disarray—a veritable health violation smack dab in the middle of your home. You can't, and may not want to, see the floor. In the rush of the morning, you won't be able to find certain items, like a book bag, a jacket—and maybe your child. Instead, you'll discover yesterday's half-eaten apple or a half-empty glass of milk now green with mold. While not *all* children fall into this mode, preadolescence is a time of emotional disorder, and "the room" often reflects, in ways you can't miss, just how up and down your kid feels.

While you're probably disgusted by your preteen's taste, you undoubtedly soften when it comes to his social life. An obsessive concern over "fitting in" first shows up in fifth and sixth grade. Cliquishness becomes a problem for many kids, and the jockeying for position in the social order often brings with it feelings of exclusion and hurt. Other kids can be downright cruel, and it's not easy for most parents to watch their children go through it (especially because most of us remember our *own* heartaches at that age). The hurt feelings have a domino effect, too, causing children to lash out at younger siblings, or at their parents. (Getting preteens to open up to you about this is covered in Chapter 6.)

The flip side of the social dilemma is the making of a "best friend," a hallmark of preadolescence. Usually, it's a child of the same sex. They talk about "real" matters: new and sometimes disturbing feelings never before experienced, a growing interest in the opposite sex, a recognition of jealousy, competitive experiences, rivalry—all of which can be confusing and embarrassing. Sharing these deep thoughts with a chum can be a lifesaver to a preteen, and the benefits last throughout adolescence. Such friendships are a safe haven; the chums create a private world in which there is deep, abiding loyalty and intense and exclusive bonding with another human being. These friendships sometimes seem "weird" to parents, but they go with the territory:

> *Paul and Michael, both age ten, created a shrine in their back yard inside an old toolshed. They carefully arranged statues and small objects, each of which had its own special place and significant meaning. They created a language that no one else could understand. The boys spent hours working on projects together or simply talking about whatever was on their minds. Thirty years later, Michael still remembers his afternoons with Paul at their "shrine" and in retrospect realizes how much the companionship and solace meant to him.*

On the home front, your preteen's morality changes from the latency-aged child's sense of fairness to something resembling "Let's Make a Deal." In almost every confrontation, you're faced by a legal barracuda, and everything—*everything*—requires negotiation. You budge a little, he wants more. You resist, he launches a full-scale frontal attack. His energy is limitless, and you may find yourself giving in simply out of fatigue. Absolutely nothing gets accomplished, especially on the chores and responsibilities front, without constant haggling.

Preteens also begin to comment on everything you do. It's like having a TV commentator in your midst, reporting on *you*. She watches you; she studies you; she knows you better than you do! (Not surprisingly, I've never met a preteen who can't predict with uncanny accuracy everything a parent will say and do in a given situation.) None of this is done *quietly* or with tact, mind you. She tells you *out loud* every flaw she sees. You were once a hero; you are now a "geek," a "nerd," or a "dork." It's like living with a mini-version of Don Rickles or Andrew Dice Clay—except you can't go home after the show. This *is* home with a preteen.

The sarcasm is not just reserved for you; these kids spread their bad cheer around. Almost invariably, their jabs are aimed at younger siblings: Eleven-year-old Amy and best friend, Jody, absolutely refused to listen to her mother's warning about keeping quiet so that three-year-old Kelly could sleep in the back seat of the car. They kept laughing, pushing the electric windows up and down, slamming the ashtrays open and shut. Of course, little Kelly woke up. The girls naturally denied doing anything on purpose; instead, they quickly took the offensive, accusing Mom of being "too serious." Didn't Kelly have to get up when they got to their destination? What was the big deal?

To say that such interactions wear a parent down is an understatement. The jibes, the teasing, and the constant put-downs get so unbearable, many parents simply give up. One mother took to walking around with headphones on to drown out her preteen's background commentary!

How to Be a Parent Chum

How does a parent connect with a child and keep the empathic envelope intact during the up-and-down years of preadolescence? Even as we must be the cops who reign over these unmanageable little people, they also need us to be Parent Chums. Especially in the face of the fragmented family, being a Parent Chum at all ages, not just the middle years, is increasingly important, although children don't always make the need seem obvious. On the surface, preteens are not usually alone; they're plugged into TV, and they've got tons of activities after school and on weekends. So, many kids don't look as if they need a chum. But try not to be fooled. Chumship at home is vital.

Easier said than done, you say, especially with a child whose every move says "Back off!" But a Parent Chum isn't fooled by an unruly preteen. A Parent Chum knows, in fact, that despite it all—the haggling, the sarcasm, the running commentary, and the increased interest in activities outside the home—the bottom line is that preadolescents still need parents to *do* things with them.

I often hear parents—both in the city and in the suburbs, complain that they're "losing" their kids earlier and earlier to peer groups and the pop culture. One way to slow this down is by being a Parent Chum through shared activities, even if your child *says* he doesn't want to. Don't listen to his initial objections. Don't worry about letting up on being the parent, the enforcer, the teacher of values. There's plenty of time for that.

Preteens need flexibility. For example, a mother who objected to violent movies nevertheless gave in and went to see

Diehard 2 with ten-year-old Jason. He balked at the idea at first (who wants to be seen around the mall with his mother?), but ended up loving it. It gave them something to talk about besides chores, homework, and beating up on his brother. Another mother described a weekly backgammon game with eleven-year-old Bobby. They shut the TV off and let the answering machine pick up the phone calls. Although neither of them addressed it as such, the game gave Bobby a set time when he knew he could talk to his mother about the things that were going on in his life. Maybe once a month he actually said something important to her, but in the world of preteens, that's not bad.

You may have to push at first, especially as these kids approach adolescence, but once convinced, preteens usually have a good time. Preteens particularly love one-to-one time with a parent. In fact, the same kid that complains to me about a parent not allowing him enough freedom—to get out of the envelope on his own—will tell me in touching detail about going to a movie with Mom or to a new restaurant with Dad.

Preteens need us to be as flexible and spontaneous as they are—although their behavior feels erratic, even schizophrenic at times. One minute they're capable of good deeds, empathy, and affection, and the next they're putting you down. A Parent Chum goes with the flow, always remembering that these kids need firmness *and* connection

> *When twelve-year-old Letty called to ask about going to a friend's house after school, she first tried to cajole her mother: "Mom, I promise I'll do my homework as soon as I get home. No TV. I swear." And when Mom said no, "Oh, Mom, you're so stupid. I only have forty-five minutes of homework. . . . " Despite Letty's whining, Mom held firm. And despite her insulting tone, Letty signed off with "I love you,*

> *Mom," and came home only a couple of minutes after*
> *she was supposed to—again, not bad for a preteen.*

A Parent Chum has to learn to dish it out, too—mix it up with your kids. Forget being the supportive therapist/parent. Forget the current emphasis on validation and positive regard. When your child calls you a geek, zing a few one-liners right back. Because of the changeable personalities of most preteens, being reasonable or self-conscious about coming up with the appropriate response, seems *phony* to these kids. If we always speak in the calm, reflective, therapeutic tone that works very well with younger children (and is advised in many child-rearing books), preteens look at us as if we're nuts! They don't *feel* us around them. After a kid acts like a sarcastic pain in the you-know-what, don't you think he *knows* what he's been doing? He can see right through your calm, cool, collected exterior! In fact, give the preadolescent too much "niceness" and there's a good chance he'll provoke you even more—until you do loosen up, react, and he feels *held*.

Parent Chums should share their feelings with their kids, too. Talk about your own past, about problems you either solved or couldn't deal with at all. The "right" answer doesn't matter; the act of sharing with them—being a chum —does. They need us to be open, to be more open about ourselves, to be not quite so protective and gentle with them, to react honestly, and not to treat them so preciously. They need us to make mistakes—and to admit them—and to be willing to move back and forth between being an enforcer and a best friend.

Finally, remember that preteens may begin to look and sound like adolescents, but they still basically think their parents know what's best. They don't think you're "out to get them." They'll question you at times, and you've got to be firm. At other times, they'll have blind faith in you.

They'll rank you out one minute, and evidence undying loyalty and respect for you the next. They'll flip-flop between abuse and tenderness, sarcasm and endearing humor, but there's a basic trust that keeps them from getting into an us-against-them rut. It's not war yet. They want to loosen the envelope, ruffle it up a little bit, but, deep down, they want to trust in your *realness*. Being a Parent Chum is one way to keep honing that trust—even when you least suspect that it's there!

Adolescence (thirteen to sixteen): **Let Me Go!**

"My parents are fools! They have no idea about what's really going on!" Beneath the contempt, when I hear a teenager say something like that, I get a sense of deep *dis*connection. A child who feels that his or her parents simply don't know what's going on in the "real" world has separated too much from her parents. She's gotten too far outside the envelope, and I get concerned—not by the anger, but by the *distance* between her parents and her.

In all fairness to parents, however, part of the problem is that in early adolescence there's often a sudden, dramatic push to get outside the container. We seem irrelevant, expendable—of course, except when they *need something*. The details of their lives are purposely vague. Their social network, into which we have virtually no entry, is very intricate and constantly changing. It's mind-boggling to try to keep up. Telephone conversations are plentiful but hushed, somehow you only hear the words that worry you! (What's that she said . . . something about "trouble," "don't tell your parents," or "swear on your life"?) Doors to rooms are closed with signs like, "Top Secret" or "Keep Out or You'll Be Shot." And you're not sure whether you might, in fact, risk your life if you do enter.

The adolescent push to get out of the envelope and to get out on their own is so sudden, you feel yourself doing the shameful things just about all parents do to break through the wall of secrecy: You listen in on phone conversations or lurk behind doors. You scour their rooms to find clues as to what's going on. You read their mail. There are no depths to which the parent of an adolescent won't go in order to be let in.

Adolescents not only stretch the envelope by keeping you out of their emotional lives, they also struggle literally to get out of the house. They want to "hang out" constantly, at friends' homes where parents aren't around, at the mall, or at other places where there's no supervision. They make plans and change them last-minute, so you can't keep up with them. And they're constantly "double-talking."

Your teenager tells you he's going to a hang-out, and you're supposed to pick him up at 10:00 P.M. What you *don't* realize is that the minute you pull away, he's off to a whole other place—perhaps a friend's house. Unbeknownst to you, he spends the whole time there, returning to the pick-up spot only minutes before you arrive. You may find out later, of course, but for that time, he's kept you in the dark and off balance. The upbeat lawyer/negotiator of preadolescence has become a real pro by now—cynical, shrewd, a tough cookie. You're constantly embroiled in a match of wits. You're exhausted.

So with all this going on—the pushing away, the secrecy, the feeling that you're not wanted—is it really so important to maintain a connection with your recalcitrant teenager? I say most definitely *yes!* Don't mistake rebellion for disconnection. Don't listen to traditional theories about separation. Remember: Though they want to create their own personalities, teenagers don't ever want to completely break the connection with their parents.

In fact, recent studies shatter the myth that teenagers simply want separation and that, despite the way they make you feel, they don't want anything to do with their parents.

In one of the largest studies, conducted over a period of four years, 1,049 adolescents ranging in age from twelve to nineteen years were asked about their relationships with their parents, their feelings of obligation toward them, and their conflicts. Contrary to the belief that teenagers must "emancipate" themselves and therefore separate from their parents in order to become adults, the researchers concluded that "the bond to parents is not severed so much as it is transformed." Indeed, the teenagers themselves report that *the most important relationships they have are with their parents.* But what is this connection between parent and teenager based on? It's based on being a Parent Realist.

How to Be a Parent Realist

As kids work their way into the double digits, Parent Realists are pragmatic about their teenagers' ever-expanding range of activities and demands. For example, while I personally don't approve of adolescents drinking beer, there's a difference between saying to a kid, "I absolutely forbid you to have a beer" (an unrealistic expectation, since you can't be with him every minute of every day and night), and making a strong statement that expresses your values and expectations: "I know that I can't control you every minute. I don't want you to drink while you're at this party, because . . . *(insert your* reasons—the empathic envelope is made up of *your* values). If you come back, and I think you've been drinking, I can't trust you to go out next weekend, so you'll be grounded. But in the end I can't magically stop you tonight." Don't hold back on your reasons; don't soft pedal; don't be phony. But somewhere, you've got to be realistic about your power to control it all. Your genuineness and clear vision will help you stay connected.

You can't stop your kids, but you *can* try to set up environments that protect them. You *can* be sure there's adult supervision at the party. You *can* pay attention to details and ask questions. What's the occasion? Who's going to be there? You can *insist* on talking to the parent in charge. But even so, remember that you can't control what goes on behind a chaperon's back. That's an unrealistic expectation, and, as such, it separates you from your child.

I realize that saying, "I absolutely forbid you to . . . " may *sound* good, but it's unrealistic and, therefore, it breaks the connection. You will seem foolish and arbitrary; and it just won't work. The second approach, which *is* realistic, actually draws the teenager closer to you. She recognizes that at least you know what's going on. Out of that, there's a chance of your opening a dialogue about peer pressure and helping your child make decisions independent from the crowd.

Parents who say, "Not my kid," can't possibly stay connected to their children. They're not acting like Parent Realists. You have to pay attention to details and become acutely aware of what's really going on in your children's world during these years—dress, music, drugs. Ask yourself: What do you *really know* about the kinds of drugs that are available in your kid's school? What are the kids in the neighborhood or in your teen's class up to sexually? What are your kids seeing in the movies? What goes on inside a concert hall—what's the experience like? Have you listened to the words of songs your kids listen to? Or is all this "off limits," because your teenager's first response is, "Leave me alone!"

The truth is, most kids *want* parents to listen to their music and care about their idols. They know it offends you, and at first they'll think you're "weird" for being interested in kids' things. But in private, kids tell me they're happy their parents know what's going on. They want to know that you take their world seriously. It makes them feel connected. One mother whose son was into heavy metal music bought a record for him when she was on a business trip in London. She hated it; but her son was thrilled. She listened to the words and was disgusted with it, but at least she acknowledged his interest. And he never failed to point out to friends where he got the prized record.

Again, don't expect your teenager to let *you* know he's happy that you're interested. Another mother who went to college during the '60s marveled at the fact that her teenage son was "discovering" groups like Chicago and Hot Tuna. Of course, her son only rolled his eyes and grimaced when she told him, "I used to listen to the same music." Only when she overheard him telling a friend what a "cool" record collection his mother had did she realize that he felt differently than he acted toward her.

Finally, Parent Realists must be *honest about themselves*. If you have problems of your own and try to push them under the rug, it's deadly to teenagers. They can't tolerate hypocrisy. It causes a major disconnection—a break in the empathic envelope. If you're not "holding" yourself, nurturing yourself, how can you hold your child? Like it or not, adolescents have radar when it comes to our unspoken or unaddressed problems. And much of their acting out is because we're not being realistic about *ourselves*.

For example, one day thirteen-year-old Craig shoved himself away from the dinner table, stood up, turned to his parents and exclaimed, "You disgust me." Questioned about his reaction later on, the teenager could only focus on his annoyance at the sound of his parents' forks clicking on the china during dinner; it made him very uneasy. As it turned out, it wasn't really the tapping sound; it was the deafening silence. His parents—who always exhorted *him* to talk and tell them about his life—weren't talking to each other.

Melissa, fourteen, was sloughing off school, refusing to do

her homework. All she wanted, it seemed, was to have a social life. Her mother, a single parent, was beside herself. Try as she did, she couldn't get Melissa "motivated." The mother didn't realize she, too, was stuck—for many months after the sudden death of her beloved mother, she had been unable to get herself back to work. Once the mother started working on *her* life, Melissa's attitude started changing, too.

It was that way for Manny, sixteen, who was thrown out of school for drinking. The teenager showed no apparent remorse in the face of his trouble, until one day he broke down in a family therapy session. He admitted he was worried about his father's drinking. When the father joined AA and took care of *his* problem, Manny's "drinking problem" mysteriously abated.

Actually, it's not a mystery at all. It's a matter of being realistic about your life. Clearly, it's not easy to look in the mirror, but if you don't want your teenager to *become* your mirror, ask yourself some questions: What *is* going on in my life? What am I not dealing with? Am I carrying leftover grudges, unfinished business, unresolved problems into my everyday dealings? What's the state of my marriage (or my relationship with a live-in), my career, my relationship with my own parents, my friendships? Have I recently made changes that have caused upheaval in my life—or am I avoiding making changes because I'm frightened? Are my actions really giving my teenager a "do-as-I-say-not-as-I-do" message?

In summary, adolescence is a time of change and becoming more realistic about the world. Teenagers move back and forth between grand dreams about themselves and hard-nosed reality. In order to stay connected to our teenagers, then, we have to do the same thing. We have to be Parent Realists who can see past our own grandiose ideas about how much we can control our kids and control who they are. We have to focus on what *is*: who they really are (whether we like them or not), what *their world* is about, and who *we* are.

Putting It All Together

As I mentioned earlier, no one way of being with your child is appropriate. No matter how old your child is, there are times you have to be a Parent Protector, times that you have to be a Parent Chum, and times that you have to be a Parent Realist. Here are some basic guidelines:

Be a Parent Protector

1) When your child is frightened, be the Parent Protector *first*, and take care of other things later.
2) When your child asks you to intervene with another child's parents, take him up on it.
3) When your child is being picked on, by anyone in the school setting, first give her a chance to work it out on her own, but if there's no change, you intervene. She'll forgive you.
4) When there is any significant life transition, prepare your child for it.

Be a Parent Chum

1) When you can't remember the last time you did something one-on-one with your child, do *something*. Even fifteen minutes makes a difference.
2) When you've been involved in a cycle of fighting without any let-up, call a truce and spend just a small amount of time doing something else together.
3) When you can't remember the last time *you* enjoyed yourself with your child, do something *you* like to do, and take your child along.

Be a Parent Realist

1) When everybody is telling you something about your child, and you just can't believe it, stop sticking your head in the sand and try to hear what they're saying.

2) When your child starts "hanging out" with another child or a group of kids who have worrisome habits, start being concerned. Your kid is probably doing it too, or at least considering it.

3) When your are persistently anxious about something your child is doing, you're probably right to be anxious. Start asking questions, and find out what's *really* going on.

5

The Myth of "Between You and Your Child"

How the Family Dance Comes Between You and Your Child

The title of one of the most widely read books on child-rearing techniques, *Between Parent and Child*, describes another significant myth of parenting: the idea that what you—and you alone—do with your child is all that matters. That might be true if you had no spouse, no other children, no brothers or sisters, and no parents of your own!

Families are systems, interconnected like webs. Even when it comes to communication, which at least on the face of it seems to be between you and your child, it's still in the context of the whole system.

Let's say you've spent almost no time with your nine year old for several days, except being "a cop," getting after him about his room, homework, chores. So, recognizing the need to be a Parent Chum, you suggest playing a couple of Nintendo games with him. Does your six-year-old leave the two of you alone—or does he push for equal treatment? Do the two of them end up fighting over who's going to take the joystick?

How about your thirteen-year-old, who has been pushing against the empathic envelope to go out next Friday night to a party? Being a Parent Realist, you press for details, asking what the party is for, who's going to be there, who's in charge, and whether adults will be there for the duration of the party? Your daughter hits you with a barrelful of teenage double talk. The "story" just doesn't add up, so you tell her she can't go. What are the chances that she'll accept your decision peacefully? Isn't there at least some possibility that she'll go to Dad and work the other side of the street until *he* gives in?

Finally, suppose your seven-year-old is upset because his teacher is mad at him. Somehow, he's gotten the idea that the teacher hates him—he's even worried that he could be kicked out of school. (Believe it or not, young kids sometimes *do* worry about these things in our accelerated era. Only recently, when I asked a seven-year-old what "wish" he'd like to have granted, he answered, "To get into a good college!") Naturally, you want to be the Parent Protector, to calm, soothe, and reassure him. But isn't it possible that someone else in the family—like your spouse—is going to accuse you of "babying" him, of being "too soft" with him?

In each of these situations, other people in the family got into the act. And you can bet it was definitely not the first time the *exact same sequence* happened in these families. It seems inevitable: We start out with good intentions, we do what we're advised or what we think is best, and despite it all, we keep doing the same old family "dances"—habitual patterns of relating. In the end, we walk away frustrated, angry, or confused, if not all three.

And it's no wonder: No matter how good a swimmer you are, you always have to be aware of the undertow in the ocean. Likewise, in family life, these dances, as well as "programs" and "scripts" handed down from the past, can get in the way. They can rupture the empathic envelope and make it harder for you to connect with your child.

Why? Because whether you realize it or not, you are rarely talking to just your child. The room is often crowded with other people, either in the form of old scripts from your parents imprinted in your mind or in the form of everyone else in the family putting their two cents in. Not only is your head chock full of ideas about what's right and wrong, so is your kid's head filled with images about "ideal" parenting that she's picked up from other kids, TV, and the movies.

With all this going on, you and your child react reflexively to each other. You're both on automatic pilot. And within seconds any incident can turn into a full-scale no-win dance, a repetitive pattern in which you all play roles you can't easily break. The dance undermines any attempts to connect inside the empathic envelope. After all, how can you be compassionate, set clear limits, or communicate when you are stuck in rigid patterns with each other?

On the other hand, if you learn a little about how families operate, become aware of the dances your particular family favors, and learn to anticipate the dances that keep you stuck, you *can* keep the empathic envelope intact and enrich the connection between you and your child.

The Family Ecosystem

No one in the family system is ever totally apart from the others. Neither distance, divorce, nor even death can ever really separate family members. Much like environmental systems—ecosystems—the family is sustained and kept afloat by a complex interplay of elements. If you alter one factor, the system is thrown off balance, and the whole picture may change.

The dances in families create a kind of delicate balance, which family therapists call "homeostasis." Any type of change—like someone trying a new "step"—reverberates throughout the family system and has an impact on each of its members. It doesn't matter whether it's a happy event, like a parent getting a job promotion or the birth of a second child, or a sad event, like a divorce or the death of a grandparent.

The concept of homeostasis also explains what happens when you watch a TV program or read an article or book about child raising and decide to try a new technique. Your new strategy may work once or for a short time; but more often, it's met with resistance. That's because families are upset by change, and they react against whatever threatens the old, predictable order. Because everyone is usually so uncomfortable with something new, the whole family gets into the act.

A mother who'd been reading a lot of child-rearing books told me that she had recently decided that it was time to set stricter limits with eight-year-old Gabe. For years, her husband had been calling her too soft-hearted and overprotective. Swallowing her hesitancy, she now accepted her husband's approach and decided that the next time Gabe acted up, she'd mete out stronger punishment. Within a few days, Gabe had a water fight with a friend and soaked her new bathroom carpet. Punishment: Gabe couldn't invite this friend over for a week, and he had to pay a small percentage of his allowance to chip in for a professional rug cleaning.

When her husband came home, she proudly told him about the punishment. But out of nowhere Dad suddenly took the other side. He said the punishment was too harsh and defended his position by saying, "Boys will be boys."

What went wrong here? The advice was good. It was a logical consequence. Gabe wasn't even complaining. The truth is, nothing went "wrong"—except that Mom wasn't anticipating that to change the dance, she would run into resistance. So in the end she became thoroughly discouraged as parents often are when they try a new technique at home, because it didn't work.

Even a change that's seemingly a private matter runs into family resistance. Look at how everyone in this family of four—a mother, father, and their two daughters, eight and four—managed to stop the mother from trying to make a change in *herself*: At her doctor's suggestion, Mom decided to lose weight. Her husband was also overweight, as was the seven-year-old. After several failed attempts, the woman figured out why she had so much trouble. She couldn't take the guilt! What guilt? The husband and the older girl started to "hate" her for losing weight. And the younger girl always got into trouble and seemed to need more attention whenever the mother dieted. It was easier to risk her health than risk her family's resentment for rocking their boat.

As you can see, family dances get just about everyone into the act. Everyone goes on automatic pilot, reacting reflexively to each other. With all these distractions, then, how is a good, powerful connection possible between you and your child?

The Family Two-Step

Even though your family recognizes that changing the old order might help make things better, they won't thank you for coming up with new techniques. It's like a body rejecting a new heart. After doing it so long, no one wants to learn a new dance. That old two-step—where one steps forward and the other steps back—is just too comfortable. Everyone has repeated the dance over and over, so it's familiar and predictable.

By the time children are seven or eight years old they're already aware of their particular family dance. If you ask an eight-year-old what happens if you don't turn in your home-work, he can probably do a perfect imitation of his mother's or father's response. Children know exactly what each parent will do and, intuitively, they react accordingly.

For example, ten-year-old Paul came home from after-school activities habitually late. Each time, his mother would yell and ask him why he was late. Paul knew that the explanation, more than anything else, was important to her, so he'd have one ready, tailored to Mom's particular mood on a given day. Since he was prepared for her yelling, he just tuned her out. His mother's reaction had no effect on Paul—he became immune to her anger—so he continued to come home late. And Mom wondered why her "discipline" had no effect!

Parents always give children cues: tone of voice, body posture, certain facial expressions. A father's eyes widen when he gets angry; a mother puts her hands to her forehead when she's dismayed; they utter predictable lines that have been replayed in scene after scene. It's the same old story on the same old tape.

Dances We Learn from Our Parents

Not only does the current family dance affect how connected and effective we can be with our children, but we also carry with us memories of dances we learned from *our* parents, which influence the connection as well. These old dances represent repetitive patterns of behavior in your family that may be generations old.

For example, Ellen is feeding her nine-month-old baby, Sara. Her own mother, Dorothy, looks over her shoulder, beaming at the sight of her first grandchild in the high chair. After a few spoonfuls, Sara spits out a mouthful and balks at taking any more of the green mush.

Though Ellen doesn't ask her mother for her advice or her

comments, Dorothy offers, "Didn't I tell you that one day you'll understand what it was like to have a fussy eater? I was the same way as a child and I certainly got paid back with *your* bad eating. And now you'll know what I went through. Sara's just like you were. Don't force her."

"Ma, leave me alone. I know how to take care of my own daughter," Ellen retorts, trying to force another spoonful in the baby's mouth.

Ironically, Ellen once swore she'd never force her child to eat. Now, even when her mother's not literally looking over her shoulder, Ellen becomes nervous around mealtimes with Sara. She loses the connection with Sara and can't figure out when to stop feeding her and when to offer more. She's the unwitting participant in an old family dance around eating that had been passed down to Dorothy by her mother and, chances are, to her mother by *her* mother—and generations before them as well.

These dances are "in our bones," and without realizing it, we end up hoofing it to our families' oldies-but-goodies tunes. Whether family members *actually* butt in or whether you're just carrying old family melodies about child rearing in your head, most likely a dance is in progress. In order to put this book (or any parenting advice) to good use you need to learn how to identify the family dance that comes between you and your child.

How You Know When You're in a Dance

No one escapes these dances. They are part of being a parent. They're not necessarily bad. The trouble is, dances can also become repetitive and reflexive and done without thought. Not thinking means not connecting; automatic pilot means not connecting. The best way to avoid getting stuck in the same repetitive dance—with your child and family—is to become more aware of how you behave. Here are some ways to recognize that you're in a dance:

You "see red" when you deal with your child. If your child can always push your buttons, pay attention to the feelings. You may be in a dance. Ask yourself if how you feel is really because of what the child is doing in the here-and-now, or is she hitting on an old "sore spot," a leftover from your own childhood? Does the incident vaguely remind you of something or make you more tense or angry than the actual situation calls for? If so, perhaps the "button" she's pushing is one you need to become aware of. After all, when you see red, you can't see your child clearly. Besides that, kids are phenomenal experts at figuring out where our buttons are.

For example, Billy's father had a real "thing" about lying. Because his own father had been convicted of tax fraud several times, he believed that telling the truth was central to being a good person. This was not lost on eleven-year-old Billy. Whenever Dad didn't come through with something Billy wanted, he would call his father "a liar" or "a fraud" and bring Mom into the fight. Every time Billy did this, Dad exploded. But, wanting to do the "right" thing, the father also gave in. The dance went on for years, with Dad feeling obligated to do all sorts of things he had just mentioned casually. No one was happy—not even Billy—who told me privately he wished his father would not be so "good" once in a while. When Dad understood the dance, he finally put his foot down with Billy, and the two began to have a real give-and-take connection.

You're convinced that your child is just like you. When you think you know exactly what your child is thinking and feeling, you're in a dance. You're reacting, not connecting, and you're certainly not seeing the child clearly.

Arnie, the father of nine-year-old Alan, was picked on as a kid, because his legs were misshapen from a serious episode of polio. When Alan developed a learning disability, Arnie was sure he knew *exactly* how the boy felt. He became overly worried about how self-conscious Alan was and, as his own parents had done with him, he did the Pep Talk Dance. He constantly tried to shore up Alan against what he thought was the same experience he had gone through. His intentions were good; but Alan was *different*. He didn't feel the same way, but Arnie was so used to doing the old family dance, he couldn't see his son clearly.

Alan's reaction in the dance was to hide his feelings of discouragement from Dad and confide only in Mom. She would listen to his experiences without probing and would then get mad at Dad for not being sympathetic enough. Arnie felt more and more disconnected from Alan. Ironically, he *thought* he knew exactly what his son was going through but ended up unable to talk to him about it. When Arnie finally recognized the dance, he stopped himself from giving Alan pep talks. He simply listened and began to see the differences between his own past and Alan's situation. Alan began to open up to his father about his school frustrations, and the two developed an interest in computers—which gave them something to do together and, not so incidentally, also helped Alan with his learning problems.

"If It Was Good Enough for My Parents, It's Good Enough for Me"

Perhaps an old family dance has become so much a part of you you're humming the tune without realizing it. Without any forethought, you do essentially whatever your parents did. "It was good enough for them," the unconscious message tells you, "and it's good enough for me."

Let's say your parents didn't allow you to go to a party until you were fourteen. No matter what, you're not going to allow your child to go to a party until she's fourteen either.

That would be fine—if you had your own reason for coming up with that policy. But if you're doing it reflexively, simply *because your parents did*, without any thought to whether it works for you and your child today, then there's a good chance you're going to miss connecting with your child along the way.

Often the rupture is quite serious: When Fred, thirteen, came home wanting to pierce his ear, his father was appalled. "My father would have died if *I* ever came home with anything remotely like an earring when I was a boy," the father stormed. "If you *ever* do that, you're out of this house." It didn't matter to the father that Fred was an excellent student, that he was one of the best players on the basketball team, or that the boy was an all-around "good" kid.

As it turned out, Fred didn't disobey his father. Dad got "his way," but at a terrible cost to their relationship. Not only did the dance continue for months, but there was endless tension in the house and blow-ups over seemingly trivial matters. And when Fred's team played in the all-city basketball tournament later that month, his father refused to go.

When Dad finally recognized how the memory of his own father kept intruding ("He'd turn over in his grave if I let Fred get away with this"), he adopted a less rigid position: "When you're fifteen, we'll talk about it again." With this change in the dance, things settled down immediately. By fourteen, neither Fred nor Dad cared much about the earring anymore.

*"I'll **Never** Be Like My Parents"*

Now let's look at the people who swear, "I'll be exactly opposite from my parents." They go to the other end of the continuum—or so they think—and then are baffled by the results. I've identified several "exactly opposite" themes that reflect this phenomenon:

1) "My parents never listened to me, so I'll be receptive to my kids at all times."

2) "My parents were strict and arbitrary. I'll always bend over backwards to be fair and democratic."

3) "My parents were sexually repressive. I'm going to really encourage discussions about sex."

4) "My parents had rigid rules about everything. I'm not going to press my values onto my child."

5) "My parents never fostered my creativity. I'm going to give my child every opportunity to develop his creative side."

Now, what's wrong with these goals? At first glance, they seem understandable, even admirable. Unfortunately, when doing the exact opposite of what our parents did becomes a goal unto itself, it is a reflexive formula, and we are caught in a rigid dance. We stop acting on what we really believe in the moment—*our instincts*—which may, in fact, be something not so totally different from our parents', nor such terrible parenting:

"Enough already! I know I want you to speak freely, *but I can't listen to another word.*"

"Democracy has its limits. You're doing this because *I'm the parent!*"

"Culture is important, but you're so overscheduled already, just sit home one afternoon and *watch some cartoons on TV.*"

How can you tell when you're caught in the "I'll-be-exactly-opposite-of-my-parents" dance? Your child has become just like one of your parents! I call this "the boomerang effect"—and it's one of the great paradoxes of human behavior. The more you're locked into a dance that's based on *not* being like your parents, the greater the chance that the past will come back to haunt you, and your child will sound just like the parent you've done everything to be different from.

A woman whose mother had been very demanding of her and very autocratic decided she'd be different—endlessly "fair" and not very strict—with her daughter. When the child was four or five she was a little whiney; by seven or eight, she was a self-centered kid and had a hard time following rules; by the time she was thirteen or fourteen, she became a despot. Eventually, this mother found herself battling with her daughter the way she had fought with her own mother when she was a child.

Similarly, the daughter of an alcoholic father had been ignored and unappreciated by her dad. Consequently, she went out of her way to bolster her child's self-esteem. She praised the boy for everything he did. The problem was, he became deaf to her compliments; he didn't believe them. He felt she was phony and unable to see him realistically. Eventually, he tuned her out and withdrew into his own world—not much differently than her self-absorbed alcoholic father.

In another family, Mom and Dad were determined to create a home life that promoted good taste and culture in their child, Eric. This was a reaction to what they experienced as the "cultural wasteland" of their youth. They were so determined to maintain their exact-opposite enrichment program, that by nine years old, Eric was a lowbrow of monumental proportions. Eric had become the neighborhood expert on slasher films, heavy metal groups, and funky clothing. (And they thought *their parents* had no taste!) As happens so often with the exact-opposite mode of parenting, we end up reliving the very situation we tried so desperately to get away from.

Déja Vu: "I've Been Here Before"

In case you don't recognize yourself in any of the above examples, I've identified a number of familiar parenting dances that I repeatedly see in family therapy sessions. Of course, most people join in on more than one particular dance, but if you really look at yourself, chances are you'll see that one particular type predominates.

The Organizer Dance   In our full-throttle world where no one's attention span is greater than thirty seconds, and we're juggling job, house, kids, and commuting, it's easy to understand why we parents get stuck in the Organizer Dance. Believing that children need constant scheduling and predictability, we move our kids along from one activity to the next. We feel that routine is essential to a child's sense of security, and it's the only way the parents survive as well. There's a certain amount of reward to this dance, because things *do* get done. Routine becomes an end in itself: Every four o'clock, the kids are going to be watching "Tom and Jerry"; at exactly six, supper is served; at seven, they're doing homework; at 7:45, brushing teeth; and at eight, they'll go to bed. If this dance is predominant, kids either dance right along or they rebel continuously and never get in step. Either way, when routine and consistency become the main dance, spontaneous connection is often lost.

The Cop Dance   There are days and weeks we constantly monitor, control, and scold. We can't get out of the Cop Dance. How can it be helped, especially when there's more than one child (even worse, two boys close in age)? One mother reported to me that in the space of an hour, her two boys, nine and eleven years old, managed to tease the cat, eat the entire contents of the refrigerator, leaving all the plates on the table, and threaten to destroy each other's posters and Nintendo games while actually breaking the toilet. Without wanting to, she realized that 90 percent of the time, she was imposing limits and levying punishment. Several months or years of this and it's hard not to get into the Cop Dance. The upshot here is that kids who are constantly facing The

Enforcer eventually go on automatic pilot themselves: Shouting leads to more shouting. Kids become immune to threats. The beleaguered parent wonders, "What *else* can I take away?" And everyone is locked in a disconnected struggle.

The Praise Dance   In modern child rearing, a heavy emphasis has been placed on praising kids. But there's a risk in *overdoing* the Praise Dance. It cheapens encouragement. If we praise children because we're supposed to, doling out compliments for everything and anything, it doesn't sound terribly real. There's also a certain precious tone of voice that goes with this dance—too empathic, too understanding—a cross between a therapist and a teacher. The upshot: Like any other overdone dance, kids tune it out, and often they don't pay attention anyway. We feel phony and unreal, not connected to the very kids we compliment so profusely.

The Negotiation Dance   In our entrepreneurial world, we've been taught we can bargain for anything. We carry that over into child rearing, thinking we can't simply demand something of our children or can't say "no" without giving something in return. I'm no one to talk: When my daughter was three and a half, to entice her into taking a bath, I'd float an Oreo cookie on her Popeye boat! Few of us are immune to this dance. The melodies in our head are the commercials and jingles we hear on TV and radio, and we believe our kids will only dance if we play them the tune they want. Does this dance actually give us greater control? No. We end up feeling resentful and ineffectual, while our kids feel like they can talk us into just about anything—certainly no basis for a heartfelt connection.

The Therapist Dance   With so many TV talk shows, magazines, and books disseminating pop psychology, we've all tilted a little toward a therapeutic version of parenting. If you've read a lot of advice books, watched Donahue and Oprah whenever they had shows on child rearing, joined self-help groups, taken Parent Effectiveness Training and other parenting workshops, it's hard not to do a little of the Therapist Dance. We've come to believe that being like a therapist is the right model for being a parent. We try to use all the right phrases; we "validate," "name feelings," and "clarify"; we are empathic to a fault. In the end, of course, this dance is unnatural. For the most part, our kids don't want us to "relate" in this manner anyway. As one kid said to her mother, "Okay, Mom, I get it. You've been putting your hand on my shoulder and looking deeply into my eyes every time we talk, because you've been to another one of those communication seminars. Get *real*, Mom!"

The Worry Dance   Who can help this one? Sometimes it seems that parenting is nothing *but* worrying. Even happy times are injected with concerns. The family is frolicking at the lake, having a wonderful day, and we start thinking, "It's getting late. The kids are going to get cold. They're going to get sick. Is that a rain cloud on the horizon? What if there's lightning, too? Someone's going to cut himself on those sharp rocks. I've got to check later for ticks. Shouldn't they be getting ready for dinner? Tomorrow's a school day. We don't want to get them back home too late. Did Celia finish her class project?" Mind you, this is on a *good* day—and they're not even adolescents yet! One parent I know who became aware of his doing the Worry Dance suddenly realized, "I shouldn't have a family—I should belong to a health plan!"

In part, this goes with the turf of being a parent, of course. But automatic worry often leads to two automatic reactions from our kids: They get the jitters and learn how to worry along with us—or they go to the other extreme, leaving *all* the worrying to us and taking unnecessary chances to prove their independence. Either way, the worry dance leads to struggling and disconnection.

The Silver Lining Dance   On the other hand, there are parents who *never* worry. Everything is upbeat. If something bad happens, they immediately see the bright side, the silver lining. Nothing can get these parents down, and, in fact, most of us envy them. However, worriers should take heart. There *is* a problem with this dance. Kids whose parents do the Silver-Lining Dance eventually learn that if they express depression or discouragement, it only leads to an immediate "solution" and a pep talk from Mom and Dad. Over time, kids don't respond to this. They can't help but clam up; they feel something is wrong with their downbeat feelings. They have a hard time—as most of us do—expressing the sadder, more vulnerable, poignant aspects of life.

The truth is, of course, that *most* of us do the Silver-Lining Dance at least some of the time. We love our kids, and it's hard to listen to their upsets without trying automatically to help them feel better, to make the bad feelings go away. But by too quickly moving to the bright side and trying to fix bad feelings, we rob ourselves and our kids of a natural connection in life: accepting bittersweet experiences that are part of living.

The One-Up Dance   As a friend of mine pointed out, when you look at your neighbor's yard, the grass actually *does* look greener. It's only when you cross the fence that you see his grass is much the same as yours! In this age of eating right, looking good, having it all, getting into the right schools, who doesn't do the One-Up Dance? We're steeped in early testing, enrichment programs, flash cards for infants—in short, our whole culture represents the pressure to succeed. Everything our kids do is compared to other children: how fast they grow, walk, run, what they eat, how soon they read. Like the Rick Moranis character in the movie *Parenthood,* we all want superbabies. The pressure on us and on our kids makes it easy not to see who they (and we) actually are—their real skills and weaknesses. This misperception only leads to distance between us and our kids and heightens our concern that somehow we're failing as parents.

What You Can Do

Recognizing your family dance is the first step in turning off the automatic pilot, so you can actually get through to your child and vice versa. But if none of the dances I've outlined seems familiar, below are several ways of keeping track of them. Remember, it's impossible not to be involved in some sort of repetitive dance routine with your child and family. You just need to know *which ones,* so you can try to avoid being a one-track parent. And so you can keep up with your child who, I assure you, knows all the steps by heart.

Keep a parenting log. Write down the things you do and say during different interactions with your kids. Do it for as long as you can manage—a day, a couple of days, a week. At night, before you go to bed, write down what you say, what he says in return, your response, his response, what happens next, and who else gets involved? If you're honest, you begin to see what comes up. What kinds of things do you say to your kid? Does your child remind you of your own parents? Are you sounding just like *your* mother or father? Do you think you know exactly what your daughter or son is thinking? What does your child do to make you see red? Do you often have the feeling you've been here before? If you can follow through on this technique, you will *definitely* find patterns to the interaction, patterns you intuitively knew were there, but now you can see them on paper, in black and white.

Tape-record family scenes. If you can't manage to jot things down in log form, then leave a tape recorder in a room where the family congregates. Wait a few days, until the tape recorder gets lost in the rubble of everyday household clutter and no one seems to notice. Then, one night, turn it on for a few hours. Later, in the privacy of your own room, listen to it. Having done this many times myself, I must warn you about how shockingly clear the merry-go-round becomes when you hear it on tape. The dance will be impossible to miss.

Ask for outside input on how you behave with your child. Have another parent you trust (*not* your spouse—he or she is too involved in the family dance to be objective) spend an afternoon or two observing you and your child. Ask the person to jot down what he or she sees in the interactions. You may have to do this one or two times to become less self-conscious. Also, the discomfort can be eased if the two of you agree to be partners and switch off with one another. (Besides, we all informally notice just about everything that other parents do anyway.) The information gathered from this kind of sharing is invaluable. Doctors, lawyers, teachers, nurses, and administrators all consult with each other. Why shouldn't parents?

Observe how other people act toward your children. If none of these approaches feels comfortable, you can use more indirect methods. Researchers Sroufe and Fleeson discovered that *other people's* behavior toward your child is often a reflection of what *you're* like with your kids—and it's extremely accurate. They found, for instance, that teachers tend to "baby" or rescue certain children and are much tougher with others. There was a direct correlation between dances teachers get into with children and dances that go on at home. Of course, don't draw conclusions from one teacher, but if several teachers get into the same dance routine with your child, you can be sure it's a mirror image of a dance at home. Pay attention, and start watching your own interactions more closely.

Look at the kind of behavior your child is "stuck" in. Interestingly enough, if you're overdoing one particular dance, there's a chance your kid will get stuck in the opposite direction. As I mentioned above, when we overdo the Worry Dance and constantly say, "Watch out! Watch out!" our child may become a risk taker. Children whose parents are specialists in the Organizer Dance often have trouble "getting it together." The Therapist Dance often produces kids who aren't introspective at all. In fact, they're totally tuned out— or turned off. As one kid told me, "Why is she always asking me questions? Can't she see I'm just a happy little zombie?"

In short, looking at those "character traits" in your child that you can't seem to do anything to change may give you clues about what dance you're overdoing. So just fill in the blanks: "If they never or always _____ (watch out, give in, feel good about themselves), then it may mean that I _____ (worry, negotiate, praise) too much."

Changing the Dance

Modern children in our action-packed, strobe-lit world need parents who can move quickly and create many different ways of connecting with their kids. It's not that any one parenting dance is necessarily bad, but any one that becomes rigid and puts you on automatic pilot can prevent you from maintaining a healthy, enriching alliance with your children. You don't get their attention. They don't hear you or even notice you anymore. And you can't see them clearly either.

Rather than have the dance work against you, arm yourself with knowledge. Once you learn to recognize that you're in a dance, you're in a position to change. You can make a choice to do something different that gets everybody off the merry-go-round. Because we are so deeply interconnected to each other, a small change by you makes all family members dance to a different tune.

For example, eight-year-old Andrew's chore was to set the table each night for dinner. However, on many evenings Andrew procrastinated, and Mom would end up doing the Cop Dance, reminding, nagging, invariably screaming—at which point Andrew would yell back, "Stop bugging me!" Finally, after leaving a tape recorder in the dining room, Andrew's mother recognized the dance and decided to change her part in it. One night, when Andrew hadn't set the table, she stopped cooking and wouldn't serve dinner to him or anyone else in the family (his two sisters and father). The dance changed radically, with both sisters now cutting in and pressuring Andrew to get the job done. Mom stopped being the Enforcer. And she got Andrew's attention long enough to talk to him about how badly his noncooperation made her feel.

Let's take another look at our fussy eater, Sara. The Worry Dance, handed down for several generations, had made mealtimes a nightmare for both the child and her mother, Ellen:

"Please, one more bite."

"No!"

"You haven't eaten enough—you'll get sick."

"No!"

Ellen's anxiety skyrocketed as Sara became more and more upset. I suggested that the mother change her dance steps just a little. Instead of focusing on how much Sara ate at each feeding, she should focus on her *own level of anxiety*. When Ellen began to feel herself get upset, *that* was the time to offer one last spoonful. If Sara said no, that was the end of the meal.

This wasn't an easy dance to change, because Ellen had old melodies in her head that had been passed down for generations, not to mention the fact her own mother, Dorothy, was on hand to remind her in case she forgot the tune. So the room was pretty crowded! But Ellen finally mastered the new dance step and stopped feeding Sara whenever she felt anxious. What happened? Soon there were fewer struggles at mealtime. Sara ate no more, but meals actually became pleasurable for both of them—a time to be loving with each other. Ellen had managed to change a generations-old dance, and, in the bargain, strengthened her connection with Sara.

One final example: Whenever eight-year-old Ian violated a family rule, his mother did the Therapist Dance. She was eminently patient, asking reasonable questions, which Ian promptly shot down with a dismissing tone. After keeping a log of her conversations for a few nights, the mother changed the dance by doing what she *really felt* in those moments. What was that? She screamed her head off in a totally un–psychologically sophisticated way! Everyone, of course, was stunned at this new step in the dance. And she got Ian's attention long enough to establish some no-nonsense rules and consequences. Soon after that, Ian cooked his first meal without any coaching from Mom.

Be Prepared for the Counterreaction

Remember that I said at the beginning of this chapter that no one in the family likes to change the dance. No matter how painful, it's more comfortable than learning a new step. So if you're going to change the dance, be prepared for what happens next!

In the examples above, things didn't go as perfectly as the summaries would suggest. But this book is about reality, not myth, and you should know about the counterreactions each of the parents initially experienced from their family members: Andrew's sisters (and father) were at first crazed when Mom didn't cook dinner. The girls screamed at her; and Dad took her aside and gave her a lecture about her responsibilities. Sara actually ate *less* for a while, prompting Grandma Dorothy to worry more and imply that Ellen was being negligent with her little girl. And when Ian's mom "hit the roof," her husband, who had been after her for years to be tougher with the boy, began defending Ian.

You've got to be prepared for the counterreaction. It is the point where almost every parent *backs down* from even the best child-rearing advice. Because your family is comfortable with the old you, the familiar dance, they'll push to get things back to "normal." They're not mean for doing this, just uncomfortable about having to dance to a different tune. On the other hand, if you're *prepared* for the counterreaction, and you mobilize the other forces within your family, you *can* change the dance, as the following example shows:

> *The mother of seven-year-old Sam had a daily fight with her son about his tardiness—getting up, getting dressed, and getting out to school. Every morning, Sam dawdled. The mother tried to move along the process, handing Sam his clothes, monitoring his routine—all of which made her progressively more angry. Often, the father got involved, too, yelling at Sam, but at the same time getting angry at the mother for babying the boy, and ruining what the father had wanted to be a quiet breakfast time.*
>
> *One morning, after the mother kept a log of the interaction and discovered herself doing the Organizer Dance, instead of getting into the same old fight, she finally did something different—to change the dance. She said to Sam, "I'm losing it. You're not getting off to school any earlier because we fight. So, you take responsibility for dressing yourself. If you're late to school, you're late. It's not my problem." With that,*

*she walked out, went into her room, and closed the
door.*

*We had talked over the fact that she had better be
prepared for the counterreaction. Sam might have
just sat in his room and done nothing; or, he could
have gotten enraged, which is what happened. He
screamed and cried and banged on her door. Again,
the mother might have caved in, getting back onto
the dance floor to do the Organizer or the Cop
Dance. Instead, she put on a favorite tape and listened to it through headphones, so she wouldn't hear
him! That was the toughest part, but she knew that
ignoring Sam wasn't putting him in jeopardy. At
worst, he would have been late again or even missed
school that day.*

*Predictably, when Sam couldn't get a rise out of
his mother, he ran to his father for support. But this
time, the father was also primed in advance, so
rather than get into an argument with his wife—
which always allowed Sam to get away with his behavior and perpetuate the dance—the father said,
"Sam, you heard your mother. Go back to your room
and get ready for school." Within moments, Sam was
back at his mother's door, but this time, he slipped a
note under it: "I'm ready."*

I believe good parenting begins with awareness: when you
understand the unique emotional climate of your family. A
particular dance routine, as habitual and repetitive as it is, may
feel familiar, but it's a habit, a box you're all trapped in. It's not
a connection. Moreover, the dance destroys the empathic envelope, a firm but flexible container that allows you to foster the
connection with your child and, not so incidentally, enrich and
enhance both your child's and your development.

In short, the three C's—compassion, communication, and consequences—help maintain the envelope. Rigidity breaks it. If you realize that you're stuck in a self-defeating dance and everyone else in the family is always dragged onto the floor, change the dance, and be prepared for the counter-reactions. In the end, it will increase your options as a parent, which is what the rest of this book is about.

II

*Everyday Myths
and Everyday Skills*

6

The Myth of Sensitivity
How to Help Your Child Open Up Without Turning Yourself into a Therapist

"How can I get my child to talk to me?" is the single most frequently asked question I hear from parents—not just parents of adolescents, but parents of all school-aged kids as well. It's not that their kids *never* talk. It's that we don't often have particularly "meaningful" dialogues with them. You know how the old scenario goes:

> *Parent:* What happened today?
> *Child:* Nothin'.
> *Parent:* How did you do in school?
> *Child:* Fine.
> *Parent:* What did you do when you went over to your friend's house after school?
> *Child:* Uh . . . we played.

Given the increased need for connection in our over-scheduled, somewhat isolated lives, today's parents are even more aware that their kids don't open up very easily. (I don't think that kids actually talk *less*; I think their parents notice it *more*.) This is what one father told his eight-year-old son in a parent-child workshop: "Son, I don't mean to pry into your life when I ask how school was. I just feel like we've been off in our own worlds all day. I've spent hours commuting in the car. And when I ask you what's happening, it's just a way of making contact again."

This modern-day urgency to communicate also helps explain the popularity of child-rearing books that offer various ways parents can help their kids "open up." They address a real need in modern families. We don't get much of a chance to be together, and after spending so much time lost in our separate worlds, we don't know how to connect.

The problem is, many of the approaches suggested in these books are based on the therapist/patient relationship and then applied to the parent/child relationship. They are the so-called skills of "sensitivity" popularized in the human-potential movement of the 1960s and the "client-centered" psychology of Carl Rogers. The emphasis on sensitivity can also be seen in the enormously effective and popular works of Haim Ginott and Thomas Gordon's *Parent Effectiveness Training*, better known as "P.E.T."

You are probably familiar with the buzzwords of sensitivity: "name," "reflect back," and "validate" whatever your child is feeling. Always remain calm and somewhat neutral. Give your child "space," and don't overwhelm him with your opinions and emotions. Following is an example of such an approach:

> *Alice:* I wish I could be pretty just like Susan.
> *Father:* You're feeling kind of bad.
> *Alice:* Yes. She gets a lot of attention and I don't.
> *Father:* You really would like to get more attention.
> *Alice:* Yes, I really feel bad when I'm not being noticed.

Father: You don't like it when no one notices you.
 Alice: Yeah, I hate it.
Father: You really hate not being noticed.

Please, don't misunderstand me. I think these are great listening skills to teach parents. However, the model of parent-as-therapist has a narrow range of effectiveness. It works best when children are younger and more regularly need you to be the Parent Protector. In fact, if you look at these books, a majority of the examples are about younger children. It is also useful when a child of any age is in a crisis or is very fearful. But the rest of the time, for *everyday* living—with kids who aren't big talkers, or when you don't see each other that much, or when your kid seems more plugged into the TV or pop culture than to you—the "sensitivity" method alone doesn't go too far. Especially nowadays, with children growing up so quickly, they're very savvy. They can see right through any kind of controlled, or preprogrammed, talk. My experience has shown that parents of children over seven have a hard time using these "sensitivity" techniques with their kids unless there's a crisis.

Also, remember what we said about the same old two-step: If we always do the Therapist Dance with our children, we become predictable—and a lot of spontaneity is lost. A nine-year-old told me: "Whenever my mom or dad gets that sweet, monotonous voice, I know they're doing their shrink thing, and I immediately want to clam up."

Twelve-year-old Brian put it this way: "My mom is so into the importance of communication, if I just *open* my mouth, she'll *pounce* on me and want to have a *talk*. It makes me feel like *vomiting*, and I immediately try to get away."

Now that's a pretty violent reaction, so naturally I asked him why he felt so strongly: "It begins to feel like talking is *more important to her* than it is to me."

What are these children saying? That an emphasis on

therapy-like communication just doesn't feel *real* to them. That when we twist ourselves out of shape by being so "sensitive," they don't experience us as genuine. In fact, parents have an equally difficult time with this model. We forever berate ourselves:

"I know I shouldn't have expressed such strong feelings."

"I should have given her more space."

"I blew it. I couldn't listen immediately when he wanted to talk. We won't ever have that conversation."

"We've got to make time for more family meetings to share our feelings with each other."

It almost seems as if having a child who talks to us has become as valued as having a child who is "a good eater" was in our parents' generation. Whenever a mother in one of my workshops says, "I don't seem to have trouble in this area—my kid talks to me all the time," the other parents look at her with a mixture of awe, disbelief, and envy. She instantly becomes an expert on children, much like Muriel Alport in my old neighborhood, whose son Bobby "eats everything I put on his plate!"

Maybe TV contributes to this pressure. Week after week on "The Cosby Show" or "Family Ties," or even earlier on "Father Knows Best," within their allotted thirty minutes' worth of air time, the precocious kids in those families always seem to open up to their parents and come out with the most heartfelt words imaginable. Perhaps the more recent popularity of shows like the "The Simpsons" and "Married . . . with Children" reflects an impatience (and boredom) with families so much more perfect than our own.

Whatever the reasons, the therapy model of parenting creates an empathic envelope that's strained. We parents turn ourselves inside out to be receptive, and our kids respond by clamming up and just wanting us to "get real!"

So forget being oversensitive to a fault. Forget about doing the Sensitivity Dance. The emphasis in this chapter won't be just on getting your kids to open up, but on helping you feel more natural and "real" with them. In the end, *your* comfort will help your child open up and help you feel more effective. But first, you need to be the Parent Realist and develop more sensible expectations about how much talking between parents and kids is actually possible.

Why Parents and Children Don't Have "Conversations"

After listening to thousands of families trying to talk to each other, I've gotten a pretty good idea of the essential reasons parents and kids have trouble communicating. Let's be realistic:

A lot of what kids have to say is boring *to parents!* That may not sound very sensitive, but it's true. Despite the fact that Art Linkletter once impressed us with the idea that "Kids say the darndest things"—which they often do—in everyday life, we're really *not* always interested in what kids actually talk about. Some of it, in fact, is downright repugnant to our ears.

Are you really interested in Teenage Mutant Ninja Turtles, Nintendo, slasher movies, horror flicks, or children's opinions about designer clothes? Even when children talk about the details of peer relationships—such as who's "in" and who's "out" or who said what to whom—it isn't always riveting, especially if you've just put in a twelve-hour day!

Moreover, what's important in your children's lives often goes against the values you've been trying to promote in them. Your child's interests are not only offensive, but you've put energy into teaching her just the opposite sensibility. So how excited can you get about your six-year-old's infatuation with a Metal Head action toy, your nine-year-old son's obsession with Wrestlemania, a huge poster of a half-naked punk rock star on your eleven-year-old daughter's bedroom wall, or your fourteen-year-old's latest idea of putting a red streak in her (or his) hair?

Damon, an eleven-year-old boy I know, talks about nothing but Dungeons and Dragons, which absolutely drives his parents out of their minds. Another parent complained that for a year her fifteen-year-old son was obsessed with the notion of traveling cross-country that summer to attend an Anarchists' convention! Do you really think those parents relished *conversations* about these topics with their kids? Even understanding parents who realize that children one day grow out of these stages, in the meantime don't always want to *listen* to children discussing such things!

There's less time and fewer moments of opportunity for conversation between parents and children. The average child spends an unprecedented amount of time in front of the TV. Through high school it adds up to 15,000 hours—more time than the 11,000 hours they spend in school, and therefore, certainly more time than they spend with their parents! Also, many kids these days are overscheduled: homework, sports, dance, computer, scouting (and that's just on Monday!). Both parents may have jobs and commute long hours day in and day out. Between all of these activities, when you get right down to it, how much time is there to actually *be* with each other?

How much do people talk to each other, anyway? Mothers and fathers don't seem to find much time for conversation either! After ten years of marriage, the average couple talks just a few minutes during the course of a day. There are a spate of books out for parents about improving communication with children, but there are even *more* that relate to adult conversation—how to talk to a lover, how to talk to the opposite sex, how to say what you mean, how to get the other person to "open up."

So it's not surprising that it's hard to have conversations with our kids. It's hard to have conversations with *anyone*. And to find the time to do so. When you factor in the pressure to be "sensitive," no wonder parents are so self-conscious about how they talk and what they say. Given so few opportunities, we want to make sure we do it "right"!

Well, there is no one right dance. In order to communicate with your child, you've got to move back and forth, between being a Parent Chum, a Parent Protector, and a Parent Realist.

Being a Parent Chum: The Art of Parallel Conversation

Being a Parent Chum is appropriate for living with everyday, close-mouthed kids—a category which includes many, if not most, children at least some of the time and kids who were never big talkers to begin with. The Parent Chum mode of communication also works best in situations when a lot of time is spent on logistical squabbles around the house (about the "room," getting ready in the morning, cleaning up common areas, etc.), or when you just don't see each other all that much. What can you do to increase the chances of communicating without becoming a quick-change contortionist?

In order to have everyday conversations with kids you've got to rid yourself of some cumbersome luggage we adults carry around about the proper way to "relate." Think about the best conversations you've ever had with your child. Chances are, they've been talks you didn't *engineer*. They just "happened"—while driving, walking to the school bus, doing the laundry, tucking your child into bed. You probably weren't even looking directly at each other. You weren't concentrating just on each other. You weren't straining to be intimate. And other things might have been going on at the same time. You had what I call a *parallel conversation* with your child. You weren't focused on each other, and the conversation came out of the moment, unplanned and unexpected.

Let's start at the logical and most crucial point—the beginning. What you do or don't do at the outset will either allow the conversation to progress or stop it dead in its tracks.

Say you're taking a short drive in the car (under ten minutes is best, because on longer trips we all tend to drive each other crazy!). You're not looking at each other. The radio is on; nothing is happening between you.

All of a sudden, your child brings something up. As thirteen-year-old Brian put it, the main thing is not to "pounce on it!" In fact, if you've been a "pouncer," I'd recommend putting your kid off a little. You might say, "Wait until this song is over," if the radio is on, or if the route is unfamiliar, "Just a minute, I need to concentrate on these directions." Unlike the Therapist Dance, where you're immediately and unconditionally "there" for your kid, you'd do better to make yourself slightly *in*accessible at first. Don't stop what you're doing immediately because your child decides, "Now I want to talk." You might even turn the volume of the radio *up* a little. Don't worry—the truth is that children are often able to be more intimate when there are distractions around; they don't feel quite as self-conscious or exposed.

However you do it, the essential thing is not to give your child the feeling that the conversation is more important to *you* than it is to him! If you do, he won't feel the conversation is "his" anymore; it somehow belongs to you. This, in turn, may lead to a power struggle. If he feels you swoop down and grab up his words like precious stones, he may clamp down or spite you by not talking or by getting defensive. So give it a few moments and then ask him to go on.

Once the conversation begins, continue to avoid falling into the Therapist Dance—that should be reserved for your child's more troubled moments, not for getting ordinary reticent kids to open up a little. Here are a few vital points to keep you from becoming overly sensitive:

Don't "name" the child's feelings. Kids who are in a panic and don't know what they're thinking need this therapeutic technique. But in ordinary situations, saying to a kid, "You must be feeling angry," or "You must be feeling sad," and so on, almost guarantees her closing up. For example, nine-year-old Eddie tells Mom that the teacher openly criticized him in front of the other kids at school. If Mom responds immediately by saying, "Oh, that must have made you feel very angry," there's a good chance that Eddie will answer, "Uh-huh," and go no further. But what should you do instead?

Ask specific action-oriented questions. Who was there? What happened then? What did you do? What did he say? What did you say? What did he do? How did it end? All questions aim at the action in the story—not just the feelings. You have to have faith that your child's emotions are going to emerge from your *interest* in what happened to her. It has been said that "love is focused interest." Focusing on the action lets her feelings come out naturally, without your editorializing or analyzing.

Don't ask why. This is a big temptation for sophisticated parents. Yet when you get right down do it, even adults who have been trying to figure themselves out for decades don't really know why we do a lot of things! And most kids don't have a clue either. One day, while sorting socks, Daphne told her mother that a group of kids made fun of her at dancing class. The mother was tempted to stop their parallel conversation, sit her daughter down, and ask, "Well, *why* didn't you walk away or tell the teacher?" That probably would have been a dead end in the conversation. Instead, the mother went on with sock sorting and asked action-oriented questions and stayed focused on *what actually happened* in the class.

Respond—*do not hold yourself back*. This is crucial. If you look at the "therapy" model, a parent is supposed to be somewhat laid back, so as not to overpower the child. But, in fact, kids don't feel listened to or "held" until they feel us *respond* to them. This is totally opposite to the idea of giving kids "space" to "have their feelings."

The need for emotional response is apparent, even with younger children. When my daughter was three, I noticed that if she stubbed her toe and I was composed and tried to be soothing, she got more upset. If I said in a therapeutic tone, "That must really hurt," she cried harder—as if I hadn't even said anything. But she actually calmed down if I exclaimed, "Oh, my God, this is terrible. I can't stand it when that happens!" Why? Because I responded in an honest, emotional way, which truly validated the experience better than any therapeutic technique could have.

Likewise, when Daphne finished relating her story, her mother, in a most untherapeutic fashion, expressed her honest reaction: "That's *awful*! I *hate* that girl for picking on you." As soon as Daphne felt responded to with genuine emotions, she felt heard. Sock sorting continued, and later that evening Mom and Daphne sat down to figure out how to handle the problem.

Being a Parent Chum II: If You Can't Beat 'Em, Join 'Em

In the course of normal events, parallel opportunities don't always present themselves. You often have to make an effort to join in an activity your kid loves. The simple act of joining in creates more opportunity for communication than you suspect. The activity serves as a buffer between you and your child (much like being in a parallel position with each other), and conversation slips in without much direct attention paid to it. Your child's interest provides a common language through which she can express herself and through which you can participate naturally.

The problem, of course, is what I mentioned earlier: Who can be genuinely interested in the kinds of things that fascinate our children? And, even if we could force ourselves to get into Nintendo, kids' fashions, violent movies, baseball cards, and so on, what worthwhile conversation will emerge from such preoccupations? Believe it or not, over the years I have discovered that plenty of conversations develop out of these interests. It doesn't require much time either. And it's often the only way to find out what's going on inside your child's head.

When Seth became a rabid baseball fan, his mother realized that the only way she would be able to communicate with him would be to learn a little about the game herself. This was a leap for her since she had always thought sports to be silly. So she made it her business to put aside fifteen minutes every Sunday morning. During this time, she and Seth would go over the week's games together. This not only got them talking, it also made the mother get to know her son better—on his turf.

For example, during their conversations about baseball, Seth always focused on certain players who were considered underdogs and who weren't performing up to their potential. The mother soon realized that Seth, despite his misbehavior in school, might consider himself an underdog, too. As it turned out, she was right: She had him tested and discovered that he had a learning disability. The school had missed it. Seth certainly had no idea about it. But Mom's attention to his interest gave her the necessary clues.

Remember Damon, who was so immersed in Dungeons and Dragons? He was thirteen, both his parents had recently remarried, and Damon was having a hard time adjusting to a new regime in each house. It was chaotic for him, but, of course, he never mentioned a word to his parents. Whenever he was home, he lost himself in D & D.

Ironically, it was his stepfather who was best able to communicate with Damon, because—despite the stepfather's boredom with D & D—he learned some of the rules. The more he learned about the intricacies of the game, the greater the bond between him and his stepson. Even more important, through their conversations about D & D, the stepfather began to learn Damon's beliefs about how an orderly home should be run. He began to realize that the families had been too loose with Damon, that he needed stricter limits. The two homes got together on rules, and Damon had an easier time.

Lilly, ten, had become "clothes crazy." Dad was pretty turned off by her superficial interests and rarely got involved. With my encouragement, he spent just a couple of minutes a week asking her about different clothes she had—what goes with what, why is this skirt special, and so on. It didn't take long for Lilly to lead the conversation from a discussion of clothes to the "in" and "out" groups in fifth grade. For the first time, she shared with her father her worries about fitting in. This kind of talk had always been reserved for her mother.

In each of these examples, the same sequence occurred. The parents put aside their reservations about their children's interest and got involved in the *specifics*, without probing for deep conversation. This took only a few minutes at a time, no more. In the course of talking, the children brought up a great deal about themselves with relatively little effort and virtually no self-consciousness.

Whether it's through parallel conversation, action-oriented questions, your genuine responses, or some small involvement with an interest of your child's, being a Parent Chum does a great deal to help kids open up.

Being a Parent Protector: Communicating During Difficult Times

Parent Chums are great for ordinary day-to-day living around the house. But life isn't always so orderly or neat. It plays tricks on you. Whether we wish it to be so or not, a great deal of communicating happens while your child or you is in turmoil—having a bad time. There is no way around this fact of family life. You just need to be prepared and know that communicating happens . . .

. . . *When There's a Crisis:*   Sometimes it takes a crisis to break down a child's resistance to talking. For example, nine-year-old William and his younger brother, Robert, seven, fought a lot. During one stretch of time, things really got out of hand, until Robert broke down to a teacher one day in school. William came in with his parents to see me, and because of all the pressure on him, he admitted, "I fight all the time with Robert, because if I don't, then instead of screaming at me, Mom and Dad will scream at each other. And I'm afraid they'll get divorced." This incredible statement (which William had felt for years) would never have been expressed without a crisis. His parents were horrified, but they began to realize how much their fighting affected the kids.

. . . *When They Hurt and Disappoint You the Most:*   Kids tend to open up just when they've gone totally against the values you've tried to instill in them. Often, when you're most disappointed in your kids *and* are unable to restrain your honest emotions, the potential for real communication is maximized.

A mother told her children, Adam, fifteen, and Nick, eleven, after they had moved to a very ritzy new neighborhood, "The last thing I want in this fancy neighborhood is to ever be publicly humiliated." *The next day*, the cops pulled up in her driveway! Her kids had gotten caught trespassing on someone else's property—a minor infraction, but Mom was livid. In reaction to her rage and disappointment, Adam and Nick finally admitted that they were angry too, at having been uprooted so many times to follow Dad in his jobs. They had never talked about it before—it only came out when Mom was the most disappointed in their behavior—and let them know it.

That's typical of adolescents, but as seven-year-old Bart's story demonstrates, it can happen with younger kids, too. Bart was caught stealing a toy car from another child's house. His parents were appalled, hurt, and disappointed; they regarded honesty as a very important quality. But out of the angry, upset confrontation that followed, Bart—a very bright, articulate child who kept his feelings to himself— started talking about how jealous he was of his younger brother. The clash and their genuine response seemed to jar his feelings loose.

. . . When You Are Embroiled in a Terrible, Escalating Battle: Thirteen-year-old Anna wanted to go to a party. But her mother thought it was too late to be out. They first got into angry words, which turned into a shouting match, and then it was all-out war. They screamed at one another; Anna threatened to run away. Finally, Anna's mother actually lay down in front of the door, blocking her exit.

It was a horrible scene, but after it was all over, they finally sat down and, in tears, Anna came forth with what really had been bothering her: Having a learning disability, she had to struggle constantly to fit into the high-pressured private school she attended. Unbeknownst to her mother, the other kids in school had been making fun of Anna for being "stupid." And the party was a way of trying to belong. It might have been months before she admitted this. Or, she could have raised a "red flag" by getting into more serious trouble. But the mother/daughter fight became a catalyst that helped them get to what was really on Anna's mind.

As I said, communication in real life often occurs during intense, hot moments—whether it's out of a crisis, being disappointed in your child, or a battle over some detail of everyday life. It's not only important for children to get their feelings out, it's vital for parents to express themselves as well.

I can't stress this enough: When you're in a confrontation with any school-age child (children less than six still need us to be gentle with them), don't act like a therapist. You have feelings, too. Be honest and be real. Don't shield children from your emotions—disappointment, frustration, sadness, anger, upset, whatever. Everyone has to cleanse his or her system, so to speak.

However, in the name of "expressing your feelings," certain lines should never be crossed:

1) It shouldn't become physical.
2) Don't threaten to cut your child off from her friends.
3) Be careful of name calling.
4) Don't humiliate your child in front of friends or, if possible, in front of siblings—to "drive home the point."
5) Don't threaten never to speak to him again.
6) Always take seriously threats to hurt themselves or to run away.

Being a Parent Protector II: Making Space

At the end of a crisis or confrontation, you child doesn't need a Parent Chum. He still needs a Parent Protector. Regardless of how old your kid is, the messy, sometimes frightening situations we all get into with our children require a calmer space afterwards. This is the time to apply the therapy-like skills so widely popularized by most child-rearing experts. Somehow, the explosion just past clears the air and a great deal of communication can now happen. At these times, talk calmly; look directly into your child's eyes. Don't bombard her with many questions or *your* reactions at this point. Now is the time to give her that proverbial "space" and reassurance we've all read about, so she can open up and let you know what she's feeling—what the crisis was about in the first place.

The Parent Realist: Offering Guidance

Whether your child opens up to you through parallel conversations, shared interest, or as a result of an intense crisis, just listening—empathy—is only part of the picture. Another part of the empathic envelope is guidance. Regardless of age, everyday arrogance, or disdain for authority, *all kids want advice*. No matter how close-mouthed or how stubborn, children need to feel your compassion and then your beliefs, to feel held in the empathic envelope.

Yet, how do you get past the paradox of kids who supposedly need guidance, but act so "adolescent" from the time they've begun school? The answer is in the packaging. The Parent Realist needs to package advice in ways that modern kids can absorb.

Be brief. These are highly charged times. Your child has

been brought up on "Sesame Street," commercials, and MTV—like it or not she has an attention span based on sound bites and ten-second commercials. You've probably got three to four sentences to make your point before your kid's mind begins to wander. If you repeat yourself or take too long, you'll lose the window of opportunity. I guarantee your kid won't hear a word—your service will be cut off, the line disconnected, and all you'll be left with is a dial tone and a dead-end conversation.

What are the signs that you're talking too long? She's got that empty expression; her eyes have rolled up to the ceiling. She may appear to be paying attention, but if you look closely, she's actually studying your chin or your nose or your forehead. A good rule, therefore, is never to repeat your advice more than one extra time. Don't be provoked by her lack of reaction into trying to get through.

Keep 'em wanting more. The Parent Realist doesn't linger, doesn't treat each conversation as if it will be the last opportunity to talk. So, *you* be the one to end the conversation. As the old show business expression goes, keep 'em begging for more. Remember the bottom line is that communication shouldn't seem more important to you than it does to your child.

This is easier said than done. Understandably, we want to hold on to the moment. It may have been the first "good" conversation in months; we want to savor it, so we try to make the conversation last just a little too long. And our child then moves farther away again. Therefore, when a talk is over, let it be over. Keep these points in mind *after* the conversation:

Try not to bring up the conversation again. Certain postconversation questions are deadly: "What did you think about what I said?" or "Have you been thinking about what I said?" or "Wasn't that conversation we had yesterday great?" You're looking for trouble, and you'll probably feel hurt when your child looks vacantly into your eyes and says, "What are you talking about?" He won't remember half the time—or he'll tell you that anyway. Regardless of age, children live in the present. They don't relish good communication; they just grow from it.

Don't expect thanks. If you're lucky, when your child is around thirty, and he has his own children, perhaps he *might* thank you, but don't hold your breath! Ironically, the sign that a conversation has worked is that life simply goes on. Your child seems to have forgotten about it. So should you.

Try not to expect greater closeness. As mentioned in Chapter 4, nothing is logical or linear in families. Close moments don't necessarily lead to consistent harmony. So be prepared. The same child who was crying on your shoulder two hours ago could be locked in mortal combat with you two hours later over buying a new video game or favoring a younger brother.

It's unwise to fool yourself into thinking that one conversation—*the* conversation—will make a "big difference" in your relationship. At best, these conversations add up and let children know they have an honest, caring adult they can turn to. Ultimately, the gradual accumulations of open moments in the midst of everyday tension, boredom, crises, and our mistakes, keeps the empathic envelope intact and strengthens the connection between you and your child.

Parent Realist II: Taking Concrete Action

Too often we forget that the final part of a conversation with a child is *action.* And the more tangible your help, the more your child feels the protection of the empathic envelope. The need for action holds for kids at all ages. Don't be fooled by pseudo-mature school-age kids. Just as much as younger kids, they often need us to *do* something after they open up. Here are some concrete actions parents I know took in response to their children:

Eleven-year-old Mark borrowed his older brother's letter jacket for a dance but somehow came home without it. Mark first tried to lie his way out of the tough spot, saying that another kid stole the jacket. His brother went nuts. Eventually, after a long conversation with his dad, Mark admitted that he had been intimidated by the boy and had *given* him the jacket, but he had been too frightened to ask for it back at the end of the evening. Dad, seeing Mark's pain, listened at first—he was the Parent Protector, giving him space and reassurance. Once he heard the truth, and recognizing that Mark was not the type of kid to be careless, he went with the boy to several different houses until they found the jacket. Mark never forgot how his father was able to put aside his own reaction to listen to him and, equally important, to concretely help him solve the problem.

Twelve-year-old Eva was being ostracized by a particular group of kids in school. She, in turn, was taking it out on her mother, while refusing to open up about her problem. Like clockwork, whenever *she* had a bad day at school, her mother got it at home. Finally, Mom blew up. She wept openly at how mean Eva was being to her. As so often happens, after this confrontation, Eva opened up about the school situation. The two of them figured out a plan, the last step being that Mom would contact the ringleader's mother if nothing else worked. In the end, she did have to contact the other mother. The bully didn't become Eva's friend, but at least she stopped harassing her, and that was enough to end the crisis.

Interestingly, the same situation in another household called for the exact opposite concrete action by the parents. Eight-year-old Harold was being picked on by the boys in his class. They were teasing him about being fat and calling him names. Mom and Dad were concerned and had already contacted the school. But it hadn't helped. One day, while driving in the car with his father, Harold told him he felt that being called a "Mommy's boy" was worse than being called fat. He was very upset, and Dad just listened and thought about it.

Later that night, he approached Harold and promised not to interfere unless he was asked. Harold didn't say anything back to his dad, but teachers reported that he was less touchy around his classmates. The name calling slowly eased off.

The Art of "Indirect" Conversation

This section might also be called "How to Have a Conversation with Children Without Their Knowing It!" You can use these techniques—having conversations that are meant to be overheard, using metaphors, and writing letters—with kids of all ages. These strategies will come in handy when you need yet another option of getting your point across.

Let Your Child Eavesdrop   All normal kids are a little sneaky. It's part of their nature; they want to know everything that's going on. Indeed, part of growing up means cracking that secret world of adulthood. Therefore, you can be sure that if your children are in earshot, they'll not only "overhear" what the adults are talking about, they'll absorb the information even better than they would in direct conversation.

So use this to your advantage: If there's something you *want* your child to hear, have a conversation with your mate or a friend. This is especially good with kids in a car. They may seem to be fast asleep in the back seat, but the minute you start talking in a low tone, they'll pick it up. (Remember this, too, when you *don't* want your children to hear you!)

They won't feel the intensity or even humiliation of being directly addressed. The key, of course, is to leave it at that. Don't be tempted to bring up the topic directly at another time.

For example, Samantha had been acting in a very nasty, hostile manner toward her mother, and they had gotten into several screaming battles about it. Nothing her mother said directly seemed to get through. Then one day when Samantha was in the back seat of the car while her parents were driving, Mom said, "I feel so hurt by the way Sam talks to me. I hate it when she calls me 'stupid.' I never want to go out of my way for her when she does that. In fact, I don't even like her at those times." That was all the mother said; she never brought it up again—nor did Samantha ever call her mother "stupid" again.

Use Metaphors   Tell your child a story that has a point, but never mention it directly to the child. In other words, make up a parable about a "hot" topic, using your child's point of experience. The information kind of sneaks up on her sideways, allows her to save face and to process your point without getting into a confrontation over it.

A great example of using this tactic came up with Damon. Eventually, playing D & D became more important to him than doing his schoolwork. The more his marks began to slide, the more attractive the game became. Whenever his parents got down on him about neglecting his schoolwork, Damon said they were being unfair and abusive.

Finally, rather than directly addressing the problem, his stepfather, Chuck, who had become familiar with D & D, asked Damon, "What does a good Dungeon Master [the D & D character that leads the game] do when one of the characters doesn't follow the rules?" Now *that* was something Damon liked to talk about! He told his stepfather, "A good Dungeon Master has to make the characters feel the consequences of their actions. If they don't follow the rules, they have to pay a price. And they have to do what they say they're going to do." Chuck then asked if Damon would play with someone who *didn't* act that way, and Damon said he would, but he'd "hate" it.

Chuck never tried to translate the Dungeon Master metaphor for Damon or drive the point home by saying, "Aha! See? That's what we're trying to do with you." He simply agreed with Damon, and then sometime later came up with the idea of a "contract" that came out of that discussion, specifying the consequences of Damon's not following the rule about doing homework.

Eight-year-old Susie screamed at her mother once too often, "I hate you! I never want to see you again." Rather than scream back or storm out of the room as she usually did, Susie's mother came over to her at a time *in between* confrontations: "Listen, Susie, another mother called me and asked me something. And I want to ask your opinion about what she should do. Her daughter, who's around your age, keeps saying nasty things to her mother, and that hurts her feelings."

Susie told her mother, "She should tell her daughter how it makes her feel." The mother didn't have to say, "I'm really talking about us." Both she and Susie knew what they were talking about. But this kind of metaphor is not only face-saving, it can be a very powerful teaching device.

A few days later when Susie lost her temper again, her mother said very calmly, "You know it really hurts me when you talk to me like that. It reminds me of how my mother used to talk to her mother when I was young, and I can't bear the thought that we might be doing the same thing with each other." Susie stopped being fresh to her mother—maybe not *forever*, but at least that "round" was over.

Write a Letter   When direct talking doesn't work, when you're embarrassed, when you can't stop lecturing, when your child won't talk to you and walks out of the room, when you're stuck in the same old repetitive dance—in short, when no other form of communication works—put it in writing. Letters can be very effective if you remember these three points: Make the letter short. Don't hand it to your child directly; instead, leave it on a bed or dresser in his room. And, above all else, don't mention the letter again.

Caroline's mother wanted to talk to her daughter about sex, but because of Mom's own rather repressed past, she was too embarrassed for a face-to-face talk. At fifteen, Caroline seemed so much more advanced sexually than her mother had been at the same age, and that intimidated Mom even more. Also, the few times she had tried to have such a conversation, Caroline kept walking out on her, saying, "Ma, I know everything I need to know about this."

After Mom gave Caroline a letter in which she expressed her views about sex and relationships, neither of them ever mentioned it. However, two things happened: Caroline gave her mother a store-bought friendship card—which was obviously her version of a "thank you" note. And though Caroline still didn't talk to her mother about sex per se, she began to ask her questions about relationships and talk to her about a boy at school whom she had a crush on.

Increasing Your Strategic Options

In each of the examples in this chapter, not only did parents find ways of increasing their options for communicating with their kids, but also something very wonderful transpired between them. The empathic envelope was reinforced, and the parent/child connection was strengthened.

Obviously, however, in the real world of family living, not all situations are resolved smoothly. Communication gets bogged down because of a dance, tension mounts, and the air gets hotter and hotter until an explosion occurs. The next chapter will cover a painful issue for all parents: "losing it" with our kids—how to prevent it and how to handle it when we do.

7

The Myth of Quality Time
How to Use Everyday Drudgery to Promote Your Child's Growth

This chapter is about trying to be a Parent Chum with your child in the midst of rushed modern living. I don't know who's busier these days, you or your kids. As I mentioned earlier, your children watch an estimated 15,000 hours of TV by the time they're out of high school, a good 4,000 hours *more* than they actually spend *in* school. Add to that the fact that they're involved in after-school sports teams, art lessons, piano, dance, ice skating—you name it. They also spend time hanging out in the park, the playground, the mall, or on the phone. And in the middle of all that, they manage to sandwich in homework as well. To put it mildly, we've unleashed a generation of overscheduled children.

Your life goes pretty much the same way. In fact, when I look at parents—men and women who are supposed to be "models" for their kids—I understand why children think rushing headlong from one activity to the next is normal. All of the stressors that I talk about in Chapter 8 weigh heavily on parents these days. Most of us are overworked, exhausted, and worried about money, health, safety, and our children's future. World-weary and often tense, we're constantly battling the clock, the environment, and the odds. And making time to "be" with our kids often gets lumped in with all our other responsibilities.

Not surprisingly, then, in the "busyness" of our daily lives, we feel we have no choice but to cling to the myth of quality time: It's not the amount of time you spend with your kids that counts; it's the *quality* of that time.

It's hard to know exactly when the phrase "quality time" became a favorite psychological buzzword, but it was probably in the early '70s. The pinch of a plummeting economy and the rising tide of feminism propelled an unprecedented number of mothers into the workplace, forcing them to assume a dual burden. The quality-not-quantity philosophy was clearly an idea whose time had come. It was just what parents, especially mothers, needed to assuage their guilt about being forced to spend less time with their kids. Quality time at least made up the difference—as long as it was better and bigger and more meaningful time.

As is so often the problem, what looked or sounded good on paper or seemed to make sense when you read it in a child-rearing how-to just didn't work out in real life in quite the same way. In fact, the way that elusive commodity is defined, it's virtually impossible for most of us to fit so-called "quality time" into our hectic lives.

Dissecting the Myth

Like so many ideas about good parenting, the notion of quality time actually ends up making parents feel even *more* guilty. To understand why, we have to dissect the myth. Let's look at what most parents believe are the components of quality time:

Quality time needs to be "enriching." Many parents believe the purpose of spending time with kids is to "enrich" them —to somehow make them more competent, as David Elkind observes in *The Hurried Child*.

Quality time should be stimulating. In our world, kids are constantly bombarded by frenetic imagery. Kids *expect* to be stimulated, and parents don't want to disappoint them. We think we have to match it. So quality time translates into a Muppet Baby extravaganza for the young kids, and an action-packed theme park as they get older.

Quality time has to be "special" time and/or it has to take a lot of time; it can never be just "ordinary" time. That, any savvy parent realizes, also translates into *expensive* time! To stimulate and enrich our sophisticated kids we literally pay a high price to connect with them.

Quality time is more important for younger children. Because children seem to be plugged into the pop culture and peer networks at earlier and earlier ages, we underestimate their need to spend time with us. After all, they're straining to get out of the empathic envelope, and they *say* they want to be with their friends. So we assume that "meaningful" experiences with their parents come last on their list.

Quality time means doing something that is interesting only to kids. We are emerging from a thirty-year stretch of child-centered dogma. Everything we do as parents is "for the sake of the children." Not surprisingly, this principle has spilled into the concept of quality time. We feel we have to do things that kids will find exciting, even compelling. It doesn't matter what *we* think of the activity, nor if we turn ourselves inside out to have a good time doing it.

What Parents and Kids Tell Me

How do I know that quality time *isn't* what the myth has you believe it is? How do I know it doesn't have to be enriching, stimulating, expensive, special, and something inherently interesting just to children—and not to you? Because parents and children have told me that quality time

- is rarely scheduled;
- usually grows out of ordinary, everyday events;
- almost never costs anything;
- is often an activity that parents like as much as kids do;
- is something preteens and adolescents end up loving —even if only in short spurts.

No matter how old they are, kids never grow out of needing this kind of quality time. Often, it simply boils down to a series of quality *moments,* moments when everything else is put aside and you can become a Parent Chum to your child. These are the sparks of connection and togetherness that increase children's feelings of security and dependability in a very shaky, helter-skelter world.

Memories Are Made of This

The afterglow of *real* quality time lingers for a lifetime. I can still taste the lemon-soaked raw clams and the tangy red sauce my father used to love when I was a boy. Benny's Clam Bar was certainly nothing special, but my father's love of those slippery little delicacies was. He died twenty years ago, but the thought of those Saturday pilgrimages to Benny's will always be alive in my memory. My mouth waters just thinking about it!

Also vivid is an even more poignant picture. Every time I went to religious services with my father, he gently placed his man-sized palm on top of my little-boy hand for what couldn't have lasted more than thirty seconds. But these fleeting moments imprinted an indelible picture in my memory and strengthened the connection between my father and me. Likewise, the times I remember best were playing "horsey" on my mother's back or when she would tuck me in tightly every night.

Such reminiscences make for sweet moments in later life. Twenty, forty, or even sixty years after the fact, adults revel in thoughts of quality moments with their parents.

> *Barbara remembers falling asleep in the back of the car with her older sister, the two flopping onto each other like rag dolls. Her parents were in the front seat talking quietly about wherever they'd been for the day. Being in the car with her parents was nothing "special"—but it made her feel incredibly safe and protected.*
>
> *Delilah also remembers going on car trips with her parents. She has no idea where they went. She only remembers delighting in the tunes they sang. She remembers the connection everyone felt as they belted out "Take Me Out to the Ball Game."*
>
> *Marty remembers his parents coming into his room every night to say a prayer with him. When he thinks about it, he can still smell his mother's perfume and feel the touch of his father's hand on his shoulder.*
>
> *Melanie remembers the day her father was coming home from the hospital after a serious operation. Walking up the driveway, Dad leaned on her shoulder for support, at that moment making a frail and frightened five-year-old feel like the most indispensable member of the family.*

Spontaneous moments like these are *real* quality times, because they reinforce a genuine connection and add to the strength of the empathic envelope. They aren't particularly stimulating or enriching experiences. Surprisingly, they even reflect the old saying, "The best things in life are free."

Real quality time like this helps to heal the fragmentation that plagues families today. You don't have to make elaborate plans or spend a lot of money to make it happen. Just follow the lead of other parents and children who have created a more secure connection and reinforced the empathic envelope simply by building on ordinary, everyday experiences—by being Parent Chums for just moments at a time.

Bedtime

Bedtime is ripe with opportunities for connection. It's when kids tell me they feel most willing to open up—to talk and to spend quiet, private time just being with their parents. The lights are dim; you're usually not looking directly at the child, so it's a perfect setting for the kind of parallel conversations I described in Chapter 6. In short, it's safer for her to feel a little vulnerable with her mom or dad. And for the parent, too, it's the end of the day—relief is in sight—and it's easier for a busy parent to relax into the moment.

Before they go to sleep, little kids enjoy a soothing goodnight prayer or a comforting "cuddle." This is *not* the time for reminders or criticism. One mother told me that although his back was always facing her, when she lay on her six-year-old son's bed with him at bedtime, a protective arm draped across him, it was the best, and most nonthreatening position for "reviewing" his day.

Just let your child talk, and you'll find out what's important to her. For example, after a long day's outing in England with my four-year-old Leah, when I asked her what her favorite part of the day was, I was shocked. "The shoes!" she exclaimed. "The shoes, Daddy!" Insignificant as it was to me, buying a pair of inexpensive "jellies" from a street vendor meant more to her than all the sights we saw, the buses we took, the people we met. I'd have never known that if it hadn't been for our bedtime ritual.

By the time they're adolescents, the ritual gets turned around: He comes in to say goodnight to you. Sure, he'll balk at first when you tell him to make sure he comes in to say goodnight. But, secretly, he'll love it and remember it as a secure part of life that he can count on. By the way, once children get accustomed to this face-saving way to make a connection, don't be surprised when your twenty-year-old comes home from college years later—and asks for a goodnight kiss.

Morning Time

Or if she bounds into *your* bed on a weekend morning! Many parents and kids have fond memories of Saturday and Sunday morning pile-ons! Some kids use this time to talk about the dreams they just had. But even if the child doesn't wake you, and just lies at the foot of your bed watching TV, it's a secure time, and a connection is made. Like bedtime, it's an opportunity for parallel conversation.

I don't believe there should be any rules about when this morning ritual has to end—that is, when kids are "too old" to come into the parents' bed. I don't think there's such a thing as an official cut-off date when it comes to connecting with your children in this way. As long as *both* you and your child feel comfortable, allow it to happen naturally.

Bath Time

With younger children especially, bath time can be an excellent opportunity to connect with your child. Most often, it happens during the child's bath. Out of that kind of time, good conversations grow organically; they're not forced.

In some families, I've heard that kids love to come into the bathroom when their parents take a bath. It's a quality moment for the parent—probably the first time of the day he's able to relax—and kids know this. If you're comfortable with your child sitting alongside the tub, and you don't feel it disturbs *your* time, it can be another nice way to spend a few quality moments with your child.

This ritual is usually reserved for the same-sex parent. Again, when to stop doing it depends on what's comfortable for you and your child. If your child begins to feel awkward having you there while he's bathing, it's time to leave the room. Or, if you're modest or don't feel relaxed having your child in the room while you bathe, it's no longer right for *you*, so don't do it.

Mindless Chores

By "mindless," I mean anything that's unchallenging, repetitive, and almost hypnotic, like washing and drying dishes, folding laundry, sorting socks, weeding the garden, setting the table. You rarely look at each other while doing such activities, so it's another great time for parallel talk. The exchanges may seem like "nothing" conversations—the sort of unself-conscious dialogues that you hear in such Barry Levinson movies as *Diner* or *Avalon*. But, believe me, for every fifty "nothing" conversations, you'll end up sharing very important moments. The content of these unexciting exchanges between parent and child is not important. For one thing, you're talking as opposed to yelling! Also, the topics that come up often give you valuable insight into your child.

Case in point: Sally's mother was washing the dishes while Sally, age eight, was drying them. They were talking about whatever happened to be on their minds. All of a sudden, out of nowhere, Sally initiated the following conversation:

> *Sally:* Dad's really grumpy a lot, Mom.
> *Mother:* He's worried about business.
> *Sally:* Is that why he's so fat?
> *Mother:* Well, when he worries, he eats much too much.
> *Sally:* I also worry. Does that mean one day *I'm* going to be fat, too?
> *Mother:* I don't know. I hope not. You're beginning to sound like me. You know how I always worry about my weight.
> *Sally:* Is that because you worry a lot, too?
> *Mother:* No, that's only because I like dessert!

After this completely spontaneous, unplanned conversation, the mother felt as if a window had opened up into her child. She began to realize that it wasn't accidental; this often happened around mindless tasks.

Mealtime

If kids tell me that bedtimes are when they're most likely to talk, mealtimes are when they're *least* likely to talk. Also, when I ask parents how many of them have good discussions with their children during meals, only about 5 percent of them raise their hands. In fact, some parents are very honest and say they prefer *not* to have meals with their kids. They'd rather have everyone plop down in front of the TV—and be entertained. Especially if there's more than one child in the family, meals tend to become a time of monitoring, not connecting.

So why include mealtimes here as having the potential for quality time? Because they *can*, particularly if you start when kids are young—*and* you remember that mealtime should *not* be:

- a time for parents to remind kids about their chores.
- a time for parents to offer constructive criticism.
- a time for children to worry that what they say might later be held against them.
- a time for children *or* parents to interrupt each other.
- a time for anyone to take or make phone calls or to be disturbed by other outside interference.

It's also crucial that during meals parents talk about *their* day as well. Conversation should *not* be focused entirely on the children. And when the children do talk about what's happening in their lives, please don't fawn all over them or hang on their every word. Remember: *Conversation should not seem more important to you than to your child.*

Getting the kids involved in mealtime preparation may be helpful as well. In fact, a great deal of meal preparation—setting the table, cutting vegetables, making a salad—falls under the category of "mindless chores," another good opportunity to connect.

In reality most parents *can't* eat with their kids every night of the week and most don't. So it's important to actually *schedule* one or two dinners or a weekend brunch, so that weeks don't fly by without including any family meals.

Going Out to Dinner

It may be surprising—it was to me—but kids of all ages, including adolescents, love to go out to dinner. They remember every course with great relish (pardon the pun). What means most to them is one-on-one time with a parent. Especially if you have more than one child, it's often a good idea to use dinners out as an opportunity to spend time alone with one of them. Of course, remember to observe the guidelines above for mealtimes at home, being particularly vigilant about *not* enforcing "shoulds."

Sometimes going out to dinner with a child can be just what you need to stop a negative dance. Rob's father had been battling for days with him over the typical preadolescent conflicts—homework, his room, his smart-ass retorts. The father really believed that this eleven-year-old kid would stop at nothing to irritate him. Finally, I suggested that the father call a truce and do something unexpected, like take the boy out for dinner. Remembering what I had said in a lecture, about avoiding face-to-face positions, Dad sat next to his son in a booth (a counter would have accomplished the same thing). Instead of getting irritated by his kid's table manners or the fact that the boy talked with his mouth full, as was usually the case, Dad was amazed by what happened: He enjoyed dinner! Why? Because for the first time in weeks, the pressure was off and the dance was interrupted. They actually *talked*—first about game scores, but then about how difficult it had been for both of them over the last week. Rob even asked him afterwards, "Can we go out to dinner again soon?"

Getting Help with a Special Project

Most parents tell me that getting their kids to do chores around the house is a constant battle. That may be true, but even the most obstreperous first-grader or the surliest adolescent is flattered when we genuinely need them. It's a chance to switch roles—put Mom or Dad in the "helpless" seat. Kids love it, because it makes them feel important and useful.

Now, I'm not talking about asking them to vacuum the living room floor because you've had a hard day at work. Although vacuuming might come under the heading of "special chore" if you're rushing around getting the house ready for a party. More often, though, a special project involves asking the child to do something you *can't* do—like dealing with a high-tech problem or doing something else that the child is better at than you are!

Serena, ten, and her new stepmother, Roberta, were struggling to develop a relationship, which is quite typical in an early remarriage situation. However, each time Roberta, who was all thumbs, asked the very mechanically adept Serena for help—to figure out what was wrong with her word processor, to connect her new telephone answering machine, to set up the VCR—it helped fortify their budding relationship. I know how much this meant to Serena because every week when I asked her about her home life, *that's* what she'd report.

When twelve-year-old Andy's overweight father had a false-alarm heart attack that scared him into losing weight, he asked Andy, an excellent athlete, to help him out by becoming his "exercise coach." Andy made a deal with his father that if Dad lost weight, he would have to pay Andy twenty-five dollars for his coaching. Was the money all that important to Andy? No, it was merely a way to disguise a tender feeling—Andy was worried about Dad and wanted to help him. They worked together three times a week. Dad lost weight and, more to the point, found a new way to connect with his son.

Eight-year-old Tommy was extremely neat and orderly, unlike his thirty-five-year-old father, who was a consummate slob. When Dad's new chest of drawers arrived, he asked Tommy for help organizing his clothing. Tommy did a great job and was thrilled because he "helped Daddy," and it was the best time they had together in months.

What makes these times work? The project has to be something *genuinely useful*. You don't have to pay your child anything. You have to curb any impulses to be a back seat driver, though. *Really* let your kid help you, no matter how young she is. Obviously, you have to figure out age-appropriate requests. But even a four-year-old can help you sprinkle spices during cooking and still feel she's an indispensable aid in the kitchen. And with older kids, make sure you really *need* the assistance, they see right through feigned helplessness. At the same time, don't assume that an older child will be unwilling or resistant. Although you're at war with an adolescent, he may still be eager to help out if you *really* need it.

Seth, who was fourteen, had become a reclusive boarder in his own house—a typical "dark" teenager—and his mother was at a total loss. She had tried everything to get through to him, like hanging outside his room, waiting to pounce with all the requests and reminders she had saved up from a week of never seeing him. Of course, the constant lecturing only drove Seth farther into his own world. I suggested that she stop the Pouncer/Organizer Dance and think of something that he might help her with. She was sure that he'd never do anything, since he couldn't even stand to be in the same room with her.

As it turned out, for her job, she needed multiple copies of a form letter printed out and envelopes addressed from a mailing list, which she didn't know how to program. Seth, on the other hand, was a whiz with computers, so she asked him to word process the letter for her. Where she expected him to say no, Seth jumped at the idea. Mother dictated the letter, Seth typed it into the machine. She left the format up to his judgment. Seth did a great job for her, and, not so incidentally, his mood suddenly changed.

I've heard similar "conversion experiences" from other parents of teenagers; we're so used to being in different dances—the Organizer Dance, the Worry Dance, the Cop Dance—asking for your child's help takes them aback, and it changes the dance. When you turn the tables and make the child the expert, it often relieves the tension. Of course, because life always moves along inside the empathic envelope, no change lasts forever, but it's at least momentary relief for us, not to mention a meaningful connection.

Rituals

When it comes to creating a connection with your child, rituals should be high on the list. No one could make this point any better than eight-year-old Mandy, who was making candy caramel apples with her mother for Halloween and said, "This is really good family bonding, isn't it? Let's be sure to do it again before Thanksgiving and Christmas."

In our fragmented world, rituals are absolutely necessary to maintain the safety of the empathic envelope. Especially today, everything around the family that once stood for security has been diluted or destroyed. So we have to firm up the envelope ourselves and make it more dependable. We can't always count on outside structures—the church, the neighborhood, the extended family—the burden is on parents. Given all the stresses and strains of modern life, then both the smallest expectable everyday routine and the largest, most significant rituals represent major quality time.

We sometimes underestimate the importance of rituals, until we don't have them anymore. And then we feel that "something's missing" in our lives. We also wrongly assume that because kids seem to fight them as they get older, they don't want to partake in rituals anymore. Don't believe them.

It might be something small, predictable, and mundane, like Sunday morning brunch (even though you eat the same thing week after week). It might be the bedtime story that a parent reads every night. A father I know made up his own adventure story, and like a soap opera, he kept it going for months. His kids loved it.

One family had a mandatory time together every Saturday afternoon. They didn't plan what they were going to do; they just congregated in the living room. One week they played Trivial Pursuit; another week they looked through the newspaper and decided to go to a museum. Some weeks it just didn't click, and everyone retreated to his or her own room, but at least family time allowed something to develop, and when it did, the good feelings lasted for days.

The bigger rituals—religious rites and/or holidays—are equally important today. In a world where it's so hard to connect, these occasions may be some of the only times you're actually *together* and can forge greater connections. Little kids obviously love these special times, but don't underestimate how much older kids—even when they object to them—still need to partake in meaningful rituals.

The way you celebrate may have to change as kids get older. When your child is young, she may not be able to sit through long ceremonies, so shorten the ritual. Of course, you may come up with the same attention-span problem when she hits adolescence, too. Or she'll complain that she wants to hang out with her friends, so let her bring a friend to a holiday dinner. The important point is that while you might adapt a ritual to keep it going, if it's important to you, *stick to it*—no matter what your child says.

Sometimes the strength of a time-worn ritual can be a

surprising asset when your child hits the double digits, and becomes a preteen. For several years, thirteen-year-old Sandy had been going to a homeless shelter with his mother on Thanksgiving mornings to work in a soup kitchen. They were in the middle of having a horrendous fight that year, but Mom insisted that they not give up their tradition. As in years past, they went to the shelter and gave out the dinners as they had always done. The fighting continued—now over the fact that they were doling out meat (Sandy had recently announced he was a vegetarian), but the ritual changed the dance between them. It provided a connection in a time when they were barely on speaking terms.

Parent's Little Helper

This is one area that's bound to increase the connection between parent and child, and yet few of us ever think of it: bringing kids to your place of work so that they can observe first-hand what you do. With parents spending longer hours at work away from home, what they actually *do* for a living is a mystery to many kids. Parents may not realize this until it happens by "accident."

One day when Rebecca, seven, was sick—not seriously, but enough to keep her out of school—her mother was out of town on a business trip, and her father, George, couldn't get a last-minute sitter. He had no choice: He had to take his daughter to the office with him. As it turned out Rebecca was a pleasure. She spent the day coloring, using the photocopying machine, and charming George's co-workers. She also got to see what Daddy's office looked like and what he did while he was there; and she met the people George worked with. Despite her bad cold, she came home that day in the best of moods. She felt connected.

George had inadvertently stumbled on a new way to enhance his relationship with Rebecca. Realizing how important this was, from then on every so often when Rebecca had a day off from school, he took her to the office. She developed real relationships with his colleagues, too, which also strengthened the father/daughter connection.

Kids always tell me how much these types of experiences mean to them. Ethan's mother was a music teacher and a critic, and from the time Ethan was old enough to sit through a recital—around seven or eight years old—his mother began to take him to hear previews. They talked about music, bought records together, went to concerts. Not surprisingly, Ethan developed a real interest in classical music that grew over the years and enhanced the mother/son connection.

Jackie's mom was in the shoe business, and every year she took Jackie to the shoe show. Now, you might ask, what would a nine-year-old *do* at a shoe show? It doesn't matter. Jackie got to be with her mother and spend *real* quality time. Jackie was able to see what her mother did and to watch her in another role, interacting as a businesswoman with adults other than Jackie's father. Opportunities such as these are very important for modeling adult behavior—not just parental behavior—for your kids.

Doing Things You Hate

Although I said that quality time doesn't necessarily mean standing on kiddie show lines every Saturday or doing only what interests the children, every now and then it's important to cast your own taste aside and do something you would never dream of doing if it weren't for your children. Every once and awhile you share your children's passions and enter their world. It's a way to bridge the chasm between your interests and theirs—otherwise your worlds are too far apart.

Doing something you hate is especially useful when you're locked in a negative, escalating cycle. Howard, nine, was on his mother's bad side because he had been particularly relentless in picking on his five-year-old brother, Peter, calling him names, taking his toys, hitting him. Feeling badly for the younger child, the mother invariably got into fights with Howard about his bullying behavior. They were at each other's throats constantly.

I suggested that regardless of what was going on between them—just *once*—the mother should do something with Howard that he absolutely loved, even though she hated it. In Howard's case, the passion was wrestling. Of course, it was excruciating for the mother to be at a wrestling match, but at least she was *there*. She could see first-hand what her child was so enamored of—the arena, the bout, the stars Howard read about in his wrestling magazines.

After that, for a few days at least, the air was cooled down between them. So the mother decided that she'd take Howard to other wrestling matches—not many, mind you— maybe two or three times a year. Their relationship started to improve, and interestingly, each time after they went off together, Howard's fighting with his younger brother noticeably lessened.

Davy loved Nintendo, but it was driving his mother crazy. He procrastinated about doing *anything* else—playing outside, doing his homework, taking care of chores around the house, seeing friends. His mother lectured him constantly about "bettering" himself, rather than playing "that stupid game," but Davy just told her to leave him alone.

I asked the mother if she knew anything about Nintendo, which, of course, she didn't. I suggested that it might tone down the Cop Dance if she were able to show even the slightest interest in the game, and every few weeks try to play it with Davy for fifteen minutes or so. My sense was that even a little bit of interest would go a long way. At a loss for anything else to try, she finally asked Davy to teach her the game.

Did she like it? No, not particularly. Did she ever get very involved? No, she spent only a few minutes every now and then. But she actually began to understand something more about Davy's interest in Nintendo. More important, Davy told me that it meant a great deal to him. Those sporadic games were important moments of connection despite the battles.

The father of ten-year-old Megan was appalled by his daughter's values. She was obsessed with "designer" clothes; he hated it, and he found himself pulling farther and farther away from her. His wife reported to him that on shopping excursions, Megan battled with her constantly over the fact that Megan had to have the right "label." Meanwhile, the father stood on the sidelines, disgusted and removed.

I suggested that they change the family dance. Despite his disapproval of her taste, the father should take Megan shopping instead. He allotted a certain amount of money which he and Megan had agreed upon in advance. Megan told me that at first it felt "weird" to go shopping with her father, but eventually they developed a bond over these twice-a-year expeditions. She shopped *differently* with her father; they developed a common "language" out of the experience; and the fights over clothing began to de-escalate in that household. Also, the father/daughter bond improved.

And a Good Time Was Had by All

You can see the common threads in these experiences. Quality time doesn't have to be a lot of time—a hug, a pat, a reassuring chat at bedtime; an experience fifteen minutes once a week; an event once every few months. Quality time doesn't need much more time than that. And it's not about high stimulation or special effects. It's about the everyday, mundane, and often unplanned events in life that can lead to greater connection.

Equally important, quality time is a DMZ in the war between the generations—where you call a truce to the inevitable battles between you and your child. It's free of criticism, lectures, complaints; in short, it's not a time for doing old dances. If a dance begins—say, you start being a cop or a teacher instead of a Parent Chum—there's no point trying to have quality time. So you might as well just stop.

Children repeatedly tell me that they most enjoy activities that they see their parents enjoying, too. They don't need Chuckles the Clown; they don't need you to twist yourself out of shape. During moments of real quality, on the contrary, parents and children are *both* having a good time. Despite the generational differences, they're on the same level, sharing an event from their different-age perspectives. Unlike other times in the parent/child relationship, you are neither controlling your child nor acting as if you are superior. In other words, quality time brings equality into the relationship.

Finally and most important, one of the often-overlooked reasons that quality time is so important is that *it gives something back to us parents*. That's why most often it has to be something that you like. Even a few precious moments of quality time can keep you going for weeks. It's sustenance for all of those exhausting, draining, stressed-out times that you spend with your children. In fact, the way I see it, you don't have to wait for old age for your kids to be a comfort to you, as the saying goes. There are an infinite number of opportunities to create these connections with your children *now*.

How to Protect Quality Time

It's very important to understand what quality time is *not*—so that when you see it going badly, you can put an end to whatever you're doing. For example, if you're at the dinner table, giving your child a bath, or doing a mindless chore, when you feel yourself step into the same old dance, when you are distracted, or when you slip into criticizing, reminding, hassling, haggling, then you, as the parent, have to take the responsibility to move on. Stop whatever you're doing. Put an end to the activity. When those old dances get going, not only won't you be sharing quality time, you'll feel disappointed as well, because it started out as something supposedly "good."

It's not anyone's fault when quality time turns into something else. Either one of you can get into a familiar dance. If a fun activity like going out for dinner always turns into a time of your offering constructive criticism, can you blame a child for having an aversion to being in intimate places with you? On the other hand, if you go out to dinner one-on-one with your child, and your child nevertheless misbehaves, I'd suggest not doing it for a while afterwards. Tell your child, "I don't enjoy doing this when we fight, so we're not going to do it for a little while. We'll try it again in a few months, and if it works, great. If it doesn't, we won't."

Never ask about quality time afterwards. Don't bring up how great it was, or at least don't be excessive about it. You can mention how much you loved it, but the more you do, the more your child feels the pressure to tell you how much he loved it, too—and that detracts from the experience. The best thing is to just have the time, be in the moment, do your best *not* to make it a struggle, and don't bring it up again, except as an offhand comment that you liked it. Cherish and relish those moments secretly, in the privacy of your own mind, or share the feeling with your spouse or a friend. It may take your children thirty years or more to admit it, but trust me: They love it, too. Just think back to whatever precious moments you shared with your own parents, when all problems were temporarily put aside and you were chums for just a little while.

The Myth of the Angry Parent
What Your Anger Is Really About and How to Cut Down on "Losing It"

Why We Lose It: The Anger Hypothesis

Angry mothers, furious fathers, parents in a rage over kids who don't listen. Countless books, magazine articles, and talk shows that address parents' anger. The experts help us set limits, discipline more effectively, stay in charge. Reading between the lines, it would appear that to be a parent is to be forever angry.

Of course, there's some truth to that. Almost every day, we *do* find ourselves angry or annoyed at least some of the time—especially if we have more than one child. And, more often than we like, we end up "losing it" with our kids.

Despite our good intentions, losing it disrupts the connection with our kids, especially with the younger ones, and strains the envelope. I've asked hundreds of children of all ages, "If you could change *anything* about your parents, what's the one thing you'd pick?" Their first response is almost always some version of, "I just wish they wouldn't yell at me as much."

The question then is, why do we yell at our kids so often?

Are the articles and books on the subject right when they point to frustration about discipline and "not getting through" as the main culprits? In many situations, that seems like the most obvious answer.

You've all been there: The kids start fighting in the back seat of the car while you're driving. A minute ago, they were giggling; now they're hitting, insulting, each blaming the other for "starting it." You warn them to stop, but it doesn't make a dent in their behavior. Your words have virtually no impact. After several minutes (that feel like hours) of being bombarded by their shrieks and their "he said/she said" accusations, you just can't take it anymore. So you blow up. You say things you didn't mean to say. You even whack the hand of the child who happens to be sitting within reach.

Clearly, angry frustration is a major cause of losing it. However, after talking to thousands of parents every year and watching how families operate, I think it's just the tip of the iceberg. I have also become convinced that getting better at discipline goes just so far toward reducing frustration and anger around the house. It helps, but it doesn't do the whole job.

In truth, as long as we subscribe to the myth of the angry parent and think of parents as essentially angry, frustrated people who are not able to control their children, the more we don't do justice to the complexity and poignancy of being a mother or father.

I have witnessed the touching drama of parenthood for twenty years. Almost every argument that starts along the anger-frustration continuum ends up with parents expressing something quite different:

> *"I feel exhausted. I can't keep up with you."*
>
> *"I feel taken for granted when you're so inconsiderate."*

"I feel rejected when you don't kiss me hello."

"I feel scared—you always seem at the edge of being out of control."

"I feel left out between you and your mother."

"I feel depressed that I can't give you more of what you want."

"I feel totally confused. I don't know what to do a lot of the time."

"I feel lonely. We're becoming strangers."

"I feel suffocated. You never leave me alone."

It seems natural for children, close friends, spouses, or lovers to have feelings like these. But we're not used to thinking of mothers and fathers having such *unparentlike* feelings. Yet explosions are frequently a dramatic signal that just these unparentlike emotions are working beneath the surface.

To cut down on losing it, then, we need to see ourselves not just being angry, ineffective, manipulative, depriving, guilt-provoking, and selfish—as traditional psychology has so often labeled parents (especially mothers). Instead, we need to see ourselves as three-dimensional human beings, subject to the extraordinarily wide range of emotions that come with child rearing.

The traditional, somewhat negative view of parents, which does absolutely nothing to help us cut down on explosions, is compounded by an unfortunate fact. Most well-intentioned parents understand much more about their children's complicated needs than about their own psychological condition. So, because many parents have such a narrow view of themselves, I have included a half dozen less-talked-about reasons that mothers and fathers lose it with children.

The Exhaustion Factor

One of the primary reasons we lose it is the exhaustion factor. As a parent and a psychologist, I am stunned by the fact that child-rearing books rarely mention one of the most common states of parenthood: sheer exhaustion. Only recently have I seen this phenomenon talked about in print. It was most eloquently reported in the best-selling book, *The Second Shift: Working Parents and the Revolution at Home.* Sociologist Arlie Hochschild spent several years observing couples in which *both* partners had jobs. She looked at who does what *after* work—on the "second shift," as she refers to it—which includes not only child care, but everything connected to managing and maintaining a household.

The onus definitely falls on women's shoulders. Among other trends, Hochschild noted that when you consider that over 70 percent of all mothers work outside the home, as well as assuming the greater part of the household and primary child-care responsibilities, it adds up to their working *an extra month of twenty-four-hour days per year!*

This is not to say that men don't get exhausted, too. It's clear that all parents today, but especially mothers, are overburdened and sometimes overwhelmed by their roles. And to ignore the impact of the exhaustion factor is to overlook one of the most devastating realities of modern family life: At times, we are simply too tired to be civil and reasonable toward our children.

The Domino Effect

It's also unrealistic to think that the moment we cross the threshold into the family sphere, we can simply leave the frustrations and complexities of our work lives at the door. As the old story goes: The boss yells at the husband; the husband comes home and argues with his wife; the wife yells at the kid; and the kid kicks the cat.

This domino effect is behind a lot of yelling and screaming in family life and is another reason we lose control and dump on our kids. A father comes home after his supercritical employer has been riding him hard all day long and demanding more of his time and energy. He's spent and dejected—he already feels he's giving the company his "all." Thirty seconds into the door and his exuberant ten-year-old starts pestering him to come outside for a catch, but Dad is in no mood to play. Feeling rejected but still desperate for his father's attention, the boy continues to badger. Is it any wonder that Dad finally explodes? It's no fault of the boy's, nor is it anything that the child is doing. He is simply the straw that broke the camel's back.

The Juggling Phenomenon

To be sure, these days, the "camel's back" is more burdened than ever before, which brings me to the third important factor in why parents lose it: We are all jugglers. We are fragmented, hurried, overwhelmed. As Arlie Hochschild points out, mothers, especially, are often doing three things at once: holding down a job, caring for the kids, and running the household.

Juggling is particularly trying and tense during the transitions of the day, which is when explosions tend to occur. Imagine this scene: You're a working parent—a mother *or* a father. You've just commuted home. There's been an hour delay due to a traffic jam or a late train. You have to make an important presentation the next day, so you also brought work home with you. Two children engulf you as you walk in the door. You remember that a leaky faucet needs repair, that you're running low on toilet paper, that the kids are due for their dental check-ups. You haven't seen your spouse, who's been on a business trip—but neither of you manages to get a word in edgewise, because the kids are bombarding you with their demands. You don't know which needs should be met first—the children, the maintenance of the house, or your spousal relationship.

In short, you're a perpetual-motion machine, juggling dinner while you're on the phone, coordinating schedules with your spouse while you fold the laundry, sewing on a button while trying to pay attention to your eight-year-old, who's disappointed about not getting the lead in her school play. At any moment, a child's demand can cause the machine to "tilt." Anger is only the most visible manifestation of an underlying reality: We live rushed, unmanageable, crazy lives —and our outbursts are the expression of this fact.

The Rejection Factor

Children hurt our feelings—by doing and saying cruel things, and, sometimes, by simply growing up and needing us less. It's such a reality of parenting, and yet I rarely hear it mentioned—except by parents when they admit it to me privately. We all pretend that parents are supposed to be mature about being hurt by our kids. Aren't we, after all, the *grown-ups?* Of course, but it's impossible not to feel hurt, at least occasionally, by a child's withdrawal, insults, threats, or lack of consideration. Reacting to these has nothing to do with maturity. It's only human.

Indeed, the things kids say and do *are* at times hurtful, sometimes intentionally so. One working mother—a typical juggler—had nevertheless made the time in her busy day to bake a "perfect" birthday cake for her nine-year-old. Just as the party was about to begin, her daughter threw the cake onto the floor—on purpose. Apparently, the little girl was angry about something that was going on with one of her friends. Mom was not only in a rage, her feelings were terribly hurt as well. And why not? She had put in thought, time, and energy, and it seemed as if her child couldn't have cared less. So beneath Mother's anger was hurt, and this hurt propelled her to go wild in the face of her daughter's behavior.

Likewise, a father complained to his wife after their six-year-old went to bed, "He only asks you to come in and say goodnight, not me." Although part of him was relieved at not having to do the bedtime ritual, he was also hurt. The next day, Dad lost his temper with the child over a seemingly minor incident. The hurt feelings from the night before had unwittingly translated into his subsequent "bad temper."

A mother who was a member of one of my parenting groups described the rejection factor rather poetically: "I feel very wounded by my thirteen-year-old. My heart aches from this loss. It's as if I no longer have the chum I had all those years before—this cheerful kid who always wanted to do things with me, who was affectionate, who thought I actually had something to say." From five to fifteen, the potential for hurt as well as joy is always there for the parent who cares.

Ghosts from the Past

Many of us were yelled at as children; we were made to feel small; we were verbally criticized. Some of us were physically abused. Almost all the research shows that it's hard to break the flow of negativity from one generation to the next. So if our parents regularly "lost it," we have to work extra hard to be different with our own kids. We may try never to let these old ways surface. We may even try to be just the opposite, but, despite the best intentions, under stress, we can forget. Our voice takes on the same critical tone we heard as children. We find ourselves saying just those things we swore we'd never even think. Those are frightening moments, to see the past repeat itself. This phenomenon has little to do with anger per se and much more to do with the "Dances Our Parents Taught Us" that I talked about in Chapter 5. We are creatures of conditioning, to our surprise often imitating exactly what happened long ago with our own mothers and fathers. Anger is only a very loud signal that we're doing an old dance.

The Manipulation-to-Connect Game

To be sure, easy kids, difficult kids, *all* kids manipulate parents. And that in and of itself is often what brings us to the edge of losing it. They purposely provoke us, push our buttons to "get a rise," or defy a request that one last time, knowing we've just about had it. Is this manipulation because children are mean-spirited or spiteful? No! The way I see it, our children are often making a last-ditch effort to penetrate that wall of preoccupation and exhaustion around us. In many instances, I believe, manipulation is really a child's fumbling attempt to *connect*. Unfortunately, that's not always what happens.

For example, a nine-year-old told me that when his father came home from the office in a "grumpy" mood, he would try to cheer him up by playing with him. When Dad was unresponsive or brushed him off, the boy admitted he would then attempt to get his father angry about something—not to cause the father to totally lose it, but just enough to inspire a reaction. Sometimes, however, the boy went just a little too far and the father would explode. "Why?" I asked him, "do you continue to do this when it backfires?" After some thought, this articulate child answered, "Because I'd rather see him mad than depressed."

An eleven-year-old told me that he'd provoke his mother

by picking on his younger brother when he thought Mom and Dad were fighting too much. He was frightened they would end up divorced like so many of his friends' parents.

A seven-year-old girl would wander into her older sister's room and intrude on her privacy. This often created a huge family fight with everybody yelling at everybody else. "Why in the world would you do this?" I asked her. Her first answer: "I'm bored." Second: "Nothing's going on." Third (and most to the point): "Nobody's talking to each other."

Do children really say these things? Absolutely. But do they think ahead about their actions? Absolutely *not*. They're reacting intuitively to a disconnection they experience or a worry they have about someone in the family. Again, "losing it" is a signal that something much more important is going on.

Kids manipulate their parents to get a reaction. They don't want their parents to lose it, but they *do* want to connect. What often happens, however, is that they push the parent too far, and the manipulation backfires.

When Losing It Doesn't Work

Considering all that parents live with—exhaustion, rejection, stress, juggling, ghosts from the past, and manipulation—it's not hard to see why anger is only a small part of the story when it comes to "losing it."

Ironically, an explosion is often the signal that a misguided attempt at connection is happening—kids and parents trying to jump the chasm of disconnection in our daily lives. Sometimes, in fact, it seems that an explosion *is* the only thing that can break through the complexities of modern life. And it *looks* as if it works. Momentarily, at least, the chasm is closed; your child listens; you have an intimate conversation afterwards; and things get better.

At best, however, losing it is a narrow way to connect. It is the language of families in which parents don't know how tired, hurt, and neglected they may feel. Moreover, if losing it becomes a repetitive pattern—if it's the primary form of connection—like any dance that crops up too frequently, it ultimately gets tuned out. We keep missing each other, and the empathic envelope is weakened.

Clearly, no book is going to change the circumstances of your life and your personality so much that you won't feel harried, pressured, disappointed, exhausted, or pushed around anymore. No book will forever eliminate those moments when your kids' demands come up flush against your own limitations and vulnerabilities as a human being. But, in the meantime, it *is* possible to cut down dramatically on the number and intensity of explosions around the house.

If you find that your losing it is becoming a repetitive pattern; if you find yourself screaming names that you can't take back afterwards; or if in any way you violate the "beyond-which-you-shouldn't-go" rules I talked about in Chapter 6; if exploding doesn't settle the issue that started the argument in the first place; if you don't feel closer afterward; or if you're dealing with a younger child who needs a calm Parent Protector, you may need to change the Losing It Dance. Below is a four-step method that will help you prevent losing it with your kids.[1] But remember: Anger is usually only the symptom, a signal that something else is going on. The following method will *not* heal the wounds that all parents feel under the anger, and that few talk about. But it will help calm life down in the empathic envelope and set the stage for the kinds of connecting with our children that this book is about.

---

[1] This is an adaptation, for use with children, of a technique I learned originally from Betty Carter, director of the Family Institute of Westchester.

Step 1: Detect Early Warning Signals

We usually focus totally on our kids—what *they* can tolerate, what goes on with *them*—and we often forget to look inside ourselves and ask, "What signals go on *inside me* that always precede my losing it?" Everyone has these signals. What are they?

Here are some that I've heard from parents: My jaw tightens. My voice gets higher and thinner. I start talking faster. I get a knot in my stomach. My heart beats faster. I start feeling a pressure in my chest. My breathing becomes more shallow. I clench my fist. My thoughts become scrambled.

The important thing is to stop being child-focused; stop scrutinizing your child's behavior and look instead at what's going on inside *you*. Remember: This self-awareness must happen *before* you get too angry. It can't happen when you're already losing it and are exploding. That's too late.

An example of these dynamics emerged with Nicholas, age ten. Whenever he was having trouble with his homework, he would get crazed and not want to show it to his parents. Of course, his parents would become upset, because they felt it was their responsibility to check his work. Before long, they'd become embroiled in a full-scale battle with each other. In an attempt to calm things down, Mom and Dad would focus their attention on *Nicholas's* behavior. They'd try to figure out how much to push him to see his work and what to do to head off *his* reaction. In other words, they were entirely concerned with keeping *him* from cracking.

I told them they had to shift the focus to themselves and figure out, "How much can we push him before *we* crack?" I added, "Only ask him for the homework as many times as *you* can stand it —without losing your temper." In time, they were able to learn to predict the early warning signs of their own explosions: Nicholas's mother said her temples started throbbing; his father noticed that his hands became clammy and his heart rate increased. When they felt these signals, they knew it was time to stop asking for his homework; they were getting too close to blowing up. Knowing themselves in this way was far more important than figuring out when Nicholas would crack. From then on, whenever either of them felt the signs of losing it coming, they stopped pushing.

Here are some questions that parents often ask about this step:

Why should I focus on me? After all, many parents reason, aren't I trying to teach my child to control himself? As I've suggested, we're much too child-focused and therapy-oriented in our parenting. As a result, we've lost our center. We ignore how *we* feel in many situations. Focusing on our own reactions reverses this process. And the lesson of self-control is *exactly* what you're trying to teach your child. He will learn from your example.

I don't think I have early warning signals. A lot of parents believe that they explode so fast there's no time to stop it. But I've almost never seen a person who has absolutely no warning. The trick is to keep focusing back earlier and earlier in the interaction. Keep a pad and pen around the house. Write down the very first body signal you notice when you're starting to heat up. Nicholas's dad found his heart pumping faster at the point when he just *saw* Nicholas doing his homework. He *already* began to get upset, because he expected the worst. It was at that moment that Dad needed to remove himself from the dance. How does that happen? That's where Step 2 comes in.

Step 2: Explain Your Feelings—and Exit

Announce to your child what's happening inside *you*. Again, you're not focusing on your child; you're saying, ''I'm beginning to lose it, and I don't want to." You can say whatever feels natural in your household. For example, tell her that your stomach has a knot in it, and that's always the way you feel before you blow up at her. Whatever you do, try not to say something like, "If you don't stop that, I'm going to lose it." That would be putting the responsibility on the child, instead of on *you* where it belongs.

Then you say, "I have to leave until I calm myself down. I'll talk to you when I feel calmer." Regardless of how your child responds at that moment, walk away. It's crucial that you remove yourself from that physical setting, whether it's by going into another room or by going out the door.

At this point, if you're like so many other parents, you'll think this won't work for you. One of the following questions will pop into your head in the middle of the confrontation:

Won't I lose face if I walk away? No, when you lose control and rupture the empathic envelope, you've lost control of the process and then you *are* losing face. That kind of losing control is worse than losing face. On the contrary, when you admit, "I feel myself losing it, and I want to stop," you are showing your child that in the face of strong emotion, you are nonetheless taking an active stance toward managing yourself. You're not losing face, you're modeling good emotional management for your child.

Won't my child's feelings be hurt if I just walk away? Yes. Your child's feelings will probably be somewhat bruised. He's not used to your abruptly ending this dance, and his first reaction could well be outrage, disbelief, mockery, or fear. Because of this, he may up the ante—provoke you— and try to get into the same old explosive dance everyone's used to. But don't give in. He will be even more hurt by the emotional bruises that inevitably result from your losing it.

Won't my child just follow me if I walk away? Absolutely. Almost all kids end up following their parents. This is why it's important you go to a place that your child can't get into. Try a bedroom or bathroom where you can actually close and *lock* the door.

Won't locking my child out traumatize him or her? In all the years of my suggesting this, I've never heard of any children falling apart as a result! Be prepared, however—she may bang on the door and scream as loud as she can. It may sound like the end of the world outside the door. But the message a closed door sends is ultimately reassuring. It says to your child, "I'm going to try to calm myself and nurture myself, and you're going to have to respect that."

When is it unadvisable to leave? You have to follow your own instincts. If you are at all worried about physical injury to your child, *don't* try this. Generally, I don't recommend this technique for children under first grade.

Why shouldn't I make my child leave? First of all, you want to focus on yourself and take care of yourself. Second, by sending your child out of the room, you potentially set up yet another power struggle. What if she says, "No, I'm not going"? Do you really need to aggravate yourself more by now battling over a new issue?

Why should I have to feel trapped in my bedroom or bathroom as a way of dealing with my child? Don't think of it as being "punished." Think of it as preparing yourself to take Step 3.

Step 3: Calm Down, Nurture Yourself

While you're in the other setting, away from your child, do whatever it takes to calm your insides and soothe yourself. Some parents take a quick shower and (a few) manage a relaxing bubble bath. For others, hitting a pillow helps diffuse their anger. Do anything that works. Complain about the incident to a best friend or ventilate the feelings to your spouse. Knit. Read. Clean out a closet. Get into any kind of mindless activity that feels self-soothing.

Also be prepared for the counterreaction. Particularly if you've been in the Losing It Dance for a long time, once you walk away, your child will probably push you to see if she can get back to what's familiar. In other words, she might get worse before she gets better, which is why I instruct some parents to keep audio headphones handy to drown out the yelling. Listen to your favorite music or, if you're into it, get one of those New Age relaxation tapes— the sounds of the ocean or a waterfall. Depending on your child's age, maturity, and how much she's been left alone in the past, you may even decide to leave the house. Simply tell her where you're going and that you'll be back after you feel calmer.

How long do you stay in your room or out of the house? As long as your schedule allows, or until you are calm, whichever comes first. Of course, you always have to make a judgment—both whether your child can "take" it and also whether you can withstand your own new behavior! Obviously, if this tactic puts your child in any real or potentially lasting danger, then *don't do it.* But most of the time there's no risk involved. The question may be more a matter of whether *you* can tolerate leaving the scene. If it makes you nervous, don't stay away too long. That will only make you feel more upset and, therefore, defeat the purpose of nurturing and calming yourself.

Clearly, it takes practice to implement any new parenting technique, and you probably want proof that it works. So, at first, just leave for a few minutes. When you see that the same child who screamed for five minutes miraculously calmed down after you were out of sight, you'll undoubtedly feel better about trying this method for longer periods of time.

Step 4: Modeling Good Behavior

If you employ this technique and see it through, I guarantee you will get your child's attention. Equally significant, you're also saying to your children, "Controlling and nurturing myself is important to me." So not only do you stop the escalation, you also provide a model of behavior—so children can learn how to respect and control themselves as well. It doesn't usually happen right away, and children are often reluctant to accept the "new" you. But once they realize that even upping the ante can't get the old dance going, they have no choice: Mommy and Daddy are controlling their behavior, I'll control mine, too.

When seven-year-old Amy got no response from her mother, even though she screamed and cried and threw herself against the mother's bedroom door, she finally slipped a misspelled but nevertheless well-intentioned note under the door: "I'm sory." Even with such a young child, Mom's simple expression of her own feelings and her leaving the scene paved the way for a meaningful and different kind of exchange.

Likewise, when nine-year-old Timmy kept badgering his overworked father about watching more TV than he was usually allowed on school nights, Dad felt his jaw tighten. He knew he was going to explode, so he announced to his son, "I can't take this right now, because I feel like I'm about to lose it, so I'm going to calm myself down." With that he went to his bedroom. It was a two-phone household, so after brooding for a while, Timmy called his dad on the extension in his room. Realizing he had no other option—that Dad wasn't going to dance the old dance—Timmy brought up an entirely unrelated topic. Dad responded with, "Thanks for calling me, but I'm still upset, so I'm going to take more time to get myself a little calmer." He came out fifteen minutes later in a fresh change of clothes, and they were able to talk about what happened.

In another situation, the mother of a thirteen-year-old boy, Alvin, actually absented herself physically from the house to calm herself down when (once again) Alvin didn't do his chores. Rather than dance to the same old tune, railing and complaining as she usually did, Mother recognized her early warning signals and just left. She went to her local church, where she prayed and meditated for a while. By doing this, she averted an old, explosive dance about trying to get Alvin to be more responsible around the house. A half hour later, she came home to find that the dinner dishes had been washed and put away. Did Alvin remember to do the dishes every night from then on? Of course not! But Mom began to recognize and interrupt her own out-of-control dance. Gradually, there were fewer explosions and Alvin became a little more responsible as well.

The truth is, you can't predict exactly what's going to happen when you change the dance—neither on your child's part nor on yours. Sitting in a room, soothing yourself, will not only diffuse your anger, it will also force you to focus on what happened with *you*. Ask yourself: What's going on here? Am I under extraordinary stress? Am I preoccupied? Tired? Hurt? Have I overreacted? Did I give him or her a punishment that was out of line? If so, remember that you always reserve the right to change your mind.

Then, when you finally go back to talk to your child, you, too, will have been transformed by employing this four-step procedure. After a few times of doing this, you'll get better at 1) recognizing the early warning signs; 2) absenting yourself from the scene; 3) being able to focus on your own behavior; and 4) figuring out what soothes you. By the way, when you start to talk to your child, if you feel the early warning signals coming on again, don't continue. Stop the flow by repeating the first three steps.

What If You Can't Help Losing Control?

The truth is, this method will still not prevent you from los-ing it altogether. So let's talk about what you can do with your child *after* you've lost control. Over the years, kids have told me what matters to them when their parents explode or act irrationally, and it's quite simple: when we apologize and then "own" what it is that's really upsetting us. Kids imme-diately feel relieved that it's not *all their fault* and that they're not *all* bad; and it explains what may have been totally in-comprehensible and therefore frightening. Equally impor-tant, they respect our honesty and courage.

So if you've suffered from a temporary loss of sanity around your child, find your own words to ameliorate the situation. It should be something simple like, "I lost it yester-day because my boss was really critical with me. I didn't mean it, but I took it out on you." Or, "I was completely exhausted because I've been overworked lately. What's wrong here is not really just you—I'm not taking good enough care of myself."

Again, although parents sometimes worry that apologiz-ing is inconsistent, or it makes you lose face, that's not the case. If anything, it's exactly the opposite. Offering a sincere apology and truly expressing regret is a way of telling—and showing—children that part of growing up is to take respon-sibility for what you yourself feel. It's an extremely positive message.

9

The Myth of Consistency
Why No Discipline Technique Works for More than Three Days and What You Can Do About It

Does this sound like home sweet home? You've just finished preparing a weekend treat for the family which you've taken special pains to prepare. You call your kids in for lunch, but no one hears you.

Your five-year-old is glued to the TV, which is so loud the neighbors' kids can probably hear it, too. She's watching "The Real Ghostbusters and Slimer" zap the bad guys with their magic ray guns. She doesn't notice that she left *The Little Mermaid* blasting from the tape machine in her bedroom, nor does she seem distracted by the noise.

Meanwhile, her fourteen-year-old brother is jamming on his drum synthesizer to the latest New Kids on the Block CD while MTV explodes from the TV set in his room.

You almost forget where your ten-year-old is. He's been outside all morning, completely preoccupied with the remote-control jeep you gave him for his birthday. It's a refreshing change from Nintendo, but no less absorbing. He's the only one who hears you—just because the kitchen window happens to be near the driveway. But he's not interested in what you've prepared for dinner. He's only in the mood for a Double Whopper at the local fast-food restaurant.

Between the proliferation of high-tech gadgets and color-ful, action-packed TV programs, our kids are instantly zapped into hyperspace—or hyped-up space, as the case may be. Stores at the mall (or whatever the downtown shop-ping area looks like where you live) lure them with strobe lights and neon and rock music. Shopping is an *event* to them.

And big-name merchandisers are doing their best to keep escalating this situation. Not content just to fill kids' stomachs, McDonald's introduced a line of clothing—McKids—so they could fill children's closets as well. Appro-priately, John Whitehead, president of the new merchandis-ing offshoot, labels the phenomenon "retailing as theater." According to *Newsweek* (November 12, 1990), at the Disney Store, the entertainment giant's retail chain, animated fig-ures dance across the ceiling, sales clerks sing Disney's great-est hits, and children watch Jiminy Cricket and Mickey Mouse on an enormous video screen. The mini-shows have proven so popular that stores regularly experience Saturday afternoon "stroller jams." No wonder we find it hard to get our kids' attention—and keep them at home!

Why Kids Tune Parents Out

To modern kids raised on megastimulation, we parents can't help but seem a little "boring," which is one of the reasons it's not always effective to be consistent. Even though most of us have been led to believe that consistency is the key to good discipline, that's somewhat of an exaggeration. Consis-tency is not only overrated, but given the action-oriented, sound-bite learning style most of our kids have, it has become outdated. In fact, those of us who persevere in the same parenting mode all the time, or lock into a particular "method" of child rearing, are bound to lose our children's attention—assuming we ever had it in the first place! It's not just the influence of quick-cut TV programs and the movies. Studies conducted with infants over the last decade prove that children get bored quickly and prefer novel stimulation. Researcher Dan Stern reports that *even newborns* will go out of their way to create new stimulation for themselves. He describes a fascinating experiment in which babies were taught to suck on a pacifier that could turn on and off a tape deck. Very quickly the neonates learned exactly what rate of sucking would "program" new music for themselves.

Based on the latest infant research, then, it seems that Madison Avenue merchandisers haven't created anything new. They've just tapped an innate quality of human beings —boredom with the "same old thing" and a consequent striving for novelty.

Of course, parents don't need scientific studies to know that kids demand ever-shifting stimulation. From the day we first hang a colorful mobile over the crib and attach an aptly named "Busy Box" to the side of the crib, our child is increasingly aroused. And the older she gets, the greater her need for excitement.

TV is vivid, stereophonic, even interactional; so are all the toys and gadgets our kids beg us for after watching those riveting commercials. And every year, it seems as if the wizards of technology who bring us animation and computers and special effects are able to keep upping the ante! It never seems to end.

Given their basic need for novelty and this constant media barrage, it's not surprising that our kids have short attention spans. Nor is it any wonder that they tune us out—we have turned into so much background noise in our own homes. It's like living near a railroad or next to an airport. Eventually, you don't even hear the freight train go by or notice a 747 taking off, because you've become so used to them.

That's also why one set of child-rearing activities or a particular type of strategy or parenting advice rarely works for more than a few days. It becomes old hat; it's yesterday's news to our kids—and they quickly tune us out.

The long and short of it is that in this modern world of ours, we can't stay connected to our kids through a rigid application of consistency and repetition. For parents to stay in control, we have to increase our options and vary our approach whenever possible.

Keep 'Em Guessing

Because there's already too much out there competing for their attention, we can't possibly keep our children interested unless we put some spice into our routine and jazz up our approach to child rearing. Otherwise, we fall into the same old dance with our kids, in which everybody is on automatic pilot, going through the steps but not listening to one another. Remember that kids quickly get wise to our "steps." They can see these repetitive patterns being played out before they even happen.

The bottom line is that despite all you've learned or assumed about the importance of being "consistent," you have to, as the kids put it, "get real." *The life span of any good child-rearing technique is usually no longer than a week!* The more you're prepared for this, the less disappointed you'll be when the inevitable happens. So start mixing it up with your child. Vary the dance. No matter how seemingly "sound" the concept, no matter how good an argument any expert makes for a particular strategy, once your kid catches on, it's time to move on. You can go back to it at a later date, but for the moment you need to develop new material.

Common Pitfalls

To create an environment that is both safe and disciplined, we have to be able to be heard by our children. I don't need to tell you how hard that can be, especially during a confrontation! The hardest time, of course, to communicate with your child is when you're exasperated. In fact, when we parents are angry, we often act in ways that inadvertently *cause* our kids to tune us out. Ask yourself if any of these apply:

Do you lecture? Since modern kids often have an attention span of maybe thirty seconds, you have only a small window of opportunity. Therefore, you need to get through to your child very quickly, making your point in a few sentences. Anything more than that, and you'll probably begin to see those familiar signs: Your kid gets this glazed-over look in his eyes. He's gone; he enters the dead zone—or, as one eleven-year-old told me, "I go into my *Night of the Living Dead* stare."

Likewise, when you're talking, and your child's eyes roll up to the left or to the right, there's a good chance she's thinking about other things. Richard Bandler and John Grinder studied different forms of psychotherapy and hypnotherapy for many years. They report that when people's eyes move up to the left or right they're usually remembering past events or imagining scenes in the future. Whether it's the past or the future, it's not too likely that your child is on the same wavelength as you are. And when you see those eyes start rolling up to the ceiling, you can bet your kid has switched channels. Your little lecture is off the air, and your show has been canceled!

Some kids *look* focused on your speech, as if they're listening intently. But if you really pay attention and follow their eyes, they're staring at your nose, chin, ear, or mouth—and they aren't hearing a word. I often see this in family therapy sessions. When I interrupt and ask a child what he's thinking about while his parent is talking, he says, "Oh, I wasn't really listening. I was just looking at my father's lips move."

Do you try to analyze your child and figure out "why"? In our highly sophisticated, overanalytic culture, everyone's a therapist. Many of us constantly ask our kids, "Why?" We want to uncover our child's deeper motivation: "I'm not just interested in *what* happened here; I want to know *why* you did it." Other favorites include, "How could you do this?" and "What were you thinking of?" and "What was going through your mind?" Trying to get your child to admit the "reason" only leads to another power struggle. Besides that, she doesn't know the answer. She may know "why" a week later but certainly not at the time it happens.

Do you try to explain yourself during a confrontation? In the middle of explosions, your child doesn't care about your "why" any more than he's aware of his. I see this in a lot of democratic families where parents believe children should be given reasons for everything. That's fine, but never try to explain yourself during a confrontation. Your child doesn't care; it's irrelevant; you're too upset to explain well; and you may not even know the reason at that moment. Wait and talk about it later. Or, just leave a note on your child's bed: "This is why I got so upset before." And don't ask if she's read it!

Do you deal with your child on a one-to-one basis? Try not to reprimand your child in front of other family members, especially siblings, or playmates. Sometimes a particular circumstance, such as a family gathering or a sleep-over date, can make this hard, but not impossible. For example, eleven-year-old Mary wouldn't stop teasing her eight-year-old brother, Warren, during the ride to school; two of Mary's classmates were also in the car. Mom, who was driving, stopped the car and asked Mary to get out. She closed the car doors and windows, so that no one else could hear her, and she walked a few feet away and said her piece about Mary's behavior.

Mom made sure she let Mary know, "I am going to let your father know about this, but I'm not going to tell your older brother (who wasn't present at the time). If you want to tell him, that's up to you. But this is between you and me." Keeping communication and discipline on a one-to-one basis like this is one of the best "triangle-busters" I know.

Do you get uncomfortable with a new technique—and quit before you give it a chance to work? Sometimes when we parents try a new way of dealing with our children we become uncomfortable taking steps to change the dance. The family or child's reaction to change is unnerving. They may initially get more upset, interfere, or just keep doing the same old dance. So we don't trust the new strategy; we don't see it through. We go only half the distance, and ultimately we fold under the pressure, which is often why a new tactic doesn't work.

Michael's father fell into this trap when he tried to break his seven-year-old's annoying habit of interrupting phone calls. Dad started out on the right path, explaining to Michael that the constant interruptions made him angry and frustrated, and that Michael's questions would just have to wait until he got off the phone. To change the dance, Dad told him that next time he'd take the call in another room.

That was fine, but when the phone rang, Dad didn't want Michael to be "shut out." He hadn't anticipated feeling guilty. So when Michael put up a bit of a fuss, he let his son follow him into the next room. And, of course, within minutes, Michael started asking questions and interrupting his call again! Dad's mistake was not anticipating his own step in the dance—how uncomfortable he'd feel about turning away from Michael. So even this simple change didn't have a chance to work.

Why Parents Have Trouble with Consequences

Many of us are like Michael's father. We often revert to the status quo because we haven't anticipated our own reactions to changing an old parenting dance. So we allow our kids' initial response to push us back to a familiar but ineffective routine. Often what happens however is that we let resentments pile up, we feel hurt ourselves—ignored or taken for granted—until we finally explode, levying severe and inappropriate punishment.

Punishment is the "P" word in modern child-rearing advice. Everyone does it, but nobody actually wants to call it by that name. These days, the politically correct term seems to be "consequences." But I have to admit, after twenty years of listening to families, I still haven't been able to figure out the real difference between a punishment and a consequence.

"Punishment" does sound more punitive. It probably reminds us of having our mouths washed out with soap or being taken out to a woodshed for a spanking or having to stay after school and write a hundred times on the blackboard, "I must listen to Mrs. Howard [my third grade teacher]." But aside from corporal punishment, which I do *not* believe in, I don't think there's anything wrong with punishment. Just about all of us punish our children, and always will.

The problem with punishment is that we often cook it up in the heat of the moment and it isn't a *logical consequence* of your child's actions. The punishment simply doesn't fit the crime. It is so out of proportion it can't possibly be enforced, so your child ends up tuning it out like so much "Muzak" in a dentist's office.

Because punishments are a part of life, though, I will try to help you make them more logical, realistic, and enforceable. However, coming up with logical consequences is easier said than done. Do any of these real-life cases feel familiar?

Peter, six, spilled his milk on his mother's new rug, and she came back with, "I'm taking away your TV tonight."

Ten-year-old Carrie was rude and obnoxious at the dinner table, ruining everyone else's meal—so her father erupted in a fit of anger: "No more Nintendo for a month!"

Paul, twelve, came home late from school every day, even though his mother had repeatedly admonished him. At the end of the second week during which this behavior persisted, Paul's mother finally lost it and said, "No summer vacation for you!"

Those punishments did not fit the "crimes" the children committed. They were downright illogical. What does spilled milk have to do with Nintendo? Asked about it later, each of the parents confessed that they didn't know what to do at the time, so they grabbed at anything. They're not alone. Many of us find it tough to come up with logical consequences when our child misbehaves. There are several reasons why this happens:

We assume kids can think abstractly. And why not? They sound so precocious these days that we forget how young they really are. The problem is, no matter what their age, *all* kids under pressure become "younger" emotionally. Remember that kids don't develop in a linear progression—they actually jump back and forth between stages. So you can't expect a child you are reprimanding to be able to make abstractions—at least not in the heat of conflict. They're just not able to make that connection.

We often create punishment when we're out of control. As I've suggested, you can't come up with logical consequences when you try to do it in the middle of a melee. By the time your anger has escalated, you can't think straight! A good rule-of-thumb is to take your initial threats (like, "No TV for a week!") and divide them in half, if not a third. Darren, ten, actually told me that he *never* listens to his parents if they say anything to him when they're hysterical, because he knows they'll never be able to follow through later on! He only takes them seriously when they talk to him in a quiet voice, then he knows they mean business!

Basic Discipline: Figuring Out Logical Consequences

So what's a parent to do? In a sentence, *learn your old dance and change it!* Between confrontations, you should plan ahead. Figure out and even write down ahead of time (since we tend to forget in the heat of the moment) what you might do in various situations. Whenever possible, talk to your spouse about your intentions. After all, you're *both* locked into the dance and what usually undermines your efforts are unforeseen reactions by your child *and* by other family members.

Let's take another look at some of the typical situations in which many parents find it hard to come up with logical consequences: Of course, with each of these examples, you'll see that there's always some pressure to keep dancing to the same old tune:

In the case of a child like Carrie disrupting dinner, for instance, how do you come up with a logical consequence if your kid is a poor eater? You're probably afraid to ask her to leave the table, because you think she'll go hungry or at least won't get the proper nutrition! So have her eat in her room, or leave a plate of food out on the kitchen counter. Or, if your child is old enough to help herself, leave the various components of dinner in pots on the stove or in the oven.

Poor eater or not, the goal is to create a consequence that fits the circumstances. No movies for a month is dramatic, but what does it have to do with the situation at hand? Instead of unrelated threats, one mother I know said to her kids, "I refuse to eat dinner with you behaving like this"— and *she* left the table. Another mother went on strike, saying to her children, "I can't put my energy into cooking for you, because mealtimes have become so unpleasant."

You may lose your family dinner hour (which for many of us is anything but quality time, especially when everyone's at each other's throats). Anyway, at that moment it's more important that your child understand that what she does has some kind of logical consequence and that, in this case, her behavior has made you too upset to go on with business-as-usual.

Let's look at another common situation: When your child spills something or leaves the bathroom a mess, stop him from doing what he wants to do *next*, whether it's going to a friend's house, playing with a computer game, even going outside to play soccer, until he does what family members do before leaving the house: make the bathroom decent enough for others to use. You're not just taking something pleasurable away, you're denying him the right to move on *until* his other responsibilities are completed. Now that's more logical than sending him to his room or not letting him go to the dance next weekend.

As a consequence of his actions, a child who habitually arrives home late from school (and makes you *nervous* because of this), should have to *earn* the right to come home from school alone. For a week or two, have him go straight home on the bus or arrange to have another child be "a buddy" who'll escort him on the route home. Be concrete: "When I trust that you're responsible enough and I can relax a little, I'll let you come home alone, but until then, I'll have to treat you like a younger child." After all, a natural consequence of maturity and showing greater responsibility is that you loosen the envelope and allow greater independence. Conversely, when he acts immaturely, you have to tighten the envelope until you feel more comfortable.

Take disrespect as another example. What if your child interrupts you, talks disrespectfully, or even curses (a growing occurrence these days)? Simply walk away—don't continue the conversation. If you try to "reason" or engage in debate, you get yourself into a power struggle. If you threaten to hold back his allowance, what sense does that make to him? Instead, say to your child, "I don't talk to people who talk to me that way. You've totally turned me off."

You have to be prepared for the counterreaction, however. When you walk away, your child will probably follow. Close the door. And don't worry: You're not surrendering; you're taking charge of the one thing you can control—how *you* feel and how *you* react to your child's behavior. It's a logical consequence not to talk to someone who is being rude to you.

The importance of logical consequences for your child's behavior goes back to maintaining the empathic envelope. In the heat of the moment—when you fly off the handle with your child and you feel out of control—it's usually because you're entangled in the dance. You and your child have lost touch with each other. And the dance has put everyone on automatic pilot. The explosion is a result of not hearing each other and is one last attempt to bridge the chasm between you. At those moments, when you're groping to keep the envelope from tearing, coming up with logical consequences is the glue that keeps the envelope from ripping apart, even when the friction is high.

When his action leads to a natural consequence or punishment, your child knows that you really see him and what he's done clearly. He can *feel* you around him much more than when the old dance—the Cop, the Therapist, the Martyr, the Enforcer, any dance—is just going on and on. I think this is why children, after their initial "hot" reaction in the face of a different, but logical punishment, seem surprisingly loving. The feel held in the envelope and are calmer as a result.

By the way, a not-so-incidental by-product of all this is

that you're preparing your kids for life outside the envelope. You're teaching them real-life cause and effect. When an adult doesn't pay his monthly bill, the credit card company doesn't write letters warning that they'll put that person in jail—which is tantamount to an angry parent who tells a recalcitrant teenager that she'll never go on another date or telling a disruptive nine-year-old that he'll never be allowed to go to the movies again. The company simply takes away the credit card. Remember that every infraction your child commits has its logical consequence. If you take the time to recognize your old dance and plan *between* confrontations, you will see how many more options are open to you.

Creative Discipline: Break the Old Dance

At my parent workshops or in family meetings, when we discuss the idea of logical consequences, people agree *in theory*—but in reality, they're skeptical. They say, "It's ridiculous! It doesn't work!" And they usually give me one of these reasons:

> *"You don't know **my** kid."*
> *"Nothing I do makes a difference."*
> *"My kid says, 'So what?' "*
> *"I can't take anything **more** away from my child."*

The way I see it, when parents feel powerless, it's because they're caught in a consistent, predictable dance that they can't break. As a result, their kids have tuned them out. It happens to all of us. Often, we even know that we're stuck, but we don't know how to do anything appreciably different. So I've come up with three questions—dance-breaking strategies, as it were—that you can ask yourself when you get stuck:

1) How do *I* feel about what my child did (not what I think I *should* be feeling, or what a *good parent* would be feeling)?
2) If I act on that feeling will I endanger my child's physical or psychological well-being?
3) If my answer to number 2 is "no," then how can I put my feelings into action and thereby change the dance?

The clue to what you do next—the tricky part—is in your answer to the first question: Base whatever action you take on how you feel. To illustrate, let me give you a few instances in which I've seen parents in my groups translate their feelings into creative actions which, in turn, changed the dance —and, most important, enabled them to get their children's attention long enough to connect.

One mother, a gourmet cook whose children, eleven, eight, and six, drove her crazy at mealtimes, was at a loss about changing the Cop Dance. Each meal turned out the same way: She'd spend a lot of time preparing, making sure the meal was not only delicious but well-balanced, and then the three kids would do all the things kids of that age do at meals—argue, interrupt, grab things from each other. It wasn't Mom's idea of the happy little family dinner, especially because after she had put in all that effort, she now had to spend all of her time reprimanding them.

I asked her, "How do *you* feel about this—not what do you think a good parent should feel?"

"I feel like garbage," she told me. "And I feel that it wouldn't make any difference to them if I just gave them garbage to eat."

"Well," I said to this woman who had always been a very conscientious, contained parent, "How about it?"

Mother thought about it and prepared her husband (remember it's not just between you and your child—everyone gets into the act). The next night during dinner, she didn't yell at her children at all. At the end of the meal, she quietly scraped the leftovers from their plates onto a large platter, and she covered the unappetizing heap with aluminum foil. And the night after that . . . she fed them garbage! Well, perhaps not garbage in the strict sense, but to these kids, believe me, those leftovers looked like garbage.

In any case, it certainly got the children's attention and stopped the dance. She then was able to tell them how she really felt—that they were really ruining what was for her a time that mattered a great deal and that she wasn't going to be cooking such elaborate meals anymore if their behavior persisted. But it was her changing the dance and putting her true feelings into creative action that made them pay attention.

Another father had trouble with his nine-year-old son, Gordon, whenever it came to doing homework. The boy was enrolled in a very demanding school, he had lots of work every night, and every night was a battle. Dad tried everything—sitting with Gordon, not sitting with him, laying out his assignment, having a checklist. Most of the time, he'd be very helpful to Gordon, trying to work with him in a collaborative, noncombative way. He was locked into the Helpful Therapist Dance.

I asked him, "How do you feel about this?" Again, I stressed that this wasn't a matter of what he thought a "good parent" would feel—rather, what did *he* feel?

Without missing a beat, he answered, "I feel like I'm going crazy."

"So why do you sound so rational about it?" I asked. As it turned out, Dad rarely got angry at Gordon; he never raised his voice at home; he was a Perfect Therapist at all times. So, the next time Gordon shuffled his feet over homework, Dad did what he really felt—he went crazy. He screamed, ranted, raved—and it stopped Gordon dead in his tracks. He was stunned.

Dad's actions changed the dance, and two things happened: Gordon immediately scampered into his room and started to do homework on his own for the first time. Also, later on, the family (including the mother, who usually absented herself during homework battles) was able to have a meaningful discussion about the problem. And they actually came up with a solution that got Dad out of the therapist/ teacher role: On Mondays through Thursdays, a high school student came over after school for an hour or two to help Gordon get his work done.

Finally, there's the mother whose ten-year-old daughter, Karen, absolutely refused to get up for school. Mother, who had trouble getting *herself* going in the morning, resented the fact that she had to wake up early to constantly prod and yell and cajole her daughter—and nothing worked anyway! Karen had only one chore in the morning—to feed the dog —and in the confusion even *that* job inevitably fell to the mother. It was clear: She was stuck in the Cop Dance *and* the Martyr Dance, too!

When I asked Mom how she really felt about this situation, not how a "good" parent would feel, she said, "I feel exhausted every morning. Even before I get out of bed, I know I'm in for a struggle."

"What would happen," I asked, "if you *didn't* get out of bed?"

When she answered, "I don't know how the dog would get fed or how Karen would get off to school," I suggested that she give it a try anyway—and test what would *really* happen. So the next morning, she spent an extra fifteen minutes in bed—the most that she could do without feeling really guilty. She didn't go into Karen's room to wake her up, so she figured Karen was still sleeping.

Meanwhile, the dog bounded into Karen's room, jumped on top of her bed—and did the mother's job for her! It was a great solution, and it happened spontaneously out of Mom finally taking an action to break the same old dance. Both Karen and her mother were very pleased with the new morning routine, especially Karen, who preferred a soggy kiss from her dog to her mother's normally angry tones.

Asking for Your Child's Input

Often, just breaking the dance gives rise to spontaneous and creative solutions like the ones I've described above. Sometimes, however, you might have to take another step and ask your child's input—a parenting strategy that is often recommended by child-rearing experts. But I've found that asking for your child's input works best *after* you've broken the old dance. Otherwise, your child will just continue to tune you out. Once you get her attention, however, she may be able to listen and help you come up with a solution.

An example that a mother brought to one of my workshops involved two brothers, Derek and Bill, nine and eleven, who were constantly fighting over their toys. Mom had tried a million and one tactics to get them to stop—labeling the toys, storing them in different places, separating the boys when they were playing—but they usually ended up in battle anyway. The other parents in the workshop asked her a very good question: "Why are *you* always coming up with solutions?" Without wanting to, she had gotten caught in the Parent/Peacemaker Dance.

In order to break the dance, Mom and Dad wrote a short letter to each boy, telling them that they no longer would settle all disputes between the brothers. The letter went on to say that they were tired of constantly intervening and coming up with plans that each time would be sabotaged. They told the boys that Mom and Dad were bowing out completely and that *the kids* would have to come up with a solution to their constant fighting. In this way, they began to get out of the Parent/Peacemaker Dance. Of course, at first the boys tried to up the ante, hoping to engage their parents into doing the old dance steps again. But when Mom and Dad made it clear that no matter how fiercely they fought, they weren't getting involved, the boys finally came up with a plan of their own: allowing each to use the other's toys on alternate nights. Of course, they didn't stick to the plan religiously, but without the "charge" of their parents' involvement, the kids actually did fight less after that. Meanwhile, Mom and Dad began to see that they didn't always have to be the ones to come up with solutions.

Keep in mind two things when you ask for your child's input: One, break the consistent pattern and *change the dance first.* Two, only *you* can ultimately decide whether the solution makes sense—and you have to let your child know this up front, when you enlist his help in solving a problem. A lot of the suggestions kids come up with are downright outrageous! One father forgot this little detail when he said to fourteen-year-old Matthew, "Your mother and I are bothered that you're not doing well in school. Help us come up with something that would make this better." Matthew did just that: "How about if I get good marks, I go on a trip to Hawaii?"

Asking for Other Parents' Input

It's hard for us to see our own predictable dances, but we're experts at picking up other people's. Think about it: Can't you describe your friend's same old family dances? As I suggested in Chapter 5, it's often a good idea to ask a trusted friend—a fellow parent—to help you recognize your own dance. The input can be invaluable. Often, the friend will be able not only to recognize what pattern you're stuck in, but also to come up with a solution that you can't see, because you're too close to the situation. (Using other parents as re-sources is covered extensively in Chapter 11.)

Case in point: A group of parents pondered a dilemma raised by Nathaniel's father. His seven-year-old loved his hamster, but when it came to really taking care of his pet, the boy was less than responsible. Every week, Dad had to re-mind Nathaniel to feed the hamster and make sure it had enough water, or he found himself doing it, as well as clean-ing the cage. Dad resented taking care of the pet, and though he had tried various strategies—most of which came under the heading of "nagging"—he would always end up doing it himself.

The other parents asked, "What would happen if you took the hamster away?" Well, Dad couldn't even consider that—he would feel too sorry for Nathaniel. The other parents con-cluded that Dad was stuck in the Martyr Dance! They could appreciate (and identify with) his feeling, but they also real-ized that he needed some kind of dance-breaking (not to be confused with break-dancing) tactic that he could realisti-cally handle. They came up with a very creative suggestion:

"Tell Nathaniel that you can't do this anymore," they suggested. "And that if he doesn't start feeding the hamster and cleaning the cage, you're going to give the hamster to the school—*for a week at a time*—until he learns to be more responsible for his own pet." Nathaniel's father liked the idea—because it gave him a halfway position, being a little tougher without having to become a totally different person. Anything more stringent would have been unrealistic for this particular father. But it was enough, because it gave him a different strategy that he knew he could carry out.

Needless to say, realizing his father was a softie, Nathaniel called his bluff. To his surprise, when he didn't clean the cage, Dad actually gave the hamster to the school for a week. He knew it would be well taken care of; and he knew that Nathaniel would feel the pinch—but not feel that his beloved pet had been snatched away from him. As it turned out, when Nathaniel saw how much fun the kids at school were having with *his* pet, he appreciated the hamster even more when he was allowed to bring it home a week later.

Equally important, in the past, his father had only *threatened* to take the hamster away from Nathaniel if he didn't shape up. Nathaniel knew how consistent his dad was in not following through. This time, however, Nathaniel was fooled. Dad actually made good on his threat—because other parents had been able to come up with a realistic idea to help him do it.

Remember Paul, the ten-year-old who kept coming home late from school? Thanks to the input of another parent, Paul's mother was able to throw him this curve ball: Instead of haranguing him with the usual, "Why did you do this again?" and making idle threats—all of which Paul invariably knew were part of the Paper Tiger Dance—the other mother suggested that Paul's mom totally disarm him by acting as if nothing happened!

The next day, when Paul came home, his mother had already set the table, she served him his favorite meal *and* his favorite dessert, and she made no comment about his being late. She reported that Paul was dazed, confused, and bewildered at this unexpected state of affairs. Finally, he couldn't take it anymore: "Ma, I promise I won't be late again, but *please*, don't you want to talk about what happened?" She ignored him and left the room.

Paul kept following his mom, trying to get her to start up a conversation about his being late, but she kept changing the subject. Finally, when Mom knew she had his attention, she said calmly, "Look, Paul, this really upsets me. I get frantic. We have to figure out a way so that I don't end up worrying so much." Paul's mother had at last found a creative, new "pitch" that got both of them off automatic pilot, so that they could try to solve the problem together.

Finally, a very dramatic suggestion came from a group of parents who listened as twelve-year-old Jeffrey's mother bemoaned the fact that she just couldn't get Jeff to keep common areas clean. She didn't ask for him to be immaculate, mind you (nothing that Felix Unger, the compulsive cleaner in "The Odd Couple" would want to call home). Just a little more orderly. She had tried everything: yelling, bribing, even tidying it up for him, hoping that Jeffrey would appreciate how great a clean house felt. But nothing worked, and they were constantly doing The Odd Couple Dance.

After talking about it to the other parents, they asked how it all made her feel. She answered, "Like I live in a dump." Hearing herself say those words seemed to jar her loose from the dance. She bought a huge garbage bin—a mini-version of the dumpsters contractors use when they're demolishing a building —put it in Jeff's room and threw all his droppings from around the house into it.

Mom definitely managed to get Jeffrey's attention when he came home from school that day, and, for the first time in quite a while, they talked and didn't argue. A compromise was reached in which the "dumpster" was moved down to the basement where Mom could throw his stuff when it got to be too much for her to live with. And though Jeffrey didn't become a perfect housekeeper, his negligence was never quite as blatant as it had been before.

What to Expect

Don't expect that any one of the solutions described here is exactly right for you. You need to figure out your own family dance and work from there. But one thing to remember: When you change the old dance and come up with something creatively inconsistent, you can't be sure what your child will do next. So think about the possibilities. Jeffrey's mom had to be prepared for the distinct possibility that he wouldn't mind a dumpster in his room. And the morning that Karen's mother decided to stay in bed those extra fifteen minutes and leave Karen to get up on her own, Mom had to be prepared for the fact that Karen might be late to school. However, in almost every case, changing the dance and getting you off automatic pilot so you can hear each other is more important than the issue you're fighting about.

The opportunities for doing the unexpected are as endless as you, your child, or other parents are resourceful. The formula is always the same: Realize that you're in a dance and that you have to break it; then be creative, even daring, and do something out of the ordinary—like letting the dog in to rouse a hard-to-wake child, instead of harping on her yourself.

I keep repeating this fact: No one likes it when you change the dance, especially kids who are used to "getting over" on their parents. Children's reactions to change may be age-related, but not rigidly so, since kids jump back and forth, unpacking their developmental suitcases as they need to use old standbys they've stored away from when they were younger. So don't be surprised if your seven-year-old sulks like a teen, or your teenager says, "That's not fair," as he so often did when he was seven!

In addition to reactions from your children, when you change the dance, you may start fighting with your spouse as well. Rather than cheering you on or thanking you for being different, very often the initial reaction of your spouse, your in-laws, or your own parents is sheer upset.

They may not like the new dance—which is what happened with Gabe's father, whom I talked about in Chapter 5. Remember that he had harangued his wife endlessly for being too lenient? Well, the minute Mom finally laid down the law, coming up with logical consequences for Gabe's misbehavior, Dad did a 180-degree turn, suddenly taking his son's side against his (now) too-strict mother. Mom's mistake—one we all make too often—was not talking it over with Dad first, so he could be prepared for the change, too.

How You'll Know What Works

You can tell that a particular strategy is the correct blend of compassion, communication, and consequences because afterward you feel closer to your child—you've strengthened the connection. Here are some signs that you made the right move:

You find yourself talking about the real issue. Johnny's mother walked away from him because he had been acting fresh to her for days and she wanted to stop the Parent-As-Punching-Bag Dance. She promptly exited into her bedroom, and her actions let him know, in no uncertain terms, that he couldn't talk to her like that. Within moments, Johnny politely knocked on her door, saying, "Can we talk? I'm sorry." The two of them were able to go over what was *really* bothering Johnny: A bully in school had been picking on him, but he didn't know how to express that to his mother; instead, he took it out on her. Walking away from him broke the self-defeating trance they had gotten into, and the poignant talk afterwards validated her actions.

Your child comes out as if nothing ever happened, but somehow makes a connection with you. You suddenly realize you're no longer stuck on the subject—it disappears, as if it never existed. An older child might start a conversation, about something else, but in an entirely different tone; or, she might enlist your advice, or offer to help you with something. A younger child might simply crawl onto your lap. It happens this way quite often. Without fanfare, your child indirectly lets you know that you did the right thing.

Your child moves to a new stage of development. It's as if the issue or the confrontation had been blocking his or her growth, and once it's resolved, your child has a sudden turn-around. This phenomenon occurs at all ages. A good example of it happened when my daughter Leah was three. She wanted gum, and I said no, whereupon she immediately threw a tantrum. When my wife and I refused to give in, she ran off into her room screaming, "Nobody here gives me nuthin'!" You would have thought it was an adolescent talking! She slammed the door of her room, still yelling from inside (but even louder), "Nobody gives me *nuthin'*!" Instead of running in to make sure that she was okay—which, after ten minutes, we were very tempted to do and had done many times before—we let her cry.

A few minutes later, a strange quiet overtook the house. So I peeked into her room, expecting the worst and imagining terrible scenes. To my surprise, Leah came waltzing out of the bathroom, totally relaxed. She announced that she had just used the toilet alone for the first time. We were stunned, but this sequence—being stuck, breaking out of a dance, your child's objections, and your holding firm with a consequence or punishment that makes sense—seems to precede many a developmental leap throughout childhood. Of course, it doesn't always happen, but it does happen enough times that parents comment on it regularly.

But My Kid Is Different

This book is about being a realist, and not all stories have such happy endings. If you're like most of us time-worn parents, I'm sure you can't help being a bit skeptical. "I've tried those tactics, but they don't seem to work with *my* kid," many parents say. And you may be right.

What's more, even if you're able to break a predictable pattern and come up with a consequence that makes sense, its power seems to last for only a few days. Pretty soon, your creative new tactic becomes a tired, old dance, and your child tunes it out. He starts acting up, half wanting to get away with something new, half wanting you to rise to the occasion and be decisive with him yet again.

The answer to our ever-changing lives with children is to have more options at our disposal. The logical-consequence approach is the staple—the bread and butter of child discipline. But to be truly effective, to provide a container that is compassionate *and* powerful, you've got to be creative and sometimes inconsistent. You've got to have some dirty "tricks" up your sleeve as well. In order to raise good children, you need to learn how good parents use bribery, threats, and guilt as a part of everyday life—so read on.

10
The Myth of the Fair Parent
How to Use Bribery, Threats, Guilt, and Other "Dirty" Tricks to Help Your Child Become a Better Person

The Party

I was at a children's Halloween party recently. Twenty or so kids, ranging from around four to eight years old, were accompanied by their parents—all savvy people who, between them, had probably read every child-rearing guide available, attended parenting workshops galore, and seen their share of experts on the talk-show circuit as well.

For three hours, I watched us all interact with our kids. I'm sure you can guess what happened. For the entire afternoon, not one kid paid attention to *anything* any parent said the first time, the second time, and even the third. Not one!

In situation after situation, kids were pressing parents up against the wall on just about *everything*! And to get our children to do what we wanted, every one of us sophisticated, high-tech, modern parents ended up resorting to those old-fashioned stand-bys—bribery, threats, and guilt. At first, we were embarrassed and a little sneaky about it. But by the party's end, all pretense had disappeared, and we were down in the mud of "unfair" tactics with no holds barred:

> *To a four-year-old who wanted to go out in the cold with her tutu and nothing else on: "If you put a jacket on over the tutu, I'll figure out a way to sneak you an extra party grab bag."*
>
> *To a seven-year-old whose mouth and pockets were stuffed with chocolate candies: "If you eat one more piece of candy, there will be no dinner for you tonight."*
>
> *To an eight-year-old boy who wouldn't let other kids share in a game: You've got to stop this. You're embarrassing me in front of everybody."*

Nobody gave a second thought to these tactics, because everyone seemed to be in the same boat. The fact is, today's precocious kids—armed with the knowledge that their parents are committed to psychological growth and to being "fair"—can give us all a run for our money. It happens way before adolescence and comes with the territory of being a modern parent. Given this state of affairs, I don't see how any of us can get by without using those tried and true methods—bribery, threats, and guilt!

If that sounds like outrageous advice from a child-rearing expert, let me explain: The problem is not that parents do such things (we always will). It's that we don't know how to use bribery, threats, or guilt in *effective* ways with our children.

Why Parents Need Dirty Tricks

In Chapter 9, I laid out a number of fair ways of trying to develop logical and creative consequences for your child's actions. The truth is, in moment-to-moment parenting, it's not so simple. Some situations defy logic, creativity, and even fairness. Especially for today's kids—steeped in media images and pop-culture portraits of bumbling, ineffective parents—there's a bit of an us-against-them attitude that children absorb.

Recent publications echo parents' concerns over the growing trend of anti-authority themes in the media, especially on TV, where parents are often portrayed as absolute boobs and kids are the savvy ones!

> *Many adults have never heard of it, but there's a new force dominating children's culture—Nickelodeon. . . . More youngsters watch more children's shows on Nickelodeon than on* **all three major networks** *combined. . . . Some critics argue that Nickelodeon's effort to make kids reign supreme goes too far, becoming anti-grown-up at times and teaching children that talking back is cool.*
>
> *"There's a kind of aggressive attitude towards adults, a kind of little wise-guy kid on Nickelodeon, said Peggy Charren, the founder of Action for Children's Television. . . . "I don't think you have to attract kids that way. Teaching kids to get involved with their parents and brothers and sisters is not a bad thing. The idea that you're only with it if you push them away is kind of sad."*
>
> *Symptomatic of how far the network pushes that idea—and how it can go awry—was a promo for an all-kids weekend, advising children to* **send their parents to their rooms** *[italics mine] if they tried to watch. The campaign was quickly pulled after a complaint that it was divisive to families.*[1]

Nickelodeon, of course, isn't unique. Somewhere between "Father Knows Best," "Married . . . with Children," and

---

[1] Excerpted from the *New York Times*, Sunday, October 21, 1990.

"The Simpsons," two different and divided worlds are usually featured in TV families—the dopey, out-of-it parental world and the hip, sometimes painful world of kids. No wonder we so often feel that we're on the front lines of a generational war in which we feel further and further removed from our children.

What makes this situation more unbalanced, with parents feeling pressed by kids at earlier ages, is the pervasive message of pop psychology extolling the values of being *fair* with our children. But what's a parent to do? We're under constant pressure from our own lives, exhausted and confused about what the "right" approach really is. So when we're faced with a Let's-Make-a-Deal kid who is constantly upping the ante, it's just not possible to be fair all the time. The emphasis on fairness in all its forms—democratic families teaching kids to ask questions, letting kids have as many choices as possible, being hesitant to impose our values onto children—has had significant positive effects. It certainly is an improvement over repressive child-rearing techniques of previous eras. But a rigid adherence to fairness can weaken the family.

After all, in any family, the most important element in the empathic envelope is *who is in charge of the dance.* And it should *not* be the children. When kids control the dance, they end up feeling too big. They don't feel us as a solid presence to rub up against. They don't feel contained. And as I've said repeatedly in this book, kids *must* feel "held"; otherwise, they'll go elsewhere to get that support—usually to their peer group, sometimes, as they get older, to gangs or other marginal groups. Parents who subscribe to the myth of fairness are clearly at a disadvantage. Which brings me back to the theme of this chapter—the effective use of bribery, threats, and guilt. I've just about never met a modern parent who can get by without these old-fashioned tools. So you might as well learn to use them to your advantage.

I must warn you, however. If you're totally committed to fairness, this chapter may not be for you. "Dirty Tricks" is about being the Parent Realist—and *winning*. It's about increasing the chances of getting the upper hand in the daily battles we have with our kids. It's for a good cause—strengthening the empathic envelope—but for some parents, the us-against-them flavor of this chapter may make it a good one to skip.

To Bribe or Not to Bribe?

When you think about it, the concept of bribery shouldn't be such a dirty word in child rearing—it's a part of life. As adults, we call it a reward, an incentive plan, the carrot compared to the stick. Life wouldn't work without it. Try to imagine never making statements like these to you kids:

> *"If you hurry up and get dressed, you'll have a few extra moments to watch TV before we go."*
> *"I'll let you play Nintendo when you finish doing your homework."*
> *"Get this chore done, and you'll be allowed to talk with your friends later."*
> *"I'll give you five dollars to clean out the basement."*

The problem with bribery is that, like anything else, it can become repetitive and habitual—and it turns into the Bribery Dance. It becomes the major way we have of motivating our children.

If you're not using bribery effectively and you're stuck in the Bribery Dance, the signals are clear: 1) Your child demands something for *everything* he does; 2) you feel *resentful*, and you end up giving more than you want; 3) you feel that you can't ask him to do something for you *without doing a favor in return*; and 4) you begin to feel that your child is a basically *selfish* person. In essence, you have become a hostage to your own child.

What can you do? As always, the first thing is to *recognize* and *change* the dance. With ineffective bribery, there's usually no other answer than to go cold turkey, and (to borrow from Nancy Reagan) "just say no"—long enough that you start to be taken seriously.

Of course, you'd better be prepared for the counterreaction. When you suddenly cut off a child who is used to the "drug" of being given *something* for every chore, demand, or favor, there's a kind of transition period. Things will probably get *worse* before they get better. Your child will definitely sulk or become even *more* argumentative and demanding. Ineffective bribery is difficult to change—you need all the help you can get. So to bolster yourself, team up with a spouse. If you and your spouse don't see eye to eye, at least agree that you can experiment a couple of times without interference.

If a partner is not available (or willing), team up with another parent who also wants to break the Bribery Dance. (It's usually best if it's a parent of one of your child's friends. Kids take it less personally when "everybody's doing it.") Support one another and monitor each other's dances. Call the other when you're about to capitulate.

In changing the dance, it's also important to do something *openly selfish for yourself*. This tells everyone in the family that you mean business—that you're no longer in the practice of making deals and only giving to everyone else or focusing on what everyone else in the family needs. Surprise them. Depending on how much of a "giver" you have been, you'll have to come up with the appropriate gift for yourself. Buy yourself a present, or do something that you normally wouldn't do. *And be sure they know about it.*

For example, one mother, who had tremendous difficulty taking *anything* for herself, prepared her own favorite dessert, fully aware that no one else liked it much. Because of who she was, that one act completely stunned the rest of the family. And she felt stronger just saying no to her nine-year-old's demand for an expensive piece of designer clothing.

A New Form of Bribery

Once you begin to break the cycle of the dance, you have to substitute a new, more effective form of bribery. This has two components—how often you bribe and the nature of the bribe. The first consideration—how often—goes back to a principle I was taught twenty years ago in my training which has proven to be one of the most useful pieces of information I picked up along the way. Researchers, exploring various theories of learning, discovered that behaviors are quickly given up if they're rewarded *every time* they happen. As soon as one or two rewards are skipped, the learned behavior diminishes or stops. Parents see this phenomenon every day. Kids who are given something for everything *expect* it—and immediately stop what you want them to do when you withhold the reward.

On the other hand, a person can go many times without receiving anything in return if he believes he might, at some point, get rewarded. (If you need proof of this, just watch people at slot machines.) Thus, if the frequency and timing of a reward varies—sometimes you get one, sometimes you don't—the learned behavior *persists*. In terms of child rearing, I know it sounds unfair; it certainly sounds inconsistent. But you will have far greater power if you *occasionally* reward your child for a job well done, rather than rewarding him each time.

Nonmaterial Bribery

If you are able to change the dance, from constant bribing to occasional rewards, the question always comes up as to *what* constitutes a good bribe. We often think that the only kind of bribes that are effective are those in "the material world," as Madonna so aptly put it. That's not true. Intrinsic, emotional rewards work just as well as material goodies, but we have to wean our kids (and ourselves) away from the notion of giving only *things* as incentives, and help kids develop an appreciation of other types of rewards.

The Reward of Earning Your Trust   Children tell me privately that they feel extremely good when their parents trust them. This is regardless of the child's age. Besides feeling proud of themselves, trust is such a valuable commodity for kids because it is associated with expanding privileges. The more children earn your trust, the more you can open the envelope and give them greater privileges. Your faith in them is supported by concrete action—the envelope expands. This sort of trust is a reward most kids yearn for, and it is parental bribery in a most healthy and genuine form.

For example, you might say, "I will let you bicycle over to Johnny's house after school, and I'll trust that you'll come straight home afterwards and be here at a certain time. If I feel I can trust you, I will relax a little, and I can let you have more freedom. But if you stop at the video store in between or meet a friend on the way, and then come home twenty minutes late, I end up worrying and not able to trust you yet."

The standard, then, is not just your child's behavior, but whether he acts in a manner that results in your feeling relaxed. *Being able to create a more trusting and confident parent becomes your child's reward.* Emotionally, it feels good to him and concretely it leads to greater privileges. This is a tough one for child-centered parents to comprehend. We're so used to focusing on our kids' well-being that we underestimate how important it is for *us* to feel good as well—and what a powerful motivator that can be for a child!

The Reward of One-on-One Time   This may come as a surprise to parents who see their children gravitate toward high-stimulation activities like computer games, peer groups, and the movies. Because of this we assume that children won't think of one-on-one time with us as a reward worth going after. But children, even modern ones, still have the needs of children. They really value one-on-one time, no matter how short it is. Parent Chum activities with no other family members present are powerful and very effective bribes.

I have seen parents cut down on sibling rivalry simply by increasing the amount of one-on-one time with the kids—especially with the one who appears to be starting most of the fights. It doesn't take much effort either, usually about an hour a week. And, of course, one-on-one time is the kind of bribery that helps foster the connection between you and your child—unlike material gifts, which many times do very little to strengthen the parent/child bond.

The Reward of a Favorite Food   Nowadays, with increased awareness of eating disorders, we are all extremely cautious about using food as a reward. But as long as eating issues haven't become a combative dance in your family, food can be a powerful—and nurturing—incentive for your child. It's worth noting that the aromas and tastes of special childhood dishes are remembered by many adults as one of the sweetest "gifts" they ever received.

Modern parents, with our increased sophistication about the misuse of food, are in danger of leaving behind this old-fashioned tried-and-true reward. And yet, food as a sign of nurturing and appreciation continues to hold its special power, even after kids go off to college. One mother, for example, whose connection with her two children is now limited to college vacations and semester breaks, nevertheless lets them know she's still very much "there" by sending care packages of goodies she used to bake for them when they were younger.

Whether it's a vegetarian delight, hot apple pie, or a Double Whopper with everything on it, food treats are powerful incentives. They can't help with everyday chores, but for the occasional times you need to lean on your child, don't leave food off your menu of bribes.

The Reward of Praise   Praise, when it's not given all the time, has more power per square inch than any other form of reward. Unfortunately, praise is both underrated as an effective bribe—even the most hardened kid is softened by genuine praise—and yet overused. How could that be? Over the last ten years, in our pop-psychologized culture, so much fuss has been made about being sure to praise our children that many of us have overdone it. We praise whether we feel it or not. Unfortunately, a child too consistently praised soon learns to disregard or disbelieve compliments. Praise then loses its effect as an incentive.

The idea is not to praise your child each time she does something (remember the principle of *variable* rewards). Nor is there any rule that dictates praising your child every day. Praise her *only* when you really feel it. I trust that if you realize how important genuine praise is, you'll know when those times are.

Also, praise can come out of the blue—not necessarily following something your child does. In fact, try not to compliment your child exactly when she does whatever it is you're proud of. For instance, later on or even the next day, when she's involved in something totally unrelated, you might walk over to her and say, "Remember when you did so-and-so? I really thought that was great." Or, you could tell it to your spouse, letting her hear the praise, without saying anything directly to your child.

The important point is not to be excessive and not to think you have to follow any particular Rule of Regular Praise. This type of consistency is not effective; it doesn't feel real; and it doesn't work. Keep 'em guessing just a little, and you won't get tuned out as often or taken for granted. Praise is too good an incentive to squander—be sure your child *earns* it.

The Reward of Your Child Knowing You Can Depend on Him/ Her   Many parents don't realize that children love to know that you can depend on them. I believe kids have a basic desire to nurture and to help their parents. I've seen this need to be helpful in children as young as two or three. Often, we don't recognize it in our kids, because we're too busy concentrating on being *The Parents*. But what a great reward it is for them to know that we can truly depend on them once in a while—when we feel bad or when something goes wrong in our lives.

Naturally, whenever anything becomes a dance, especially parental dependency, it is *not* healthy. As many recent books with the word "codependent" in the title hasten to point out, we certainly shouldn't depend on our children more than they depend on us. Nor should our children think the reason they exist is to help us to get through life. But those are extreme cases—the kinds that find their way into parent-blaming books like *Toxic Parents*. So, let's not throw the baby out with the bath water. Strong families are interdependent—members know that in a pinch they're there for each other. *Everyone* chips in, in ways that are age-appropriate. With kids being as naturally self-absorbed as they are, it's easy to forget that the gift of helping a parent is a powerful incentive on its own.

The feeling of giving to parents is so satisfying to children that saying to them, "I need your help" is a nurturing form of bribery. Not for chores, of course, or everyday demands. It's only effective when you really need their assistance for some emotional reason—like when you're completely stressed out or feeling badly about yourself or if you're sick in bed. When we forget our own human needs, we are robbing children of a chance to pay back their debt to us and to feel good about themselves. Allowing children to help us is another incentive that makes everyone feel more connected.

• • •

As with all the strategies I've suggested in this book, any one form of bribery won't work if it's used consistently. You need to mix them up—praise, favorite foods, time together, asking for help—or else you will lose your effectiveness. You need to be agile, to move back and forth between material bribes and offering more intrinsic, emotional rewards. Finally, you need to remember that being consistent and fair—rewarding *all* things your child does correctly—will reduce you to background noise and lessen the possibilities for connection.

Threats: Your Rights

No matter how enlightened we are as parents, there's no way to raise kids without threatening and, at times, punishing them. If we don't have the capacity to deliver effective threats and follow through when necessary, we lose control of the dance—which, as I have suggested, is the key to keeping the empathic envelope whole. However, most of the time when we're ineffective in our threats, we don't control the dance. Instead, we get entangled in reflexive battles with our kids.

So how do we change this? As discussed in Chapter 9, the biggest problem in being able to threaten *well* is that our threats usually come out in the middle of escalations or irrational dances, so they're not particularly powerful. By eliminating lecturing, analyzing, and explaining from your repertoire, you can help increase the effectiveness of threats. But sometimes these are not enough. You also have to recognize that you have certain rights vis-a-vis your child. Recognizing your rights can help you come up with threats that have some teeth and give you real power over your child.

The Right to Slow Down the Action   In everyday life, struggles around the house happen incredibly fast. Parenting would be easier if we had the ability to go over events with an instant-replay camera, and in slow-motion at that. But since we don't, parents have to reserve the right to slow down the action instead.

Here's a typical case in point: Eleven-year-old Elliott was leaving the house one morning, and just as he was on his way out the door, he hit his mother with, "Jeremy is having a pizza party . . . after school . . . and all the kids are going to be there. . . . I'll be able to do my homework when I get back . . . it's okay? . . . right?" The kid talked so fast, you'd think he had been auditioning for a Federal Express ad! And Mom was expected to answer *ON THE SPOT.*

Kids speed up the action early. They quickly catch on, by around six or seven years old, how easy it is to get the fast answer they want from a parent who is juggling fifteen things at once. Invariably, the moment you're involved or preoccupied, they'll ask your permission to go somewhere, have a friend over, or rent out the downstairs rec room to the entire eighth grade. You could be on the phone with a client, hovering behind the bathroom door in a towel, or fixing a delicate mechanism that requires your utmost concentration —it doesn't matter. That's when kids will pop the question. And why not? Their lives hang in the balance, so you'd better hurry up and answer!

Though children of all ages use this approach, preteen and early adolescents elevate these tactics to an art form: You're getting dressed for an important meeting. You have to feed the cat, but then you spill something on your suit. Meanwhile, the phone rings, the baby's crying, the sitter is late, and *that's* when little Johnny tells you that Adriana's grandmother has a CONDO IN FLORIDA, and Adri's parents invited him for CHRISTMAS VACATION, and IT WON'T COST A THING, because they've got a SPECIAL DEAL ON TICKETS, but you've got to let Adri's mother know *RIGHT AWAY!*

In the face of these pressure tactics, you must remember who is supposed to control the dance—*you*. You therefore have the right (and the responsibility) to slow down the action. Try telling your child, "I can't say yes to this, because you're not giving me enough time." Or say, "I don't have time to figure out what would make me comfortable about your doing this. In the future, you're going to have to give me more time. For now, however, the answer is no, because I can't think it through."

By the way, no matter how old a child gets, this little phenomenon lives on: My co-author and I were surprised one day when we were involved in an intense phone call discussing the contents of this book, and her *twenty-one-year-old* interrupted our conversation on her end with some desperate life-and-death matter—that had to be settled *NOW!*

The Right to Change Your Mind   No matter how hard you try, you're going to lose it every now and then. The dance is bigger and more powerful than you and your child. You're going to say things that are crazy and that you'll regret. When this happens, rather than changing their minds, many parents get bogged down in the Myth of Consistency. They're afraid that they'll drive their kids crazy by reversing field, or that they'll lose face in their kids' eyes. The problem is, many threats have no teeth if you're unable to carry them out. As I suggested earlier, "a month of no TV" sounds powerful in the heat of the moment. But can you really enforce it, or is there a good chance you'll relent sometime during the month?

At the other end of the continuum, sometimes your threats are rationalized and talked *down* by your smart, argumentative child. A determined seven-year-old, obsessed with "fairness," can come up with several reasons why you shouldn't punish her. She will come up with arguments that, in the moment, are *so* convincing (and make you feel *so* guilty) that you will walk away with the uneasy feeling that you've just bought some swampland in Florida. Only later on do you realize you've been had.

In either case, consistency in no way means that you can't change your mind. You can always retract your initial decision by admitting, "I said that (or agreed to that) in the heat of the moment. Now that I've thought about it, my decision doesn't make sense, so I'm changing what I had planned to do with you. Here's what I've decided." You don't lose face this way, because *you're still in charge* of the process. Equally important, because you took your own threats seriously enough to reflect on them, your child will begin to take them more seriously, too.

The Right to Consult with Your Partner   Children, wanting to win power struggles, count on poor communication between parents. They also count on our isolation and our busyness, which, in many ways, makes it difficult for us to consult one another. They will especially count on parents having different opinions and will play one side off against the other. It's not that children are in any way malicious— they just want to get *their* way! But slowing the action down and taking time to consult with a spouse is your *right* as a parent.

You needn't agree. In the world of parenting, teamwork doesn't mean agreeing—it just means communicating with each other. Ideally, when you don't agree, when it comes to judgment calls, you win some, your spouse wins some. Regardless of the outcome, however, you definitely must reserve the right to consult each other. Parents who regularly skip over this step lose credibility, and their threats are viewed skeptically by children.

This includes stepparents as well. It doesn't mean that a stepparent is going to take over or make the final decision for the child, but he or she is clearly part of the household, and you have the right to get another significant adult's input before taking action.

The Right to Ask Your Child to Go Over the Facts with the Other Parent or Partner   Kids often do end runs around a parent. Here's an example: Twelve-year-old Emma wanted to go to a party that her mother was worried about, and she insisted, of course, that she needed an answer quickly. Mom decided against Emma's going to the party and told this to Dad, saying she'd not only like his backing on the decision, she wanted *him* to tell Emma. Well, these parents had been through this dance many times before. It always ended in an argument. Dad resented being asked to be "the heavy," especially because he didn't really agree with his wife.

I asked him if he had spoken to Emma directly, or was it all going through Mom. Predictably, he hadn't. We then worked it out that the next time a decision had to be made about giving Emma permission, Mom would tell her, "I'm not going to decide anything until you go over this with your father." As it turned out, when the father heard first-hand all the preteen double talk and the ins and outs of Emma's request, Dad often ended up on the same side as Mom! This one additional step got Emma to take them—and what they decided together—seriously.

The Right to Call Other Parents   This is extremely important and will be covered extensively in Chapter 11. Through fourth, fifth, sixth, seventh, and eighth grades, kids will tell you that they'll absolutely *die* if you call their friends' parents—and they'll do whatever they can to make you feel you don't have the right. They'll tell you you're the only parent who wants to call other parents, that you don't want them to have fun, that they'll be the laughingstock of the school.

The irony is that although your child may never admit it, deep down inside, she is usually *relieved* when you make these calls. It takes her off the hook. But don't expect your child to *tell* you that. Calling other parents is one of the *best* things you can do for yourself and your child. It strengthens your hand and increases the feeling of safety in the empathic envelope. And, at the same time, your sense of being "on your own" is dramatically lessened.

Punishment: Some Helpful Guidelines

The primary benefit of these parental rights is that they allow you to slow the action down, give you time to think and to threaten a consequence or punishment that makes sense. In order to be taken seriously, it also helps to follow these guidelines:

Punishment has to have a beginning and an end. It can't be vague, such as "no TV until further notice." It really has to have parameters. Why? Because with vagueness, your child will probably continue to badger you. This puts too much pressure on you to remain involved with the punishment, causing you to ask yourself, "Should I let him off the hook? Has he learned his lesson?" Why waste further time on this matter when you undoubtedly have many other things to take care of? And, if your child has developed skillful arguing tactics, there's a good chance that you'll relent before you're ready. For these reasons, your threats will carry more weight if you think in terms of clear beginnings and endings: "No TV for the next three full days—mornings, afternoons, or nights. That means no educational programs, no Nintendo—no exceptions. That's it."

Punishment should be something you can enforce. If you have a choice between making it shorter or longer, think about the benefits of each: Longer may *feel* more powerful, but shorter is usually more realistic—something you can really carry out, which, in the end will be more effective. For example, if your initial impulse is to ground your child from after-school activities for a month, forget it! You'll never be able to follow through. It would be far better to bring it down to a few days that you can really monitor, rather than have your words become an empty threat.

Don't make a threat or levy punishment that you'll resent. In the heat of the moment, it's not uncommon to come up with consequences more onerous to you than to your child—like a weekend without play dates that keeps *you* pent up in the house, too. What good is a punishment that makes you have to suffer along with your child? This is partly why you need to give yourself more time to think and to be able to change your mind. Your child will also take you more seriously as she begins to learn that punishments cause her more discomfort than you.

Reserve the right to delay your decision. Serious infractions require time for reflection on your part. Give yourself the opportunity to think over what is likely to be enforceable and effective. Simply say to your child, "I'm not going to punish you now, but there will be consequences for what you've done. I am going to think about it. Mom [Dad] and I are going to talk it through. We'll tell you our decision *when we're ready.*"

Take your time. Don't twist yourself out of shape or rush to judgment. Your child may not be happy with this delay—

she may claim it's unfair—or she'll be on her best behavior, hoping you'll forget. But neither forget nor feel obligated to act before you feel clear about what you're doing.

Even when you threaten or punish, be respectful of your child. Keep in mind the rules-of-thumb for expressing your feelings that I laid out in Chapter 6: Don't get physical. Be careful of name calling. Don't threaten to cut your child off from her friends. Don't humiliate your child in front of friends or, if possible, in front of siblings—to "drive the point home." Don't threaten to never speak to him again. And take seriously threats to hurt themselves.

Expecting the Counterreaction

No matter how effective a threat or punishment is, your child is very likely to up the ante, to try to talk you out of it, to provoke you with guilt. As I've said so many times, when you change the dance, a counterreaction occurs during the period of transition.

Here, in fact, is when you can expect The Triangulator to make an appearance. You've heard of Arnold Schwarzenegger's *The Terminator*? Well, even though it's quiet out there, you've got to be on the lookout for THE TRIANGULATOR living in our midst. The Triangulator—he can be six *or* sixteen—is one of the key reasons we "lose it." The Triangulator will pit one parent against the other and thereby take the spotlight off himself. The Triangulator will also try to wheedle himself out of a punishment by creating doubt. The Triangulator slips through the cracks between parents. The Triangulator knows each parent's soft spot. At the moment of confrontation, the Triangulator does not operate from a moral position and cares little about right or wrong—he just wants to win. So, *he keeps coming back.* This is not because kids are mean spirited. Children just go all out to get what (they *think*) they need. And pitting us against each other is one way to make that happen.

Let's say The Triangulator wants to go to the movies. Mom says, "You haven't finished writing the social studies report that's due on Monday, so the answer is *no*. I told you that was the deal." The Triangulator, knowing that his father probably won't check it out with Mom, runs to Dad, who says yes. Suddenly, Mom hears The Triangulator announce, "Dad said I could go to the movies," and she becomes furious—with her spouse. The Triangulator gets off scot-free (and possibly even ends up at the movies).

I couldn't describe The Triangulator any better than the nine-year-old who told me, "What's the point of fighting when they're not around? Sometimes, when they are, I push it and purposely pick a fight with my sister—just to see who's side they'll take."

The Triangulator can be stopped from sabotaging your discipline by planning together with your spouse—either beforehand or when you try to "slow the action down," as I described earlier. Also, to keep The Triangulator from bringing other members of the family into the fray, try not to make threats when other siblings are around—it usually leads to trouble.

One mother told me that if she disciplined her twelve-year-old Jessica when eight-year-old Christopher was in earshot, he'd invariably pipe in to defend his sister's behavior. He'd find some loophole which made Mom "wrong" and "unfair." As Mom put it, "I felt like I had an eight-year-old attorney living with us!" This can go in either direction; sometimes an older sibling jumps in to defend (or taunt) a younger one, too. In either case, a triangle is formed between a parent and two children—which inevitably sabotages discipline.

You can also change your usual triangle dance by doing something you *don't* believe in. In every family, one spouse is always more vigilant than the other one—he or she is the one more likely to remember, notice, schedule, reprimand, and so on. So, switch positions. The normally superresponsible spouse tries to lay back and let the other take over for a *short time*.

This is very difficult to do. As practice, you might first try this with something not terribly important, like whether your child should be allowed to play with her friends on Saturday before her chores are done around the house. Let the stricter spouse say "yes" for once—or at least take that position. Be sure to tell your child exactly what you're doing —so that switching roles doesn't seem phony.

I'm not suggesting that you and your partner switch positions for more than one night or a few hours at a time—that would be much too hard to do. But you'll find that trying this once in a while cuts down on allowing dangerous triangles to form. By practicing on less important issues first, your child won't easily forge an alliance with one of you against the other when something big comes up. And, of course, reducing triangles immediately makes children take us and our punishments more seriously.

Knowing When You Need Professional Help

This is one of the only times in these pages that I recommend getting a third person involved—a professional counselor— so please take heed: If you and your spouse consistently come down on different sides of issues and therefore find it impossible to make threats or try to establish consequences together, you may need professional counseling. That is, if the two of you are constantly polarized—in *every* instance, you say black, your spouse says white—chances are, you're locked in a dance that no book can help you with.

This is what generally happens: When your child does

something wrong, instead of being focused on your child, in the end, you and your spouse become angry at each other. Meanwhile, your child slips through the cracks in the envelope that are the result of your rage. You're perpetually locked in a furious battle, you can't get out of it, and your child gangs up with one of you against the other. If this keeps happening, there's a good chance that you're all locked in a dance that's bigger than anyone can handle alone. And you probably need outside assistance to break the destructive pattern. In that case, it's probably a good idea to get professional help.

Guilt: Constructive or Destructive?

A few years ago I heard Joan Rivers remark that, every now and then, just to keep her fourteen-year-old in line, she would go into her daughter's room while she was sleeping and wake her up with, "You ripped me to shreds! Now go back to sleep!" Rivers said she found it extremely effective in taming an adolescent. "Bad" parenting perhaps, but it was obvious from the hearty laughter in the audience that people recognized themselves (or at least what they might like to do).

On a more benign note, I couldn't help noticing that at the beginning of *The Wizard of Oz*, Professor Marvel convinced Dorothy to go back home by showing her in the crystal ball that poor Auntie Em was so worried her heart was breaking. Twenty years ago, nobody thought Professor Marvel was seriously damaging Dorothy by this obvious attempt at guilt manipulation.

Unfortunately, like so many other no-no's in our pop psychology (and parent-bashing) culture, guilt has become a dirty word. The party line tells us we should never provoke guilt in our children. Well, I'm certainly not recommending Joan Rivers' extreme approach, but the ability to provoke guilt, like bribery and threats, is a fact of parenting and always will be. More to the point, guilt is an important way that parents and children connect. In fact, guilt is *necessary* for children to grow up healthy—as long as parents are able to distinguish between destructive and constructive guilt.

Like any other one-dimensional approach to parenting, when guilt is repetitive and becomes one of the main ways of dancing with our kids—so that they end up feeling as if they have too much power to hurt us—that's obviously destructive guilt. Destructive guilt makes children feel manipulated and dumped on. We often get into destructive guilt trips when we allow things to build up. Rather than have yet another confrontation over the room, the homework, the "little things," we let things slide.

For example, the mother of eight-year-old Douglas had suffered a period of Douglas being especially sloppy—leaving his socks, underwear, and jacket on the floor, crumbs, plates, and leftovers on the kitchen counter, and causing a dozen other minor irritations. Finally, Mom absolutely lost it when Douglas talked back to her about going to an after-school doctor's appointment. Out of nowhere, she erupted, spewing forth a list of accusations—everything that she had let slide over the past several weeks which, nevertheless, were totally unrelated to that particular incident. It became a "Gripes of the Week in Review" session in which she piled on the destructive guilt.

That kind of guilt doesn't help children grow. Ironically, it rarely even makes them feel guilty! On the contrary, when you can show children the impact of their actions on you, that's constructive guilt. Sadly, because the Therapy Dance has become such a popular parenting mode, we think we're not supposed to really show kids how badly they can make us feel. A lot of us try to suppress our reactions, so as not to provoke unnecessary guilt.

Still, angry feelings burst forth from us during explosions. But anger and frustration are just the tip of the iceberg. We have many other feelings that we believe are inappropriate for *Parents* to express. The truth is, to be effective, parents need to express a wide range of unparentlike emotions and sometimes provoke guilt. And kids need to feel guilt toward parents in order to learn what their impact on us (and on others) can be.

This came home to me when my daughter Leah was about four years old. I had been with her the entire day; we had done a lot together. At the end of the day, she asked me to play "Chutes and Ladders," but I couldn't manage one more activity. When I told her I was tired, she threw a tantrum, kicking and screaming, *"Nobody ever does nuthin' with me!"*

I sat bolt upright. I was hurt and disappointed in her—and I let her know it: "What are you talking about? I've been playing with you all day. What's the matter—don't you appreciate that?" I didn't pretend that I was above her lack of gratitude bothering me. Leah suddenly stopped her kicking and screaming and listened with great attention. She became upset with what I was saying; clearly, she felt disturbed and guilty. Her tantrum immediately stopped.

The bottom line is that rather than waiting until we absolutely explode from the frustration of holding our feelings in (a problem in many human relationships, not just those between parent and child), we parents need to stop pretending that our kids' actions don't affect us. When kids are selfish, inconsiderate, ungrateful, or unkind, of course it bothers us. Such behavior *is* hurtful, and it's important for kids to know that—both to increase our own control in the empathic envelope and to help them understand the impact of their behavior.

Practicing Constructive Guilt

Constructive guilt takes practice—especially because many of us labor under the misconception that we have to protect our kids from the full range of our feelings. I couldn't say it any better than thirteen-year-old Peter's mother, who wrote the following:

> *I told Peter that I've sheltered him from my struggles. I didn't want him to feel the bumps. I cried and I told him that I had hoped to accomplish more than I have and that I was disappointed in myself. I had been afraid to tell him that, because I thought* **he wouldn't look up to me anymore as a parent.** *I also told him I need his support.*

You need to practice using unparentlike phrases, such as this mom's "I need your support"—expressions that you would probably not say if you were worrying about making your child feel guilty. Here are some others:

"I depended on you, and you let me down." For example, one mother I know asked her son Tommy to "fix dinner" (really, just put something in the microwave), because she was feeling sick. As many eleven-year-olds would, Tommy stalled, playing a little Nintendo, watching TV, fooling around. Instead of exploding or taking it out on him by nagging, as she normally would have, Mom told Tommy she was disappointed in him; he didn't come through for her. She turned away from him and said nothing more.

First, Mom changed the old Nagging Dance; then she didn't protect him from her hurt. Obviously, this woke Tommy up from his self-absorbed reverie, because twenty minutes later, he appeared at bedside with dinner prepared and a slightly more concerned attitude. Did Tommy undergo a personality change and thereafter become a truly involved citizen around the house? No. But at least he came through this one time, which eased some of Mom's resentment toward him.

"What you did made me feel happy all day." We're not supposed to lay a guilt trip on our kids—and, of course, if our entire happiness depends on our children, that *is* a problem. But none of these lines is meant to become your theme song. Besides, what the kids are up to often *does* give a lift to our day. A father told his nine-year-old son in front of all the other participants at one of my parent/child workshops, "You know why I ask you about school every evening? A lot of the time at work I have to do things that I consider very tedious. But when I hear about the details of your day, it gives me a boost for the rest of the night and reminds me of why I work so hard."

There was a brief moment of silence during which it seemed as if this dad had gone too far—that maybe he had crossed over the invisible border into the land of guilt-provoking parents. After all, he was implying that he works at something he hates just because of his son. However, instead of getting mad or withdrawing, the boy replied, "Dad, it would be easier to answer you if you could be more specific—like, 'What happened in computer class with that new program?' That way, I feel like you know what's happening —like you're really involved."

This poignant exchange got below their superficial anger and instantly cleared up how each had been "missing"—not connecting with—the other. And it immediately touched a nerve in the whole workshop. The usual griping that can go on between a group of third- through sixth-graders and their parents turned into a night of dramatic honesty on both sides.

"You're driving me crazy." The mother of twelve-year-old Carol told me that her daughter was pushing and pulling her in different directions about going to a party. Finally, Mom

just said to her, "Carol, you're driving me crazy! I don't know how to treat you. One minute you're acting like a three-year-old, and the next you're trying to act like a thirty-year-old. You have me completely confused and I don't know what to do with this. I feel like I'm going out of my mind." She then left the room.

Carol felt guilty—and she certainly had something to think about. In a few minutes, she came to her mother and said, "I guess the truth is that I want to be treated older when I want privileges, and I want to be treated younger when I feel scared." Her mother's honesty, which lead to Carol's guilt, got them off automatic pilot, and created a space for mother and daughter to feel something else besides frustration and anger.

"I feel beaten." This one comes under the "I-absolutely-give-up" heading! You can either say the words themselves or let your actions indicate your feelings, which is what happened when seven-year-old Carl badgered his mother about buying a new, expensive, baseball glove. She was trying to get dressed to meet an old friend she hadn't seen in years and was extremely nervous about the reunion, which she told Carl. Nevertheless, he kept harping on what *he* wanted. Mom first tried being reasonable—it didn't work. She tried bargaining—it didn't do a thing. She tried threats—to no effect.

Finally, Mom couldn't take it anymore. She put her head down on the table and started moaning, "I give up. You win, you win. I'm too much of a wreck to meet Abby now. Just leave me alone." This capitulation stopped Carl dead in his tracks. He immediately ran out of the kitchen—he *did* leave her alone. After a few minutes of peace, Mom pulled herself together and went out to meet Abby.

Did Carl feel guilty? Absolutely! Was Carl psychologically damaged? Just the opposite. For a little while, he could see the full impact of treating his mother as if she had endless patience and no needs of her own. The next night they had a great dinner together and Carl stopped badgering her about the baseball glove (for a week, anyway).

Of course, if Mom had *faked* surrendering, or if she did it every night, her behavior would provoke anger, rather than guilt, and she wouldn't have been as effective in changing the Gimme Dance.

In each of the above cases, regardless of what was actually *said*, the same sequence happened. The parents weren't afraid to provoke guilt, so they honestly expressed what they felt. Feeling some remorse was like a healthy shock to the system—it pulled those kids out of their self-involvement and changed counterproductive dances. All of a sudden, kids rubbed up against their parents' genuine reactions. This is crucial in the empathic envelope—that children experience their parents as *real people* with *real emotions*.

Furthermore, contrary to the common belief that guilt is destructive, children actually feel *less* badly about themselves, because they don't feel so big and all-powerful. Rather, they feel that there's a container around them, holding them, protecting them from completely taking over—which, despite their actions to the contrary, they don't really want to do.

When the Other Shoe Falls

As always, you need to be prepared for your child's reaction. Very often, when you express an unparentlike emotion, like dependency or hurt or disappointment, you will create more guilt than you bargained for. When my daughter Leah realized that I was upset by her claim that "nobody does nuthin' with me," she fell into a heap on the floor and started crying inconsolably. I was actually taken aback by the intensity of her response, and it was all I could do to let her feel badly—without trying to make "nice." But not acting on my *own* guilt was crucial to the process. In most situations where we don't hide our feelings, children of all ages get quite upset. You need to let this happen, without rescuing them by immediately trying to make them feel okay.

So, I ignored Leah's tears; I didn't try to take her off the hook. And, I waited until *I* felt a little better. Finally, she stopped crying, and we hugged. For the rest of the night, she played more independently and was very loving to me.

When we are honest about unparentlike feelings, children almost always respond. However, sometimes they may not show it right away. If you've been in an Angry Dance, for example, there's a chance they'll act as if they couldn't care less that you're hurt or disappointed. This is natural and you need to let it go. Even though he continues to *look* as if he doesn't care, if you just give it a chance, later on that night or perhaps the next day, he may approach you in a less belligerent manner. Guilt sometimes takes a while to work its magic. But if you're genuine about your reactions, and you don't rely on it too often, guilt almost always leads to a greater connection between parent and child. We *are*, after all, human, and it truly helps children to feel their impact on another human being whom they love.

Indirect Guilt: Dirty Tricks

Knowing that you need always to keep your parental repertoire varied, here are a few additional dirty tricks—which I think fall under the heading of "indirect guilt"—that you may want to keep up your sleeve. These are some favorites that good parents have shared with me over the years.

The Soften-'em-up Tactic   If you know that tomorrow you're going to have to convince your child to do something or go somewhere she won't like, the evening before, soften her up

—fix a favorite meal, do a special favor, or play a game she really likes. Remind her (only once), before bed or upon awakening, how much you enjoyed going out of your way. Your request will then be made in an atmosphere of relative goodwill, and you'll have a slightly better chance of getting some cooperation. Obviously, this one is good only a couple of times before your child catches on.

The Intentionally Overheard Conversation　Do you remember how Samantha's mother in Chapter 6 dealt with the fact that Sam had been extremely nasty to her lately? Rather than express her hurt directly to the child, she told Samantha's father. The conversation took place in the car, and Samantha, in the back seat, could hear every word, although Mom never addressed her directly or brought it up again. You can have these purposely overheard conversations with a spouse, another relative, or a good friend.

Purposely Losing the Game　Often mothers and fathers will tell me that they've created a battle *on purpose* that they're willing to lose—in order to win later or the next day. Thus, on Friday, they may give in about playing Battle Tech or staying up past the normal bedtime. And on Saturday, they'll find it easier to get him to clean up his room for Grandma's arrival.

A simple reminder, like, "Look, you beat me last night, so don't push it today," is sometimes just enough to do the trick. Losing on purpose isn't so difficult or even phony—we often feel like throwing in the towel because it's easier. And if doing this *once in a while* increases the possibility of getting action on something else you want, it's not such a bad deal.

Getting an I.O.U.　There's nothing wrong with having your child know that she owes you a favor. Life is really a two-way street, and family members are always in debt to one another. Occasionally reminding your child of this fact does absolutely no harm. Since children tend to move on so quickly and forget all the ways we give to them, getting a *written* I.O.U. for certain favors is an effective device:

> *Celia owes Mom one favor for the time Mom*
> *went to five different stores to find the*
> *book that Celia lost in the schoolyard.*
> > *Celia (signature)*
> > *Mom (signature)*

Mom cashed in on the above I.O.U. when she needed Celia's help cleaning out the porch one Saturday. Getting a written I.O.U. like this is constructive guilt in the best sense. Your child has a chance to repay a debt, which then makes her feel better about herself and closer to you.

• • •

A final word about bribery, threats, and guilt: As with all parenting strategies I suggest in this book (or those in any book, for that matter), you must be the Parent Realist. You must remember that good strategies are effective for a few days, perhaps a week at a time. Then you need to move on. The reason nothing ever works for too long is because your children keep changing—yesterday's perfect strategy becomes tomorrow's ineffective dance. We so easily go back onto automatic pilot; we begin to tune each other out, and the connection is lost.

When you get right down to it, "dirty tricks" help us reestablish a connection and therefore our effectiveness. The real trick is not to become boxed in by ideas of fairness or by the notion of consistency. Creativity and resourcefulness are our allies. So, go back and forth between the various possibilities suggested in the last two chapters. And make the most of all your options.

11

The Myth of the Self-Sufficient Parent
How to Connect with Other Families Before There's a Crisis

When I was around nine or ten, one day, on the way home from school, I happened to cross against a red light. By the time I got home, my mother was waiting at the front door, ready to lecture me about the seriousness of my transgression. I was dumbfounded. How long did the reach of her influence extend, I wondered? What magical powers she must have had!

When I questioned, "How did you know, Ma?" she told me that *how* she knew was not important. What I did wrong was the issue at hand. Understandably, for some time after that, I was rather careful at intersections, always wary that some agent of my parents might spot me.

Whether I liked it or not, when I was growing up in my neighborhood, the adults around me were aware of my comings and goings. This magical network, serving as extra pairs of ears and eyes and arms, was composed of a variety of adults: my parents' friends, many of whom happened to be the parents of *my* best friends as well; members of my extended family who lived in the area, too; and people who were associated with the community center or the local religious institution, who, at the first sign of misbehavior, knew where to reach my parents.

In those days, for better or worse, there was also little or no divorce in the neighborhood. Everyone knew who was married to whom and what kids belonged in which household. There was a kind of unwritten code—that parents would be there for one another, for support, to talk about problems as they came up, and in times of crisis. If sickly Mrs. Miller had to go into the hospital again, it was understood that little Ricky would come to my house or any of the other boys' houses after school; and when Freddy's father died, some of the other dads in the neighborhood became pinch-hit "uncles."

My parents and their friends seemed to have a sense of confidence about their parenting that came from being able to talk with other parents about what their children were doing and to solve problems together, offering solace and suggestions. I was thinking about this recently when I was dealing with the divorced mother of a thirteen-year-old boy who had seemingly run away. After Mother and I had been on the phone a number of times for the better part of the evening, I finally said, "You shouldn't be going through this alone, Alice. Why don't you make some calls to his friends' parents? I'm sure they will be sympathetic to what you're feeling."

"But I really don't know any one of them well enough to impose on them like that," Alice told me. What a dramatic contrast to the way things were in my old neighborhood!

Parenting Without a Safety Net

What happened to that mother is a microcosm of a very problematic modern-day situation, which was highlighted recently in the popular press:

The idea of "community" has always held a special attraction for Americans. In a 1984 speech, President Ronald Reagan celebrated America's "bedrock"— "its communities where neighbors help one another, where families bring up kids together, where American values are born." Gov. Mario M. Cuomo of New York, with a very different political leaning, has been almost as lyrical. "Community . . . is the reality on which our national life has been founded," he said in 1987.

There is only one problem with this picture. Most Americans no longer live in traditional communities. They live in suburban subdivisions bordered by highways and sprinkled with shopping malls, or in tony condominiums and residential clusters, or in ramshackle apartment buildings and housing projects. Most of them commute to work and socialize on some basis other than geographic proximity. And most people pick up and move to a different neighborhood every five years or so.[1]

That's just what Alice was up against. Her child was out there—probably hanging out with a group of kids—while she sat home alone. He was connected with his friends, most likely having a great time, while she at home was frightened, waiting helplessly by the phone, having no one to turn to— except someone she *paid* to listen. This gave the child the power. He called the shots. And the envelope was upside down.

The upside-down quality of such a scene is in direct contrast to the way many of us grew up. It also resonates with so much of what parents face today. When you get right down

[1] "Secession of the Successful," *The New York Times*, Sunday, January 20, 1991, pp. 16–17.

to it, parents are, in fact, parenting without the benefit of a safety net. We are expected to provide an empathic envelope —a container—without having one around us ourselves. We are expected to nurture without being nurtured. Further-more, even though we try to get by without the benefit of a safety net, we are faced with unprecedented pressure from our kids at earlier and earlier ages.

Am I Ready for This?

Modern parents are now burdened with decisions about matters that used to be the province of adolescence. Those supposedly "quiet" years from seven to twelve are quiet no more. Today's school-age kids act more like adolescents: seven- to-eight-year-olds begin to hassle parents with their constant wrangling and bargaining; some nine- and-ten-year-olds want to go on dates, and most of them have been exposed to an almost continuous stream of sex and violence on TV or in the movies; eleven- and twelve-year-olds hang bad-taste posters on their walls, some think it's "cool" to talk back to parents, and certainly most know about the existence of drugs.

Along these lines, I found it particularly striking to study a photo taken at a recent New Kids on the Block concert. Par-ents were waiting outside while their fourth, fifth, and sixth graders were inside the concert hall, some without parental supervision. By the sixth grade in many areas around the country there's pressure from kids to have parties without chaperons. And even if parents are present, because of mod-ern-day divorce and remarriage configurations, it's not such a simple matter to call Johnny's mom or dad in order to check out the specifics.

As one mother told me, "My daughter asked me if she could go to her friend Alissa's house for a party Friday night.

I know nothing about what kind of supervision will be there, but I feel uncomfortable calling, because her parents are separated, and it's in her father's house. Alissa goes there every other weekend, but I don't feel I have enough of a relationship with him to push for the information I need to have."

That mother was right to be concerned. Parties with preadolescents are not always the harmless affairs they used to be. "Spin the Bottle" has been replaced by "fooling around," a euphemism for everything but "going all the way," as we used to call it. (By high school graduation, 48 percent of all teenagers have had their first experience with sexual intercourse.)

In both suburban and urban areas, young teenagers' parties are likely to include alcohol—with beer as the drink of choice these days. Parents of thirteen-year-olds who leave their kids alone for the weekend almost guarantee that their home or apartment will eventually be used as a place to hang out, and, most likely, as a place to drink.

Plugged-In Kids

Several decades ago, parents of teenagers *also* complained about their kids—how they felt powerless against the enormous influence of what was then called the "counterculture"—images, icons, and ideas that were foreign to adults, if not downright repulsive. Today, those cries still ring true, but it's parents of eight-, nine-, and ten-year-olds who are muttering the same sorts of things about the pop culture. Furthermore, there's another important difference: The moving front of the pop culture knows no bounds. With the pervasiveness of mass communication, the pop culture can't be contained; it's bigger and more intrusive than most parents can handle.

In Chapter 4, I mentioned a six-year-old whose mother

was upset because she came home and asked what "oral sex" was. Well, that question signaled to the mother that something was going on with the girl's ten-year-old brother. As it turned out, unbeknownst to the parents, he and several other kids in his class had been tuning into the local cable TV sex shows. None of the parents had been aware of what was going on—right under their noses *in their own homes*! Yet all the kids in the fifth-grade class knew about the boys' midnight escapades.

Again, I am struck by the upside-down quality of modern family life: While kids are totally connected and plugged in —to the pop culture and to each other—their parents live essentially disconnected from one another. Busy in their own lives, parents are often unaware of what's going on in the families of their children's friends. On the other hand, kids get plugged in at astonishingly early ages in ways we take for granted.

With automatic touch-tone dialing, even a four-year-old can use the phone without getting a parent's permission or help. And by the time they're nine, ten, and eleven, the situation explodes. With gathering momentum, kids spend more and more time talking to each other and guarding their phone rights with a vengeance. How much did *you* talk on the phone as a kid? Yet, just try calling the home of a preadolescent or adolescent these days, and it becomes clear who is plugged in and who isn't. As kids get older, it's possible for adults to get through to each other only if you've got callwaiting or a second line. (Call-waiting, originally conceived as a helpful communication feature for people with busy lives, now guarantees that the parents of an eleven-year-old will never have an uninterrupted conversation for the next seven or eight years!)

Between movies and MTV, the phenomenon of pluggedin kids transcends regional lines and even developmental lines. How else can one explain hearing Valley Girl talk—

complete with requisite expressions like "awesome," "tubu-lar," and "grody"—while visiting relatives in San Diego, talking to the children of old friends in Minneapolis, sitting in a shopping mall in Columbus, Ohio, and eating dinner in New Jersey with a family whose three daughters go to paro-chial school.

At a recent party for a five-year-old, there was yet another reminder of how even the youngest of our kids swim in the same soup dished out by the marketing chefs who appeal to our preteens and teens. Midway through the party, someone put Mel Brooks' *SpaceBalls* on the VCR. For the next hour and a half, kids from five to twelve, many of whom didn't know each other, sat transfixed and united—members of the same secret society—all of them shouting in unison to the dialogue of the movie. (This is poetic irony for Brooks, since in the film it is suggested that "marketing" is The Force that propels all life.) Once again, the parents were not exactly "with it," but these five- to twelve-year-old kids were connected through a sort of peer group subculture that one would consider to be the province of teenagers or cult film enthusiasts.

Peer Groups for Parents

Parents muddling through on their own is certainly different than the reliable network of previous generations. In today's culture, the idea of a "peer group" seems to apply only to children, especially preteens and adolescents. For many ur-ban and suburban families, who live their on-the-go lives without the benefit of an extended family, or a real neigh-borhood, or jobs that stay in one place, there is little support for parents that is *specifically connected to their children's daily lives*. For all the reasons I've mentioned, ordinary parents going about the ordinary tasks of parenting have just about no peer group to support them.

This truly modern condition—parenting without a safety net—robs mothers and fathers of power and unbalances the natural generational hierarchy in families. The lack of daily support for parents is a main reason we often feel overwhelmed by the persistent (and mostly normal) demands of our kids.

When do parents finally get help for themselves? Ironically, when our children get into serious trouble: when there's a problem like substance abuse, an eating disorder, failing at school, fighting with peers, or when she runs away. *That's* when parents get help for themselves. Then, and only then, do parents get the support that they have actually needed all along.

In our modern culture, the proverbial child's "cry for help" now ends up getting help for the parents' own beleaguered (and previously ignored) situation. Thus, we find ourselves in the Age of Support Groups. Unfortunately, this much-needed support comes a little too late—when we're *already* in deep, deep trouble.

Support Groups as Empathic Envelopes

Fourteen-year-old Alan was compulsively making obscene phone calls—two hundred or more a month. When his parents took him to a therapist, *that's* when they got help for the problems they had. Both had been abused as children, the father beaten, the mother molested. Their experiences had left them ashamed and isolated—truly alone in their day-to-day lives. But Alan's blatant behavior couldn't be swept under the rug; it forced them to get the help they each needed, even if, at first, it was to help Alan with *his* problem. Dad joined an ACOA (Adult Children of Alcoholics) group, and Mom an incest survivor's support group. In these groups, they found other parents struggling with similar issues. For the first time in their parenting lives, they felt part of their *own empathic envelope*. And because his parents felt stronger, Alan's behavior improved dramatically. The connection may be hard to understand, but in the crucible of family life, when we adults aren't supported, we can't be effective as parents—and our children get in trouble.

In the same way, seven-year-old Dylan was melodramatic with his peers. He whined and became hysterical when he didn't get his own way. No one wanted to play with him. His behavior didn't stop until his mother and father, who had divorced several years before and were now remarried, went to a family center for guidance about stepfamily life. There they met other stepfamilies struggling with divorce and remarriage. When they finally got the support *they* needed to make this difficult life transition, they were able to be strong enough to help Dylan calm down and get along better with his peers.

Likewise, when fifteen-year-old Lynn began drinking in high school, she was sent off to a highly structured substance abuse program for teenagers. One of the requirements of her stay was parental involvement in a support group. Lynn's parents met once a week with the parents of other kids who had similar problems. This newfound support for both Lynn *and* her parents brought the girl's behavior under control, and she was eventually able to go back to school.

What helped in each of these rather extreme situations was that the *parents* received the support and guidance that they had been living without for years. As a by-product of the crisis, the children's problems unwittingly created a kind of extended family for them, a community of people with common concerns.

To my mind, support groups have become the neighborhoods of the '80s and '90s. They're the modern answer to what's missing: the extended families, organized religious affiliations, and close-knit communities many of us grew up with. Just like the reliable network of previous generations, today's support groups offer concrete rituals and guidance, a regular place to meet, ethical and spiritual values, a common language. In short, these groups offer everything that previous generations needed and could take for granted in dealing with the rigors of daily life.

Support groups for specific problems have saved millions of lives and are absolutely necessary. The only problem is that they're "sickness" oriented, and they don't happen earlier—before difficulties arise. They're not part of normal, everyday living, and, in the meantime, parents live without support *until problems develop*. Only when there's a breakdown in the family, or a crisis with the kids, do parents get the help that they've actually needed all along.

Self-sufficient parenting is not only a myth, it is a debilitating and destructive expectation. In order for parents to create an empathic envelope for our families, we need to garner support for ourselves *before* serious problems occur. We parents need to develop more of the reliable, taken-for-granted networks of previous generations—to help deal with the everyday humdrum issues of child rearing.

Extending the Empathic Envelope: Transitional Grade Parent Groups

When groups of parents bond together in response to the myriad of *everyday* problems, the communities they form are a small step toward re-creating the dependable neighborhood networks of days gone by. Started by parents whose children are in the first, sixth or seventh, and ninth grades (those difficult "in-between" years), they are called "transitional grade" parent groups. (Of course, with preadolescence happening earlier these days, it's not uncommon to see parents of third-, fourth-, and fifth-graders getting together as well.)

Transitional grade parent groups can help parents get through the typical precrisis issues that pressure us—everything from homework, chores, sibling rivalry, and hanging out after school, to drugs, sex, and rock and roll.

How Do We Get Started?   Get together with a few parents of your child's friends. It's important that you begin with parents whom your child sees on a day-to-day basis. Because you want to create the feeling of a greater presence in your child's life, you have to go where the peer group is—most often, it's his classmates.

Start small, and gradually build up. Spread outward from your child's closest friends. Or let every parent in the class know, and start with whoever shows up—they're obviously most interested in being part of such a group. The idea is to create a group of concerned parents whose kids see each other day to day.

Where Do We Have the First Meeting?   If possible, the first meeting should not be at the school, but rather at one of the parents' homes. It's more personal that way. If it's at your house, it's best not to have your child there; let him have a sleep-over date. That way, your child doesn't feel left out or talked about or threatened by seeing all the parents together. Also, you can then speak openly without having to worry if she's in earshot.

If the group is too big, you may decide to hold the meeting at a community center or at the school. Most school officials are very cooperative when it comes to supporting these groups. But at first, until you get off the ground, the group should only be composed of parents; do not include any officials from the school. This is to ensure that the motivation comes from the parents, from their desire to nurture and strengthen themselves.

How Often Do We Meet?   This is best determined by the flow of people's lives. I've found that once a month is usually *maximum*, so that parents don't feel that these meetings intrude on their already overcrowded schedules. More often, it settles down to once every two months. The idea is to be realistic; don't make parent group meetings feel like an extra burden on parents.

Should There Be a Leader?   Pick one person or two to be leader or co-leaders who will be responsible for getting future meetings going and, at first, for leading the meetings. This has to be clear. If you leave this on a vague basis, the group will never happen.

Hopefully, there will be someone in the group who has the organizational skills and determination to get this done —to make the phone calls, send out letters, put up flyers, arrange for a meeting place, and to delegate responsibility.

Someone also has to be in charge of the group process during the meeting. A person can be chosen either on a rotating basis, with each meeting run by the person hosting the group that month, or the group might agree on one person who's particularly good at running groups to be the chairperson at every meeting.

What Should Be Discussed?   Anything that deals with the common concerns of the parents should be open to discussion. However, you'll first begin with some relatively ordinary exchanges, like introductions. You'd be surprised at how little parents know about each other. If the school doesn't provide a directory, exchanging phone numbers is an important piece of business. Don't forget to include getting the phone numbers of divorced spouses as well. Agree to call each other between meetings in case you need support, advice, or assistance. After all, that is the purpose of having these groups in the first place.

To develop a concrete agenda for the meeting, talk about your expectations and common concerns. The kinds of topics that frequently crop up are: feelings about school—how much homework the child is getting, how much help the parent should give; issues of fitting in, peer pressure, and teasing; money—how to handle it with your kids; how to control the amount of TV children watch or the movies they see at the local mall; the problems of kids hanging out in houses that are unsupervised or going to parties without parents; questions about sex, alcohol, and drugs; and safety issues—in urban areas, how one deals with street crime, and, in suburban areas, the increasing threat of kidnapping.

After the meeting, someone should be responsible for writing up minutes to distribute to the attending parents. You will also need to make decisions for future meetings: who will lead them, where will they be.

Do We Need a Professional?   There are only two instances in which I'd suggest bringing in someone with professional credentials: First, you may need help in harnessing the group process. It's important to prevent any one person from dominating. That's the single biggest problem that tends to sabotage the effectiveness of parent groups. When one or two powerful and vocal parents take over, and their interests and opinions don't reflect the group as a whole, it is probably not in the group's best interest. If that happens, and the group feels stuck, you may need to bring in a professional.

The other instance in which a professional can be helpful is as a resource—to provide information about a particular topic. For example, you might want to know more about the signs of substance abuse, eating disorders, or whatever is of interest to your group.

What Topics Are Off-Limits?   Long-standing personal gripes with other parents that have nothing to do with your children don't belong at these meetings. In the same way, if your child has told you something in confidence, don't bring it up. The one exception to this rule is when you feel that your child or another child is in danger. No matter what promise your child has exacted from you, safety must come first. For example, if your child tells you that he and some other kids had been drinking beer at another parent's house, that's worrisome enough to break the confidence.

How Will Our Children React?   Younger kids either ignore or love the fact that their parents have created a support group for themselves. They're the least ambivalent about extending the empathic envelope past the boundaries of their own families. However, as kids get older—around sixth grade— they start becoming uneasy about it. They think the idea of their parents having a peer group is "weird." Of course, that's because the idea of parents helping each other with "normal" everyday life *is* a relatively foreign concept. Feeling left out, they may push for a group of their own. I'd first ignore that request (to make sure it's serious), but if they're in high school, it might be helpful for them to have a group forum to air their feelings.

Since many pre- and early adolescents (especially boys) have a hard time just sitting still long enough to concentrate on something so vague as "parent/child issues," group meetings for kids under ninth grade can be particularly chaotic. Beginning with ninth grade, however, the level of maturity has progressed to the point where kids can begin to articulate their concerns about parents in a more orderly fashion. These meetings are a tremendous source of information for parents about what's on kids' minds. Interestingly, from the meetings I've conducted with kids, what's most on their minds is— *parents*. "My parents seem *insecure*. They blame themselves for everything. They go through periods of no confidence about what they're doing—and *that* drives me crazy!" The kids are, of course, adamant that they be treated "fairly," but equally sure that they want parents who have some degree of self-esteem. And they're right. Parents with self-respect create an empathic envelope that is compassionate and secure.

I've also found that regardless of kids' initial reactions, they're relieved that you're doing something to make yourself feel stronger. Indeed, most children tell me privately that they feel *good* about it! However, they won't admit that to *you!* Most likely they'll say, "Why are you meeting like this?" Explain in a straightforward way: "We parents need to help make ourselves feel stronger and not so cut off from each other." Say that you're doing it for *yourself.* Don't turn it around and imply that you're doing it for your child.

The bottom line is that the commitment to your own nurturing is not lost on your kids. When you admit that you're not self-sufficient, you become the Parent Realist. And when we're realistic about ourselves, it makes our children feel cared for.

One mother told me a great story that reflects how much kids really favor these meetings: She had been instrumental in getting a group going in her son's class, and about a week after the first meeting was held she was approached by one of her son's classmates. This particular seventh-grader, who sported a large shock of blue hair and a black leather biker jacket, was not someone her son normally brought home after school. In fact, the mother found the boy a little menacing, especially when he came into the kitchen and announced, "I got somethin' I want to say to you." She figured she was really in for it.

The boy looked her straight in the eye and asked, "How come you didn't send *my* mother an invitation to your group?" Before she had a chance to answer, he instructed her in no uncertain terms, "Don't make that mistake again," and turned around and swaggered out of the room.

The Results

Below are the minutes of a seventh-grade parent group that discussed the topic of parties without supervision.

Minutes of Parent Group Meeting
Parties Without Supervision

1. Parents have the responsibility to chaperon and be a visible presence for our kids. Our children should not have to find themselves in the position of dealing with unruly guests at parties without parental support and authority.
2. When guests are dismissed from a party, the chaperon should be present to be sure that children are called for by their parents.
3. Children need to be picked up from parties on time. If a child is to travel home alone, the chaperon should be told.
4. Once a child is at a party, he should not be allowed to leave without permission.
5. There need to be appropriate time limits set for parties, depending on the age of the children. Some parties are just too long to hold the attention of twelve- and thirteen-year-olds.
6. Children at a party should be reminded of a few things: They must greet and thank the host. They must ask permission of the chaperon before going outside for air or before using other areas of the home or party space. And a party at home requires the same high standards of behavior as a party in a special environment.

Were all these rules carried out by the parents? Of course not. Some fell by the wayside over time and under pressure from the kids. But by providing *any* guidelines, parents took the important step of breaking the *kids' rule* that parents shouldn't get together, lean on each other, and exchange information. The mutual support derived from these sorts of discussions proved so helpful to the parents that they continued group meetings into high school. Another parent group began in first grade and actually met for ten years, the purpose of the group obviously moving well past child-rearing issues. The group became the extended family and neighborhood many had left behind.

Summarizing another of these transitional grade meetings, at which about forty parents of sixth-graders met, one of the members described the hopeful, collaborative spirit that is created: "We spent the evening talking with each other about the social issues of our children. We shared information, gave support, disagreed and agreed about our values, expectations, and differences with each other. We perhaps felt a bit more comforted by each other and more confident that we are all in this together and that we can count on each other to keep an effective net around our community."

Widening the Empathic Envelope

Once a parent group has been established and is meeting on a regular basis, it's time to strengthen and widen the empathic envelope to include the school. Although PTAs exist in most schools, organizing special events from seminars to picnics and pot-luck dinners, there is usually little effort for parents and teachers to have ongoing collaboration about issues. More often, these groups get together in the hierarchical format of parent/teacher conferences. This is not really collaboration, but more of an evaluation. The other times parents and teachers have formal contact is in response to a crisis—a death, a rumor that has spread, a difficult situation in the community. Neither of these situations—crises or open-school nights—help bridge the gap between the world of school and home. In fact, what often happens is that a chasm develops between the two worlds.

I have done many consultations in schools and have been repeatedly struck by the subtle antagonism that can exist between parents and teachers. For their part, parents often feel that they hear too little from the school, that teachers are not available enough or open to criticism. And the teachers, feeling overwhelmed themselves (just like the parents), sometimes believe that parents simply hand over to them the responsibility of "raising their children." Both groups often feel that the other has little real understanding of what they're up against.

How can such a disconnection between these two significant forces in children's lives be helpful? And what sort of coordinated message do we send our children—about values, acceptable social behaviors, competitiveness—when there's a lack of communication between life before and after three P.M.?

When you apply the concept of the empathic envelope to the school as well as to the family, you can begin bridging the gap between parents and teachers. It's helpful to follow this sequence:

- The parent groups should first meet as I have described above. After their concerns have emerged, a formal connection needs to be made with the school, describing an agenda and asking for a meeting with the teachers of the grade.
- To prepare, the teachers need to meet together and discuss concerns they have about the kids—and the parents. The idea of a parent/teacher meeting must be supported by the school's hierarchy—principal,

deans, guidance counselors—or it will not be successful. Also, the reason for the meeting needs to be framed as a way to collaborate with parents to work better with their kids. Otherwise, teachers may feel like their territory is being invaded.

- Parents and teachers then can meet together. Meetings are organized around a specific topic that both groups decide is important. For example, groups of third- through sixth-grade parents and teachers met on the subject of teasing and ostracism. They tried to come up with a united set of values and to coordinate a strategy for dealing with teasing at home and in the classroom. Another topic was homework —how to handle it, how much parents should get involved, how teachers can let parents know when there's a problem, how to tell whether schoolwork was actually getting done. A third parent/teacher meeting dealt with helping the parent communicate with the teacher and vice-versa—literally, what time of day, how often, how long conversations should be; as well as how to bring topics up with each other in nonaccusing or defensive ways.

These can also be pure information-sharing meetings, without a particular topic. After all, kids are notorious for *not* talking about what goes on at school. One such meeting occurred at a school in which a teacher had been absent for a long time. An incorrect rumor had been circulating that the teacher was dying of AIDS, so the parents and teachers got together to stop the rumor. At the same time, the incident made parents and teachers realize it was also time to figure out what to say to kids about AIDS, so that was added to the evening's agenda.

At another school—and I've seen this happen increasingly throughout the country—parents are brought in to teach classes. They talk about what they know best: A computer expert explains a new software program; a comedy writer reveals how comedy is written for television; and a chef talks about how different foods go in and out of fashion depending on the times.

Needless to say, the guest "teachers" gave the students extraordinary and personal insights about different careers. Moreover, the children whose parents were involved suddenly saw their parents in the school setting; they really *felt* their parents' presence. Equally important, it gave the parents a greater understanding of what it's like to be in the teachers' shoes—to handle twenty or thirty high-energy kids —which immediately made them less antagonistic and more empathic toward the teachers!

Finally, parent/teacher meetings are an important way to *anticipate* what issues might come up later in the year. Bring in an expert to talk about problems that don't yet exist but could come up on the developmental menu at any time. At one school, it was hard for some parents and teachers to understand the wisdom of having meetings around problems that didn't yet exist. However, several months later, when those fifth-graders made major leaps into rowdy preteen behavior, parents and teachers were well prepared and not thrown off guard by the kids. I'd hold such meetings once at the beginning of the school year.

In each of these cases, the idea was to create an *ongoing* collaboration between parents and teachers and to narrow the distance between them, thus strengthening and widening the empathic envelope and making it more resilient. Straightening out bad communication between parents and teachers is as powerful as helping disconnected mothers and fathers at home. It makes parents and teachers more effective and helps turn the upside-down hierarchy of modern family life right side up, with adults more in charge of the process and with the kids feeling more "held" by school *and* home.

Parent/Child Workshops

When bridges have been created between school and parent, it's time to bring parents, school, *and kids* together. Of all the work I do with families, parent/child workshops conducted in the school are the most rewarding and fascinating. Generally, a particular topic is chosen, taken from everyday life. I must stress that topics should *not* be about "heavy" problems; they must be about children and parents in *normal* circumstances. These are particularly effective from grades three through six.

For example, at one workshop, seventy-five parents and their children discussed, "Getting Through the Day: Keeping the Lines of Communication Open." As the parents and children talked about the hot spots in a typical day, there were very poignant exchanges around specific issues.

One father got the ball rolling when he asked his own son, "How come you never answer when I ask, 'What happened in school today?'" The son said that he felt as if he needed a time between school and home when he didn't feel he had to "produce" anything—a kind of rest period. Another child said that when her mother asked her what was going on, she felt "quizzed." Another brought up the point that it would be nice if his mother told his father what he had said, so that he didn't have to go over everything twice. It made him feel as if his parents never talked to each other. Many kids also said their parents' questions weren't specific enough. Instead of asking, "What happened in school today?" they wanted their parents to ask very pointed questions, such as, "What happened today in arithmetic with Sally? I know you told me that she was having trouble with fractions, and you helped tutor her."

The parents, on the other hand, had their point of view: One, whose comment I mentioned in Chapter 10, told his son, "You know why I ask you about school every day? A lot of the day at work I have to spend time doing things that I consider very tedious. But when I hear about the details of your day, it gives me a lift for the rest of the night." A mother said, "It's not that I need to pry. It's another way of saying 'hello,' and to bridge the gap that I feel has developed during the day."

Some other topics at these parent/child workshops have included: Life with Siblings; How to Deal with the "Gimmes": Money, Values, and Consumerism; How to Deal with Chores, Responsibilities, and Sharing Around the House. Whenever these parent/child workshops meet—generally, it's three or four times a year—there is always a burst of response. The next day parents, who had never done so before, start to approach the school guidance counselor to discuss matters about their children. And the kids actually look forward to the meetings, feeling they have a controlled forum to discuss everyday life with parents.

After his first parent/child workshop, one ten-year-old boy lamented, "I forgot to bring up something that was on my mind." Thinking about it for a moment, he shrugged his shoulders and said, "Oh well, I guess I'll just bring it up at the next meeting." Interestingly, at that point no meeting had been scheduled, but the forum obviously felt so "right" to this kid that he assumed (and hoped) it would become a regular occurrence.

Networking with Parents of Older Kids

When your kids are in ninth grade or older, it's not as easy to have parent groups comprising the parents of their friends. For one thing, you can't divulge the confidences of teenagers without their getting very upset. When that starts to happen, many parents widen the empathic envelope and get themselves nurtured by going through a Y, a community center, a church or synagogue, rather than through the school. These centers attract parents from different schools and different areas, so there's more anonymity, which their teenage children find less threatening.

Of course, similar topics are covered at these parent groups. Since the parents don't know each other, it is generally better if they are run by a professional who facilitates communication. Once the mothers (who are usually the first to respond to these meetings) realize that the aim is to create the sense of neighborhood, regarding everyday issues in their lives, fathers begin trickling in. By the end of the series, it turns out that there are always *as many fathers in the groups as mothers.* People also end up bringing their friends—even friends with kids of different ages; some bring their own parents.

Ultimately, the group—with mothers, fathers, grandparents, friends—really *does* develop a "neighborhood" feel. It becomes a place to share information and to become more effective as parents. It gives parents an arena in which they get something for themselves and take care of their kids at the same time. As one parent remarked, "I never understood just how alone I've been as a parent. How could I not have realized something as simple as that?"

• • •

Many parents feel on a treadmill lost in space, just trying to get by, isolated from their peers. They have little support against the powerful alliance of children, the pop culture, and the rush of time. Given all this, being self-sufficient is most definitely an illusion and a myth. It is a denial of parents' need to be nurtured. Sadly, most of us realize how undernourished we've been only when the kids or family get into big trouble. That's when we finally receive the support that we needed all along, that we didn't even know we were missing.

In the end, parents and kids essentially want the same thing: parents who are strong and sure. Widening the empathic envelope by building connections with other parents and with the school is one way to do something positive *before* there's a crisis.

12

The Myth of the Wise Parent
How to Deal with a Dozen
Impossible Situations That
You Can't Possibly Solve

When parents get together to share practical solutions to everyday problems, it is immediately clear that no expert is any better at coming up with solutions than parents themselves. Indeed, the child-rearing experts I admire the most have drawn much of their concrete advice about raising kids from listening to and learning from parents.

One of the immediate benefits of the parenting groups I described in the last chapter is that they give mothers and fathers a chance to share information—directly with each other. When children are included, and parent/child dialogues ensue, the amount of information shared between families is impressive. Kids, seemingly fortified by the presence of other children, are remarkably open about how the different child-rearing techniques we read about actually make them feel.

This chapter lists the most popular techniques I've collected from parents and children over the last twenty years to deal with certain "impossible" situations. They're the issues that invariably come up when families discuss daily situations around the house that defy us and are virtually impossible to solve.

Because they have been "test-marketed" by thousands of families, the solutions presented here are realistic—they offer no miracle cures. Indeed, this chapter reflects the *limits* of our parental power—the need to *think small* in order to be effective and maintain the parent/child connection. It is also meant to be a "no-frills" reference guide.

Remember the Myth of Harmony: None of the solutions offered will work for *all* situations, nor will they work for more than a little while. But the more options you have at your disposal, the more effective you'll be. So, if you can add one, two, or three extra strategies to your repertoire from the suggestions that follow, you may be able to make those impossible situations a little easier to get through.

The Morning Chaos

• *Divide and conquer.* Parents with two or more children wake up one before the other. That way they can focus on one kid at a time. Alternate which child you wake first; or, perhaps one child regularly needs a little more sleep. Parents say that the idea is not to handle both children together—even a ten- or fifteen-minute staggered schedule helps with gridlock in the morning.

• *Change off parents.* I often hear that one parent is a good morning person and the other a bad morning person. It's not effective to have a bad morning person wake a bad morning kid. Two cranky people stuck together invariably end up getting nowhere or, worse, into a wrangle. Ideally, then, a better morning parent should team up with a bad morning kid. If Mom and Dad both have trouble in the morning, it helps to alternate.

• *Get the issue of what to wear out of the way*. Some parents check tomorrow's weather and lay out clothes ahead of time. If they're comfortable they let their child choose an outfit the night before.

• *Choose clothing that involves less layering, if possible*. As every parent knows, the more layers, the more chances for procrastination.

When you know you're going to have to rush the next day because of something special, it's helpful to keep in mind that many parents simply give up. They let children get dressed the *night before* and sleep in their clothes! When it comes to children's attire, we need to ask ourselves, "Is it crucial what my child wears? Is it really going to affect her psychological well-being forever if she ends up choosing colors that don't match or articles of clothing that don't look great?" Veteran parents would rather live with wrinkled outfits than frazzled mornings.

• *Create a checklist together*. Children like this one. Ask your child to write a list of all the things that must be done in the morning: washing up, getting dressed, eating breakfast, brushing teeth, making a sandwich for lunch, getting books ready. You write one also, and then combine lists, letting her choose the order she wants to get them done. Kids are less obstinate if they can control some aspect of a task—here it's the order of the chores.

• *Spend five minutes of play time in the morning*. Because the underlying issue in the morning is saying good-bye (more than stubbornness or procrastination), even a tiny amount of time together may be enough to refuel your child, so that he finds it easier to let go and get going. Of course, you can't do this if you're still pushing things along on the sly. It really has to be play time, *without haggling*. Don't try slipping an extra sock on or reminding your child of what he has to do next. The five minutes needs to be one of connection—sitting together reading a story, finishing a brief game, and so on. Mothers and fathers who can be Parent Chums for just a few minutes are amazed at how much easier the morning is.

Coming Home: "What Did You Do Today?"

• *Leave him alone for a specified period of time.* Be a Parent Chum. Ask your child how much time he needs to unwind after school. If it seems reasonable to you, agree to a "no bugging" period. During that time, don't ask questions, don't remind about chores or homework. Let him "veg out." You've probably been trained not to bother him anyway, but now try to do it without feeling guilty or annoyed.

• *"Feed me!"* Whatever your taste—health food or junk— some kind of snack helps bridge the connection gap from the day. In parent/child workshops, kids always mention how much they appreciate a snack when they come home.

• *Tell them something about* **your** *day*. Our child-centered culture makes us overly conscious of asking kids about *their* day; part of being a Parent Chum is to share what *you* did as well. It takes some of the pressure off him to feel he has to "produce." And it helps to fight the underlying notion in many families that only the kids' lives matter—or, as one thirteen-year-old put it to his ever-questioning mother: "Mom, will you get a life?"

• *Ask* **specific** *questions*. I've mentioned this earlier, but it bears repeating. Kids hate being asked, "How was your day?" Specific questions are better, like, "Did you find any books for your report on John Kennedy?" or "How are the rehearsals for the Christmas play going?" or "Did you get along with Gretchen any better on the school bus today?" Kids say that being specific shows you're involved with what they're doing.

• *Share with your spouse what your child tells you*. Any child will more willingly open up if he knows that he won't have to go through it all a second time. And, unless it's a secret, most kids like it when parents talk to each other—the envelope feels more secure.

Dinnertime Indigestion

• *Don't* **expect** *conversation at dinner*. If you're not a Parent Realist, you'll be disappointed a lot of the time. Kids tell me they can't stand the notion of conversation being forced at dinner, and the more parents expect it, the less they're inclined to talk. Parents who more regularly have family conversations around the table make the following suggestions:

• *Start family dinners when children are young*. The younger, the better. Preschool is best.

• *No TV during dinner*. Videotape important shows that conflict.

• *Don't allow phone calls during dinner*. Make sure to put the telephone answering machine on, so "urgent" calls don't interrupt the meal.

• *Don't let kids ruin* **your** *dinner*. Expect a certain amount of fighting between siblings. However, at the point at which siblings become too rambunctious—and it's making you crazy—then leave the table, or send one of them away. Which one? The way triangles work in families—especially between a parent and two kids—conflict is never the "fault" of a particular child. So be sure to alternate which child you send away from the table, no matter who *looks like* the guilty party. Tell the kids something like: "I don't care who began it tonight. You're both responsible for ruining the meal. This time I'm sending Bobby away, but next time, no matter who's at fault, Tommy will have to leave the table." Take yourself out of the Triangle Dance (with you acting as Judge), and you might have less stressful mealtimes.

• *Dinner together is not a necessity*. It may not be worth the struggle every night. As I've heard from so many families, there's nothing sacrosanct about mealtimes. If you have two kids, consider giving them dinner at different times. Leave meals out on the counter. Teach them to prepare something themselves. Or, if it means that much to you, then make sure you have dinner together a couple of times a week, and let the other evenings go.

• *Don't be afraid of silence at the dinner table*. Kids tell me that they hate it when parents start up conversations to fill in the gaps—they know their modern parents get edgy about not communicating. Since it doesn't work anyway, try to train yourself to sit through the silences.

• *Develop mealtime rituals*. Again, start when kids are young. Once a week, for example, a family I know has a "good and new" time at dinner, when every member shares something good or something new that happened during the week. This ritual was started a decade ago, and the kids, now eighteen and thirteen, *still* occasionally ask to do the "good and new."

Rituals should reflect your family's personality and needs. One family, in which the members tended to be close-mouthed, had a tradition of everyone—including the parents—saying just two sentences about his day. But in another family, the opposite problem existed. Because everyone was so talkative, there was no need for a rule to force conversation, but rather to cut down on the chaos. So Mom and Dad instituted a red napkin policy: Whoever wanted "the floor" simply picked up the red napkin placed in the center of the table. That signaled to everyone else that the person couldn't be interrupted.

• *Don't overdo it*. Dinner doesn't have to last a particular amount of time. Many parents, believing that mealtimes should be "meaningful" and that they're one of the few times that the family is together, understandably try to hold onto the moment. But from what thousands of parents say, little quality time is created when mealtimes are artificially extended.

Surviving Siblings

On this topic, parents and experts completely agree, and I would recommend any one of the many excellent books dealing with sibling rivalry. My two favorites are *Siblings Without Rivalry*, by Adele Faber and Elaine Mazlish (Norton, 1987), and *Loving Your Child Is Not Enough* by Nancy Samalin (Penguin, 1987). Briefly, here is a smattering of lessons parents have taught me, some of which you won't find in the popular books:

• *Stay out of it*. Or, as I would say, "Cut down on triangles." Don't make yourself the judge. Believe that there is
no one sibling who started it. Understand, it's the *dance*
that has to stop. Tell them, "I'll give you five minutes to
settle this, or I'll have to separate you two." Then walk
away. If five minutes feels like too long, start out by leaving the scene for just a minute or two. The important
thing is to remove yourself without getting too anxious.
Unless you are truly concerned about their safety, this is a
good way to help break the dance.

• *Get a Walkman radio*. Parents of siblings say this comes
in handy when they walk away. It blocks out the screaming that may follow. Also, it's convenient for helping you
not have to listen to all the fighting and taunting that goes
on between kids—especially a preteen and a younger
child.

• *Treat them differently*. Parents agree with the professionals, it's a trap to feel obliged to treat siblings the same
way. In fact, it's best if you find something different to
value in each and *highlight* the differences.

• *Don't punish one sibling in front of the other*. Easier
said than done. But if you're committed to this, options always emerge. For example, when a fight breaks out in a
restaurant, take the child you're upset with to another part
of the dining room (ask the waiter or manager to watch
your other child for a minute). Say your piece quietly and
privately, and then return to the table.

• *Don't tell one sibling the nature of the other's punishment*. Parents say that a punishment is far more effective
when it's kept between you and the child it's intended for.
If he tells his brother, that's his business. But try not to

increase the possibility of messy triangles by mentioning it to the other child.

• *Spend one-on-one time with the "aggressor."* Parents report that all the techniques in the world are not as powerful as a little extra time with a child—especially the one who most often takes the bad "rap." An hour a week of Parent Chum time is often all that's needed to balance things in a better direction. I've seen this make a difference with even hard-core sibling rivalry. For example, the vicious fighting between two sisters, ages thirteen and ten, diminished significantly when Dad spent a couple of hours every month with Annie, the older, more aggressive girl.

TV Obsessions

• *Set a limit on the number of hours, per week or per day.* Do this through conversation—and negotiation. The ideal seems to be a little more than you want and somewhat less than your child wants. Be a Parent Realist. From what parents say, there are almost no kids left who never watch TV (remember those few "oddballs" from your past?). On the other hand, you have to set some limits for kids—they shouldn't be allowed to watch as much TV as they want, because it may end up being four or five hours a day. Parents agree (in theory) that one to one-and-a-half hours per school day is acceptable.

• *Make children choose programs ahead of time.* Most parents let kids choose pretty much what they want to see, but they seem to reserve ultimate veto power. Parent Realists, however, know that by around middle-school—sixth and seventh grades—it's hard to stop kids entirely from watching programs we find objectionable.

• *Take advantage of a VCR, if you have one*. If a program puts your child over her limit, or intrudes into homework or chores, tape it for weekend watching. With the proliferation of VCRs nowadays, this has become a favorite parent tactic.

• *Have a pay-TV system*. Some parents give their kids an allotted figure—you'll have to come up with the exact amount on your own—and they assign a "price" to each program. In one family, for example, the parents allotted $3.50, and each program cost fifty cents. The child could spend the money any way he wanted. However, they added one incentive to make educational public television programs more appealing. Those shows only cost twenty-five cents. In fact, it worked—the boy, wanting to get more for his money, grew to like public television.

• *Try the "Temporarily-Out-of-Order" Technique*. When parents see that it's really tough to change their children's TV-addictive behavior, they go so far as to put the TV out of commission (by removing the cable wire or some other essential, but easily replaceable electronic piece). At times the TV is operational; at times it is out of commission. This lets the child know, "We don't think you should have more than one hour of TV a day, and you can't control yourself. We can see that you can't do this on your own—you're addicted—so we're helping you out." After the initial hue and cry, children actually go about their business without much fuss.

• *Watch TV with your kids*. Despite the warnings of some experts, it seems that many parents and kids enjoy TV time together. They find it's an opportunity to snuggle up on the couch, without pressure, without eye-to-eye contact, without talking. Many parents actually slate in TV dates with kids—to pile up on the couch and refuel together.

The Homework Struggle

• *Don't necessarily send your child away to do homework.* Spend less time being a cop and more time being a Parent Chum. A lot of kids say that it's too much of a *separation* doing homework in their rooms. It's like being sent to solitary confinement—too split off from the rest of the family. If given their choice, many kids prefer to sit in a part of the house, maybe the living room or kitchen if it has a table, and spread out their papers, with other members of the family nearby. Contrary to the usual belief, parents who have gone along with this often report better homework output when children are less isolated from everyone.

• *Don't force your child to work in a quiet place.* We have it in our heads that homework ought to be done in an environment where there's no noise, no distractions, no one else around. The reality these days is that kids are used to a lot of stimulation. Much to their parents' surprise, kids tell me that they, in fact, focus *better* when the TV is on and there are other things happening. It makes them nervous when it's too quiet —"spooky," "eerie," "sensory deprivation," they call it. Feeling more comfortable if everyone's in earshot—Mom watching the six o'clock news and Dad cutting up vegetables for a salad—*more* homework is actually done.

• *Don't ask, "How much homework do you have?"* Almost all children guarantee that they will answer, "not much," "a little," or "some." Why get them into the habit of *under*estimating—which they invariably do. Just set the time for homework, and don't worry about getting an initial estimate.

• *Take turns monitoring homework*. Even if your child likes to work alone in a room, parents report that it's helpful to check in every once in a while. How often is up to parent and child, but saying hello reinforces the connection—especially if it isn't always the same parent, and if it's a chummy, "How ya doin'?" rather than a surprise inspection.

• *By all means, use bribery*. Only a handful of parents I've ever met can do without occasional bribery in the homework department. When there's a crunch or a cranky kid, parents use just about anything as incentive—TV, phone, getting involved with a sticker collection—you name it.

• *Use homework to spend time with your child and strengthen the connection*. Whereas parents are often warned by the school or experts *not* to do homework with kids, in reality, they end up getting involved anyway. It seems to be a potential Parent Chum-type connection, and with so few other times available, parents and kids gravitate toward doing homework with each other. However, sometimes it's *not* a good idea—in which case families report the following signs: 1) There are often terrible struggles over the work—she gets defensive and you get angry; 2) you end up doing the homework *regularly* for your child; or 3) the work means more to *you* than it means to her. Otherwise, doing school work together—projects, practice quizzes, reading—can be great times of sharing.

Fear of Learning Disabilities: "Oh, No! My Child Is Stupid!"

• *You may not need an expert to tell you if your child has a problem*. After all, you spend more time with your child than an expert who's called in to consult. In fact, Parent Realists can often spot the signs, if they know what to look for:

> • You find yourself saying, "He could do it—if he only tried" or "He's really smart—he just doesn't care enough (or apply himself)."
>
> • Your child's performance is uneven—he's surprisingly good in one area, and falls way below par in another.
>
> • Your child learns better one-on-one than in the classroom. In class, she takes on the role of the class clown; she can't stop herself from talking, touching, fooling around; or she is very distractable.
>
> • Your child (especially around middle years—fifth and sixth grades) starts pretending that school doesn't matter, and yet he comes from a family in which learning and educational achievement are valued.

If these signs are present, psychoeducational testing is indicated. Call in a professional.

• *Don't look at your child's having a learning disability as an intellectual death sentence*. Acceptance is key. Your child's intelligence is not affected—it's the way his brain functions. Certain processing channels—visual or auditory —simply don't work as well as others. Your child can learn how to compensate for this learning difference, and you can learn how to help him. If you stay stuck in your own disappointment or guilt (common feelings many parents express when they first find out their kids have learning disabilities), you can be neither Parent Protector nor Parent Realist to your child.

• *Educate yourself.* Find out as much as you can about learning disabilities in general (there are many good books on the subject) and understand your child's problems in particular. The fascinating thing about LDs is that no two kids are alike. For example, a child who has problems with visual processing needs to sharpen her auditory skills and learn how to take information in through her ears, while another LD child has to learn how to better utilize his visual channels.

• *Explain to your child the exact nature of her problem.* Start as soon as you find out, no matter how young she is. Parents tell me that it's important to keep talking to their kids about their learning differences, too, since new problems come up as the demands of school change.

• *Become your child's advocate.* If he's seeing a tutor, monitor his progress. If he's in a special class, keep in close touch with the teacher. Demand reports in writing if testing is done. Don't just leave it to the experts—always trust your own instincts.

• *Set realistic standards for your child.* Not too high or too low. Let your child know what the rules and limits are and what you expect of her. Tell her it's okay to make mistakes or to take extra time, but she also shouldn't think that having a learning disability is an excuse for not trying.

• *Discover and nurture your child's* **nonacademic strengths**. The truth is, many LD kids are often naturally gifted in music and art; they excel as athletes; they are mechanically adept. A little self-esteem goes a long way in helping your child build confidence in her ability to overcome a learning disability.

"The Room"

• **Create a different set of standards around your child's room.** Many parents report that after a certain age, keeping "the room" tidy is like fighting the ocean. In essence, they become Parent Realists of the highest order. They throw up their hands, forget about the room itself, and protect the rest of the house or apartment! Some parents say to their kids, "You can do whatever you want in, with, and to your room, as long as it doesn't jeopardize the rest of the house." No food in his room that might attract insects or vermin; his room can even develop that "ripe" smell, as long as the odor doesn't seep out. In other words, parents decide, "We'll lose the room, but save the house."

• **The room must be cleaned "X" amount of times.** Parents make tactical decisions—once a week, once a month, whatever they can live with. With younger kids, some parents help with the clean-up. With older kids, they give them a warning ("You have two days to get this room clean"), followed by a threat ("or else you lose your right to take care of it—which means we do it, we put things where *we* want them to be, and you also lose your privacy.") Many parents also tell me that their kids don't care if they come in and clean their rooms. It may not "build character" to have it done for them, but at least the room gets deloused every now and then.

• **Watch out if two kids share a room.** Especially when the two kids are as different as Oscar and Felix, parents try all sorts of things, and, unfortunately, *almost none of them* *work!* I'm not going to pull any punches, this is a very difficult issue. You can't change kids' personalities—some are naturally neater than others, and chronic battles are unsolvable. Short of hanging a curtain or building a wall—which helps but still requires some monitoring along the borders—I haven't yet heard of a way that people get through this without a lot of trouble. Most parents end up intervening as little as possible. Only if the kids are in some kind of danger because of a physical battle do they get themselves involved.

• *Stay out!* Whether your child has his own room or shares it with a sibling, the best overall advice from thousands of parents can be summed up in those two words: "Stay out!" Don't look into the room more than necessary; don't inhale deeply when you're standing in the doorway; don't even imagine to yourself what it looks like. It will undoubtedly push your buttons and get you crazy!

Privacy: Yours and Theirs

• *Bedrooms and bathrooms need locks.* It's no surprise that so many parents don't have locks in the bedroom or bathroom. We're afraid of not being available to our kids or not having immediate access to them. Kids also get insulted or frightened when we don't operate on the 7–Eleven model—open twenty-four hours a day. With young children, bathroom locks should be workable from the outside in case of emergencies. However, except for dangerous situations, the conclusion I've heard from parents who have tried locking their doors is that they heartily endorse it. Converts will often say that they're sorry not to have tried earlier—the kids get used to it quickly;

they're not always coming in for help and often attempt to work things out independently; and, of course, there are more private moments for parents to share.

• *Don't read journals or diaries, unless . . .* In twenty years, I've never heard a parent say he or she was happy after reading their child's diary. I can almost guarantee you'll learn information you're not ready for. And then with this new, perhaps frightening, information in hand, you'll still feel unable to confront your child, because you broke a trust.

There is a good working rule, though, that parents learn: If a diary is in a *common area* or left open in her room, where she knows you'll run across it—it's an invitation to read. Perhaps not the first time, but by the second, it's rarely accidental. She may be trying to tell you something that's hard to say face to face.

If you learn something dangerous, you *must* confront her. Tell the truth: "Several times, the diary was in the dining room, right out there in the open. I couldn't ignore it any longer. And now we need to talk about this."

• *Don't listen in on phone calls, unless . . .* This situation is similar to reading diaries. If kids don't want you to hear something, they usually won't let you. When your child is talking in a common area or shouting into the phone, it's usually *meant* to be heard by you. One parent told a group that her fourteen-year-old daughter, knowing the walls were thin and Mom was in her brother's room cleaning, kept repeating the same conversation, louder and louder. *Three* times this happened—until Mom finally told her she had "overheard" the phone call.

• *There are times you must break your child's confidence.* Whenever your child's safety or the safety of someone else is at risk, you must go against your child and reveal the secret. In these situations, parents say to their kids, "I'm sorry, but I have a responsibility to (so-and-so) as another human being." I've never met a kid who doesn't understand this—in fact, kids usually tell us secrets because they want us to *do something*.

• *The walls have ears.* Don't expect fairness regarding *your* privacy. Parents say repeatedly that kids snoop and eavesdrop all the time—and at all ages. Kids admit the same things about themselves. So, unless they're locked away, any personal letters, sexual material, medications, or drugs will *definitely* be found.

• *You have the right to remain silent.* When eight-year-old Debbie asked her mom if she ever had orgasms and how many times a week she and Dad "did it," Mom was confused about how honest to be. She had always said, "Ask me anything," yet. . . . Parents report that they find their own comfort zone by trial and error. Don't feel forced to be "modern" and more revealing than you'd like. Kids say they feel guilty when they push parents to reveal more than parents genuinely want. So, it's in their best interest to say, "I'd rather not answer that."

Allowance: Whose Money Is It Anyway?

• *Try to give allowance regularly.* This is one of the areas where parents report that consistency really works best. Most *try* to stick with a regular allowance. The range I've heard goes from once a day, once a week, to once every two weeks. Decide what feels right to you—as long as it's regular. Although if you aren't totally consistent, don't get discouraged. You're not alone. Between fast-talking kids, "advances," special events, and unexpected presents from grandparents and other relatives, the reality is far less consistent than the theory.

• *Define allowance*. There's a wide range between the way families define allowance. Sometimes it's given for daily expenses or sometimes it's just for discretionary items. In both cases, most parents still reserve veto rights on spending. They let kids spend money on whatever they want—as long as it doesn't go directly against the family's values. Even with strongly held ideas, just about all parents give in more than they'd like. For example, some parents "forbid" the purchase of guns; others are against sweets; in some houses there's a "prohibition" against anything that pollutes the environment. But *limits* on restricted items seem to be more realistic. Whatever the ideology, most veteran parents have thrown in the towel; they make it clear what kind of items are off limits, but they also try to be Parent Realists and not purists.

• *Encourage saving*. Almost all parents make a decision that some amount can be spent on whatever the child wants, and some portion of allowance will be saved. Many also like to help their child open a bank account. Of course, these days you have to hunt for the kind of account that doesn't have service fees—which are often more than your child is able to save.

But what happens when the eleven-year-old who's been saving money since he was seven wants to take a large chunk of money out of the bank? One boy who was a baseball-card collector was planning to spend $150 on a particularly valuable card. Not a bad investment, perhaps, but his dad nevertheless thought that at eleven, that kind of expenditure was inappropriate. Most parents seem to agree with this approach and usually maintain the right to be a Parent Protector and veto spending. On the other end of the continuum are children who "hoard" and never spend their money. This is absolutely normal—especially for first- to fifth-graders—and is of no concern.

• *Step in if your child spends money too quickly*. That may be a signal that your child needs more help monitoring her spending. When spending gets out of hand, many parents then decide to give money in smaller chunks— lower the credit line, so to speak. Children tell me they feel relieved when parents step in.

• *Let your child get "burned" every now and then*. Although we definitely need to have ultimate veto power, we also need to give our kids a certain amount of latitude. That's why some parents occasionally allow a child to buy a poorly made item that immediately falls apart when he gets home. It helps kids become more realistic (better than anything we can *tell* them), because it's a lesson that hits where it hurts. Since it's their money, kids really feel the pinch. Obviously, children need to be eased into learning the value of money and how to spend it. They have to be protected not only from misusing it, but also from becoming victims of consumerism. But both kids and parents seem to agree on this one—kids occasionally need to make their own mistakes.

• *Indulge your child*. All parents whom I meet, no matter what their financial situation, admit to "spoiling" children every once in a while—simply because it makes them feel good. I'm not talking about the times our kids barrage us with a campaign to buy them something, and we finally give in. I'm talking about those moments of hassle-free indulgence that are expressions of love. When it's time to indulge, however, parents say that if you want to sustain the pleasure of giving, it's best to make buying decisions quickly, without letting it turn into prolonged negotiations.

• *Say what you mean.* Eight-year-old Heidi told a parent group that she absolutely hates it if she asks for something and her parents say, "We'll see" or "Maybe later"—when they really mean "no." For their part, parents standing in the middle of Toys-R-Us often don't know whether they're going to give in. Or, they want to see if she's really serious and asks again. I think both are good reasons for saying, "We'll see."

However, Heidi has a point, too. Our kids usually know when a "we'll see" really means "no." So, if you're trying to avoid a battle by a "we'll see," your child will know it. In such situations the word from kids (despite the fuss they put up) is to say "no" right away. If you're really not sure and you want more time to consider the request, it seems better to be straightforward and say, "I don't know —I've got to think about it." When you're honest, your child's reaction may be intense, but it's usually short-lived.

• *Think about paying kids for extraordinary chores.* Experts are mixed on this, but parents are not. Just about *all* parents give something for unusual, distasteful jobs around the house. Some mothers and fathers are particularly organized on this one. They make up a job list of items that need to be done around the house and what will be paid for each one. Of course, kids bargain and negotiate about "unfair" wages, but in the end they settle on whatever is within the family's limits. I've heard this approach often enough that it's worth a try.

• *Don't leave money around the house.* It's too much of a temptation. At some point while growing up, just about all kids will take/borrow/steal money from their parents. However, just because it's normal, it should not be ignored. If money is missing, it may be a sign that your child feels deprived in some way, is perhaps trying to buy favors and friendship from other kids, or, more seriously, is using it for alcohol and drugs. Parents agree that it's wise to be the Protector *and* the Realist here—they keep close track of the money around the house.

• *Set an example*. Parents and kids always bring this up at parent/child workshops. Whatever example you set with children—disregard of money, caution, leaving it around, paying bills on time, and so on—will be noticed and absorbed by kids. No amount of talking teaches the value of money more than your actions do.

The Bedtime Routine

• *Start the bedtime ritual earlier*. On this one, parents don't easily follow good expert advice: Start the process of bedtime quite a bit earlier than when the kids actually say goodnight. If you're trying to get your child into bed by 8:30, don't start at 8:15. Parents report better results with around a half-hour preparation time. This gives your child time to calm down and let go of you and the day. Consistency is important in creating a calm space—no high-stimulation movies, Nintendo, or TV after a certain time; no physical fighting with siblings; telephone "off" period for kids (and yourself); out of clothes and brushing teeth around the same time each night, and so on. All this is easier said than done, but the crucial thing is to think of bedtime as a much *longer* process than your child's simply hopping into bed—a time you need to be the Parent Protector.

• *Come home earlier, if you can*. All your calming efforts will evaporate if one parent comes home in the middle of the bedtime ritual. It tends to rev the kids up all over again and unwittingly sabotages the other parent's efforts to get the child to bed. Of course, given the economic facts of many of our lives, choosing the time we come home isn't always possible. So, many parents report that if they get home in the middle of bedtime, they'll try to sneak in and stay out of the picture until after the kids are asleep.

• *Encourage a divorced spouse not to call at bedtime*. While it's understandable that an absent parent will want to say "goodnight," a before-bed phone call only stimulates children. The parent trying to get the kids off to sleep is furious, because a call may start things up all over again. Meanwhile, the out-of-house parent is upset because the kids have little to say. By all reports, it's really better if the conversation takes place earlier—say an hour or two before the bedtime procedure begins.

• *Let kids gravitate toward their own bedtime*. As they get older—fifth and sixth grades—most parents give up on enforcing a particular sleep time. While you should never force your child to go to sleep, you can ask kids to stay in the room after a certain hour, even if they don't go directly to sleep. Or, parents enforce *bed*time rules (not sleep rules), like staying in bed, no TV, lights out, and so on—and stop from getting caught up in the hopeless aim of forcing *sleep*. Of course, if the next day your child is zonked out, you know he's not getting enough rest. That still doesn't mean forcing him, but you ought to start bedtime rituals and quiet time earlier.

• *Read to your child*. This is one of the best ways to spend time with children of all ages before bedtime. Many parents only think of reading aloud to young children. However, as Jim Trelease, a leading expert on reading and children, points out, reading aloud is a wonderful way to connect, even for kids in the teen years. (Trelease has a series of audio and video cassettes on the subject that I highly recommend.) The only change for older kids is choosing more complicated books that can be read in installments.

• *Switch roles with your child*. Every once in a while, parents play a game and let children put *them* to sleep. Besides individual differences in sleep cycles, children report that their reluctance about going to sleep has something to do with feeling like they're being shunted aside—exiled away. Occasionally, being the "parent" allows children to get the anger out. Mothers and fathers tell me that the best games are those in which they—as "children"—put up the biggest fuss. They say this strategy gives them clues about how to handle their child. For example, one little girl tried to get her mother to go to sleep by sitting next to the bed and holding her hand. Mom realized that that's what her child needed to feel secure enough to let go for the night.

• *Make bedtime peaceful*. The idea is to help calm children down. Most of the rituals that parents use are the old soothing stand-bys: saying prayers together, singing lullabies, telling stories, just talking quietly. Bedtime is a great time to go over what happened in the day. It's parallel communication at its best—unpressured, not looking at each other, rambling, often meaningless—yet sometimes quite intimate.

Veteran parents also try to remember that bedtime is *not* a time to nag or haggle about things left over from the day or coming up tomorrow. We may be tempted, because it seems that we always have so little opportunity. However, since so many kids point to bedtime as the time they love to be together with us, protect those special moments for quiet talking, sharing—and being a Parent Chum.

After Hours: "Can I Come into Bed with You?"

• *Don't necessarily believe expert advice.* "Is it normal for my children to want to get into bed with me?" is one of the most frequently asked questions. Kids of all ages seem to occasionally need contact with us in the middle of the night. Yet just about all child-rearing experts (myself included) were taught that after a child is about three, to open the parents' bed is absolutely *wrong.*

On this matter, parents and theory seem to be at odds, with parents, I think, being more realistic. Over twenty years, I've learned that whether it's the middle of the night or early in the morning, school-age kids somehow wander in, call us in, and wake us up far more frequently than is discussed—and these are normal kids, including early adolescents.

When is it inappropriate for them to get into bed with you? The time to stop is when 1) *either* parent *or* child becomes uncomfortable; 2) if it becomes a regular occurrence; or 3) if your child can't fall asleep without being with you. The following suggestions gathered from parents and kids are designed to take some of the edge off this emotionally charged issue:

• *Don't believe everything you hear.* This is one area where parents are not particularly open with each other at first. We start fibbing about how soon our kids sleep through the night and rarely mention the little nighttime forays that happen around children's bad dreams, their difficulty falling asleep, or when they're lonely. It's too bad, because once the initial embarrassment has lifted, parents have very practical ideas about what to do.

• *Deal with the fear first.* Nighttime terrors are frightening for both parents and children. When a real panic hits your child, throw away theories. The first order of business is to calm him down. Whether this means hugging or holding or lying together for a while—even the rest of the night—be a Parent Protector. Soothe your child *first*; figure out a longer-term approach later.

• *Desensitize your child gradually.* When parents feel like their children are up too often or asking to be in their bed too much, they gradually separate, moving slowly in the direction of getting the child back into his own bed. Some parents will let their child "camp out" on the floor *next to* the bed for a while—in a sleeping bag or on a spare mattress. After a couple of nights, they'll bring the child back into his own room and sit with him—stroking or holding his hand until he falls asleep. Next, they may sit *by* the bed and stay until just before the child actually dozes off. The idea of this approach is to slowly move your child toward not needing contact in order to fall asleep—but to do it gradually, without suddenly increasing the separation.

• *Parents take turns.* Sharing this burden is obviously preferable and worth a major confrontation if your spouse doesn't see it that way. The resentment that builds when one parent is totally responsible for after-hours child care is enough to put a strain on any good relationship. Parents in workshops are pretty adamant in saying, "Don't turn yourself into a martyr on this one."

• ***Consult an expert***. If nothing can pry your child out of your bed or you're spending more time in his room than in your own, this may be a time to seek out professional help. But do so with the knowledge that you're not alone, and that few good parents have not had to deal with the same issue at different points as kids grow up.

• • •

One final note about the basic lesson I've learned from sitting with families, parent groups, and parent/child workshops: My idea of "normal" has expanded. My sense of children's resilience has strengthened. And I have come to believe that parents sharing information with each other helps make "impossible" situations easier to get through— not *disappear*—just a little less difficult to handle.

13

The Myth of Parenting Without Faith
Why Old–Fashioned Values Will Always Have a Place in Modern Parenting

Filling the Void

I was asked to do a consultation on a case that had to be every parent's worst nightmare. Fifteen-year-old Paula was out of control—drinking, not going to school, refusing all forms of help or rehabilitation. The situation came to a head when Paula accidently set herself—and her house—on fire. Miraculously, she had suffered only minor burns. Paula's mother was understandably frightened. She feared what her daughter might do next and also realized that her eight-year-old son was equally jeopardized by his sister's behavior.

Paula was finally admitted to a rehabilitation center, but her mother clearly needed help, too. The family counselor kept trying to get Mom to attend a parent support group meeting sponsored by the rehab and also to get her to start going to Al-Anon, a twelve-step program for families and friends of alcoholics. But the mother was completely immobilized by her own fear and by her deep abiding sense of guilt. Despite all the assurances of the counselor, Mother was sure that she had *caused* Paula's problem. She was tortured and paralyzed at the same time.

Listening to Mom describe the situation, it was obvious that nothing could penetrate her wall of shame and self-blame. I later took the counselor aside and asked if she was affiliated with a church or synagogue, or any type of religious or spiritual organization. If so, I suggested, Paula's mother might be better off talking to a spiritual counselor, rather than another therapist. It was clear that this woman needed reassurance and guidance from a higher authority.

I've seen this particular scene played out many times—albeit in not so dire situations—in which parents can make use of a resource that psychologists and child-development experts don't always consider. For many, many families, faith is a central part of their lives. But traditional mental health training doesn't teach us about the importance of religion and spirituality nor about incorporating these values into everyday life. While the principles of psychology and various techniques are important and often can provide us with valuable tools, in no way are they enough. They simply can't fill the void.

Where Psychology Stops and Faith Begins

It may sound heretical coming from a psychologist, but I believe that in our culture too much emphasis and reliance has been placed on psychology and not enough on the spiritual side of life. My profession has often been embroiled in political upheaval over theory and techniques, and issues of morality and faith have been overlooked. In a 1986 survey of 425 mental health professionals, Professor Allen Bergin of Brigham Young University found that only 5 percent of today's practicing therapists received any training in dealing with religious issues. For the most part, the psychiatric–mental health establishment has a very "deterministic" view of how people live—in other words, all actions are determined by inner motivation. We place almost no emphasis on a search for spiritual meaning as a reason why people do what they do and believe what they believe.

Of the psychoanalytic founders, only Carl Jung seriously regarded spirituality and mysticism as part of the process of psychic healing. For a while, during the '60s and early '70s, writers like Martin Buber and Paul Tillich tried to combine faith and psychology; and, in his theory of human needs, Abraham Maslow not only included morality and spirituality, but placed them above people's more basic needs for nurturing, love, and respect. But these ideas didn't seep into child-rearing approaches, nor did the work of Eric Fromm, who made a significant impact toward bringing social consciousness into American psychology. Only recently has Robert Coles explored the issue of faith, particularly as it relates to children, in his book *The Spiritual Life of Children*.

Fortunately, the climate may be changing. Among the 425 mental health professionals he surveyed, Dr. Bergin found that though many were against organized religion per se, and only about 40 percent attended church regularly, 68 percent —family therapists, clinical psychologists, social workers, and psychiatrists among them—said they "sought a spiritual understanding of the universe and one's place in it." Not surprisingly, at many professional meetings these days, among the list of workshop topics, a significant number combine concepts of therapy with ideas about spirituality.

Increasingly, clients—many of whom have turned to therapists as they once turned to spiritual counselors—are also bringing discussions of faith into the office, forcing psychologists to consider their spiritual selves as well as their emotional beings. This is happening, in large part, because of the tremendous popularity of the twelve-step programs, an estimated two hundred different self-help groups modeled on the principles of Alcoholics Anonymous. These programs—AA, Al-Anon, Overeaters Anonymous, Gamblers Anonymous, to name a few—emphasize belief in a "Higher Power," if not God, then at least a "force" greater than the individual.

The New Spirituality

Over the last two decades, I've also discerned a very subtle shift in families themselves—a return to spirituality and religion—which has also been well documented in both psychology journals and in the popular press. This movement has emerged as a particularly striking trend in the Baby Boom generation—more than seventy million people born between 1946 and 1964, now old enough to be parents themselves.

According to sociologist Wade Roof, at the University of California at Santa Barbara, roughly two-thirds of the Baby Boomers—always a rebellious group—dropped out of religion, but, now in their mid-thirties to mid-forties, more than a third of the drop-outs have returned. The biggest group of returnees are married with children. Interestingly, the least likely to return are couples who are married without kids.

At present, 57 percent—that is, forty-three million people—now attend churches or synagogues. The question is, why are people returning? *Newsweek* quoted one parent's answer in its cover story on this phenomenon: "I wanted my kids to have the knowledge of religion that I didn't have. In this crazy world, any kind of positive influence you can give your children is worth the time."

You can hear that mother's sense of trying to buttress the family and give some kind of essential moral fiber to her kids and, in doing so, counterbalance the effects of living in what is often a very crazy, sped-up world. "Going to church every

week on Sunday is really important for our little three-par-
ent family," said another dad, indicating that the assurance
of spending that time together was another key reason parents are returning to religion.

In fact, reforms within various churches and synagogues
also reflect the theme of this book. These institutions see that
the modern family needs connection and support in order to
exist in a world plagued by the loss of so much of what traditional families could once take for granted. The *Newsweek*
piece summed it up by describing religious centers nowadays
as "places of support, not salvation; help, rather than holi-
ness; a circle of spiritual equals, rather than one authoritative
church or guide."

Many churches and synagogues now provide much more
than services and sermons: twelve-step programs, lectures
by experts, singles mixers, and music events, as well as a
wide range of activities. For example, the Second Baptist
Church of Houston counts sixty-four softball teams, forty-
eight basketball teams, eighty-four volleyball, soccer, and
flag football teams, golf tournaments, and a family life center
complete with aerobics classes, a workout room, and rac-
quetball courts. They're providing something—perhaps the
missing community—that people seem so desperately to
want.

Why Families Need Faith

This growing spiritual movement speaks directly to the major issue I've raised throughout this book—that people need
to create a sense of connectedness, a sense of belonging
somewhere. We cannot live in isolation. It makes sense that
parents, in particular, are the people who are spearheading
the recent spiritual movement. Just as they are called on to
create an empathic envelope to hold their children, in the

absence of an old-fashioned, protective neighborhood and a nurturing extended family, parents also need to create a container to cradle and protect themselves. Religion and spirituality is one of the ways they're doing it.

In truth, psychological techniques take us just so far. Families need something more to curb the epidemic of "gimmes" that afflict our kids in this consumer-driven society and to combat the relentless invasion of the pop culture into our homes. If you have any doubts of the severity of this problem, here's a sobering thought: A study done by the National Coalition Against TV Violence found that more preteens could identify Jason and Freddy, the sexually sadistic monsters of *Friday the Thirteenth* and *A Nightmare on Elm Street* than George Washington, Abraham Lincoln, and Martin Luther King!

The more I see families in this supercharged world and ask myself what it takes to bring up children, the more I come to the conclusion that in successful families, parents give children a sense of values and ethics. It doesn't matter what your particular belief system is, or whether you embrace organized religion. The important element is a basic spiritual model for ethical behavior which, in some way, gets transmitted to your children. Whether it's a belief in God, a humanistic philosophy, a belief in the sanctity of life, or the importance of good deeds—successful families create a moral climate inside the empathic envelope that is a direct counterbalance against the materialistic world outside the container.

This moral climate gives children a sense both of belonging to a family and of having some ethical base. I don't mean "ethical" in the parochial sense—of being "righter" than other people, or that kids must always be goody-goodies. What I'm talking about is that your kids can rub up against the edge of the envelope, feel your beliefs, and know that you stand for something beyond the world of material goods. The question is, how do we do it? Below are several concrete avenues we can take to help fulfill a family's need for a spiritual life.

Maintaining Rituals

In the successful families I see, parents use rituals both as a way of spending quality time with children and to forge moral values. The parents may adapt the rituals in certain ways as the kids get older, but they nevertheless fight to maintain the observance.

Preserving rituals begins with making sure that they are not always about the "gimmes." Kids are usually in a great mood around the Christmas and Hanukkah holiday season, less because of the spiritual meaning and more often because they've simply gotten so many presents! Thus, the rituals we observe should also impart to children the underlying spiritual meaning of those significant days—the sense of rebirth and hope for peace at Christmas, the underlying gratitude of Thanksgiving, the universal story of freedom in Passover. Moreover, the various holiday rituals also provide a unique opportunity to mix the generations, to show respect and reverence—in our youth-obsessed culture—for the older members of our families.

In this view, rituals around the passing of life are often overlooked—and this is an enormous mistake. In my practice, I'm stunned by how many people have never visited their parents' graves or explained the family's roots to their children. That is undoubtedly one of the reasons so many people don't feel anchored in life—they are cut off from past generations.

Some of the most exciting experiences I have had are when I help parents and children construct a family tree. Children have a genuine interest in where they come from, and the kinds of information we take for granted about our histories end up meaning a lot to them. You needn't open up dark family secrets. But some kids don't even know what town, state, or country their grandparents come from, or what they did for a living; and they don't know about long-lost uncles or distant cousins and other bits of historical family trivia. Granted, given kids' short attention spans, you can't overload them with too much material at once, but every bit of information helps children make a little more sense of the world and feel more securely rooted about who they are. Actually going to the cemetery or lighting a memorial candle to commemorate the anniversary of a parent's or grandparent's death gives children a sense of reverence and connection—and momentarily transports them out of their often mindless self-involved pursuits.

Teaching Children to Be Charitable

You can also help your kids develop a sense of ethics through charity. From a very early age, kids in successful families seem to have a sense of generosity and doing good deeds toward others. Of course, the charity should be appropriate to your child's particular age. Little kids can gather up their old toys and outgrown clothing to give to less fortunate children. As they get a little older, they can help collect these items from other people and, with a parent's help, bring them to homeless shelters. Middle-age kids can participate in events such as the March of Dimes Walkathon or the AIDS walk. And when they get into their preteens and teens, they do volunteer work. In fact, many schools now include "community service" as a part of the regular curriculum.

I know lots of parents who insist that their kids select a charity to participate in, or even donate a small percentage of their allowance to a charity of their choice. One father I know goes to a church men's shelter with his son once a month. No matter what else is going on at home (in other words, whether they're getting along or not), the two of them spend the night in the shelter. Another group of kids started a program of handing out cards to homeless people in the winter, telling them how to find the nearest shelter or food kitchen.

The content of the charitable work needs to be decided by you and your child. As far as I can see, what you choose doesn't much matter. What's important is that *something* be done. Giving our children the message that situations and conditions outside family and self are worth some effort makes an enormous impression on modern kids bombarded by the self-centered messages of consumerism—"Gimme," "We're number one," "I gotta do what's best for me!"

Making Sacrifices

Parents who are concerned with instilling a sense of morality in their children ask them to make sacrifices. They do this without shame, without embarrassment, and without being heavy-handed about it, because they don't want their children to be motivated entirely by the need for instant gratification.

The constant "gimmes" are virtually an epidemic in our culture. Rena Karl, editor of *The Marketing to Kids Report*, notes that children between the ages of four and twelve spend about $9 billion per year on everything from Barbie dolls to Nike running shoes. During that same period, they also influence about $75 billion worth of adult spending.

Of course, many of us feel that we don't want to "deprive" our kids, so, for one reason or another, we are easily swept into that $75 billion statistic. Perhaps we didn't have the benefit of so many material things when we were growing up. Or, we might feel pressured because the other kids' parents buy so much for their kids. And at times, we're so busy—too busy to give our kids what they really need—so we try to buy off our own guilt.

In this context, the idea of instilling a sense of sacrifice in kids is perhaps more important than it has ever been. You can start by insisting that your kids do chores. I'm amazed by the numbers of parents who think of school as the only "chore" their children have; they don't press kids to do anything involving maintenance of the house, nor do they give older kids the responsibility of helping care for younger siblings.

On the contrary, in the close-knit and connected families I admire, even when their children are small, parents assign chores appropriate to each child's age. The envelope needs to increase gradually in this area, so children go through slowly expanding stages:

1) Simple chores around the house for no money or increase in allowance—setting and clearing the table, bed making, laundry.
2) Extraordinary chores that involve being paid—cleaning out the basement, washing or waxing the car.
3) First jobs outside the home, working for friends—baby sitting, mowing lawns, shoveling snow.
4) Summer jobs with adult friends of the family—being a "gofer" in an office, working in the mailroom.
5) Part-time after-school or summer work with real employers—local merchants (delivery, stock, or counter work) and summer camp jobs (being a counselor or waiter).

All of these—chores, rituals, and charity work—require a certain degree of sacrifice and delay of gratification. It's not fun to set the table or babysit for younger kids; it's not fun to sit in church for a few hours or to have a non-TV day or non-Nintendo day, as some parents do on religious holidays. It's not pleasant, but we're also not talking about any kind of heavy-handed sacrifice that takes all the pleasure out of childhood.

Clearly, instilling in children a consciousness of the greater good is an important part of family life. It's important for children to grasp that sometimes we have to give of ourselves in order to pay homage or attend to something more important and larger than one's own immediate need or even one's own family.

Reaching Outside the Envelope

Affiliating with organizations outside the envelope—such as religious institutions, neighborhood community centers, and groups like the Girl Scouts or Boy Scouts—lowers your family's isolation and increases the connectedness that you feel. This is an additional way we parents can strengthen and yet stretch the boundaries of the empathic envelope, providing another "ethical voice" for our kids—so that we're not the only ones trying to teach them values. This widening of the empathic envelope cuts down on our falling into the ("Let-me-teach-you-how-to-be") Moral Dance that so many kids (and adults) rebel against.

Since 40 percent of all Americans don't have any religious affiliations, organized religion may not be the answer for you. That doesn't mean, however, that you can't get connected to some other type of group outside the family that has as its purpose the transmission of ideals and ethics. For example, a neighborhood group that's fighting for the environment or a public service group that stands behind a particular cause gives children a sense of commitment that transcends the family.

When children are encouraged to think ethically, it is often surprising how seriously they take these matters. Recently, I was visiting a fifth-grade classroom in which the students were engaged in building a model of an "ideal" city. Besides amusement parks, malls, and plenty of fast-food joints, these ten-year-olds had designed ramps and special side rails for the disabled, parks with mobile police units so that old people could safely congregate, many hospitals, and a cemetery nearby so relatives could visit easily.

One can immediately see how crucial the school can be in the teaching of ethics. In Chapter 11, I discussed the importance of widening the empathic envelope to the schools. When it comes to helping instill values in our children, many schools already have begun to include ethics as part of the curriculum, but not enough has been done in this area. A sense of ethics, like anything else, needs to be practiced—when you don't use it, you lose it. We parents need to press our schools to teach kids about moral issues, how to explore and solve ethical problems, and to be aware of the normal differences between boys' and girls' sense of right and wrong (for gender differences in morality, I strongly recommend the work of Harvard psychologist Carol Gilligan).

To this end, some social critics are saying that in today's troubled world it is appropriate for schools to encourage discussions about morality. In *Moral Development and Socialization*, Myra Windmiller and her colleagues call for a curriculum that trains children to think about complex moral issues. The authors offer some concrete suggestions:

> *Role playing, simulated political decision-making activities, and honest, detailed inquiries into the lifestyles of others would be useful instructional activities. These activities would need to be carefully planned to produce an understanding of the relationship between social acts and social consequences.*

Visits to a jail, an Indian reservation, or a home for the aged could be outstanding opportunities for moral growth, depending on the level of moral discussion and debate that preceded and followed them.[1]

Ironically, in decades past, parents have been afraid to get schools involved in such matters, because they feared educators might proselytize; morality was best left to the family. However, as with many movements seeking to ensure personal freedom, the pendulum has swung a little too far. A vacuum was created, both at home and in the school, that ignores children's need to discuss their different and evolving views about morality.

In an age where kids are steeped in junk values and junk food, designer madness and sticker mania, material goods and Nintendo numbness, violence in the movies *and* in the streets, earlier sex and dangerous sex, pressure to grow up fast and pressure to succeed—can it possibly be bad for parents and teachers to join forces and ask kids to dig a little deeper, to think about ethics in living?

Sealing the Trapdoor

With any of these concrete ways of instilling a sense of morality and ethics in kids, the bottom line is that we as parents must stand for something. Even if children rebel against our ideals, having this kind of foundation allows them to feel held. They feel that we are providing a container for them in a pretty uncontained world.

I couldn't say it any better than Forrest Church, the na-

[1] From *Raising Responsible Children*, Children's Television Workshop, Random House (New York, 1991).

tionally known minister of All Souls Unitarian Church in New York City, who told me, "Parents have to provide a moral context for their children. Individualism is worth celebrating and cultivating, but people can find themselves liberated from every constraint and yet *all alone* in the end, with nothing to fall back on. While each individual is special, each of us is not ultimate. We may be brilliant and talented, but being brilliant and talented alone is not enough."

Reflecting about the kinds of problems families bring in today, he, like other therapists and pastoral counselors, sees many kids who can't leave home because they have no direction to go in, or, at the other end of the continuum, kids who leave home by becoming involved with marginal groups and sometimes cults. Parents always ask the same questions in these situations: "How could this happen? *We never imposed anything on our child.*"

That's exactly the problem, says Reverend Church. "So many children have no bearings. When parents let children choose everything for themselves, they aren't providing the context and the constraint for them—and the kids feel lost.

What Church calls "context and constraint," I call the empathic envelope—the container—but it's really the same idea. If we parents, under the guise of fairness or democracy, don't provide something for our children to rub up against, to "bounce" off of, they won't feel anything around them. They will drift further and further out of the envelope, until they find a group that *does* hold them.

What clergy in all faiths suggest is that part of being a parent is to address our children's deeper needs—the profound spiritual questions that all human beings have. Who made the world? What does it mean to be alive? What does it mean to die? If these issues are not raised in one's family, it's as if there's a "trapdoor" under us. And when we come up against something that's frustrating or traumatic in life, we just fall right through that trapdoor—we cannot cope.

Surely, this is a basic reason twelve-step programs have served such an important function in the last two decades. They are the containers, the providers of spiritual guidance for millions of Americans. But, as I've suggested, we need to provide something earlier—*before* there's a breakdown or a crisis.

In fact, I have seen mothers and fathers successfully provide this guidance: In families who have integrity and remain whole (regardless of whether they are intact or not), the trapdoor has a foundation underneath—it is safety-sealed. There is a palpable belief in something bigger than oneself. It's not just a sense of putting one's individual needs on hold for the common good of the family. In these families, it goes even farther. Children grow beyond a celebration of pure individualism—past "me" and even past "us"—toward a truly felt awareness of others' needs and, for many, a relationship with God or some form of a Higher Power.

Why Parents Can't Ignore God

Since the turn of the century, with few exceptions, professional psychology and child-rearing advice has ignored the place of God in children's thoughts. Just recently, however, the noted child psychiatrist Robert Coles opened up this question in his acclaimed work, *The Spiritual Life of Children*. In this study, Coles interviews children of all faiths—Christians, Jews, Muslims, Native Americans, and agnostics. As it turns out, the search for spiritual meaning seemed to be very much on these children's minds. Child after child described God in the most richly textured, flowing, and detailed terms. Cole summarizes the thoughts of nine-year-old Gil:

> *Like philosophers, he examined the beliefs of others and was becoming an analyst and critic of ideas.*

*Like them [philosophers], he was trying to pull to-
gether what he observed, read, and heard others es-
pouse—to make thereby his own system, his own set
of principles. As I listened to him and to other boys
and girls making similar intellectual and ethical
struggles, I often found myself remembering their
sometimes urgent determination to define God, to
locate Him in time and place, to know Him as precisely as possible.*[2]

The same nine-year-old, who a few minutes before was
pushing mercilessly for a new remote-control car, messing
up the bathroom with wet towels and dirty underwear, and
calling his younger brother a "stupid dork," during more reflective times may have questions about God, life, and death
on his mind. "How to Handle" child-rearing *techniques* are
not enough to connect with kids on these matters. We need
to have inner beliefs of our own—some idea of where we
stand.

Even if such questions are not on our minds, even if we
have no religious affiliation, even if we think that being the
best and most loving parent is enough to get us by, even if we
believe that good parenting techniques will carry the day,
thoughts about God and what life is all about are on the
minds of our kids. By addressing these issues in some way, we
create the possibilities for a connection with our children that
may serve them through a lifetime of good times and bad.

[2] *The Spiritual Life of Children*, Robert Coles (Boston: Houghton Mifflin,
1990), pages 146–47.

Conclusion

Why end a child-rearing book, chock full of techniques and concrete suggestions, on the question of faith? Because, as parents, we ultimately can't control everything. In the end, we must throw up our hands and have some faith in our children and in ourselves. And despite the worrisome decisions today's mothers and fathers are facing, there are a number of hopeful developments on the parenting scene.

For one thing, the rampant parent blame—directed at both mothers and fathers in different ways—that has characterized psychology for nearly fifty years will greatly lessen. The field is beginning to recognize the excess of criticism and the sabotage of parental authority that results. We've come a long way from antiquated post–World War II ideas, such as "schizophrenogenic mothers" and "absent fathers." This change is already creating a more collaborative attitude between parents and the hundreds of thousands of licensed therapists in the United States. Family counselors, family support groups, and enlightened individual therapists are fast replacing models of treatment that block parents' direct involvement with the therapeutic process.

Related to this is another revolutionary change. Over the past ten years, the idea that one traumatic incident can cause irreparable damage to children has been almost abandoned. Respected child researchers have demonstrated that what matters is the everyday fabric of life—the ongoing connection and emotional atmosphere in a family. For concerned parents, this eases the worry of making any *single* mistake that will forever harm or damage our children. Blowing those fabled one-time events—like "the big sex talk," or not responding immediately or appropriately to the one moment your child wants to "open up"—simply isn't the way problems arise. There are thousands of opportunities to re-pair, heal, and be together.

The other major change in psychology is the movement away from traditional Freudian theory to a "relational" model. Children are no longer viewed as driven simply by instincts, like sex and aggression, that constantly need to be reined in and socialized. Numerous studies by child re-searchers have demonstrated that from early years onward, children are capable of tremendous empathy; they have a desire to nurture and a real need to make others feel better. While you're in the midst of haggling over every little detail of life around the house, this may seem like the furthest thing from the truth. But a recognition of the tremendous potential for connection in all children helps fight the "us-against-them" attitude that's so easy to fall into. It also helps us envision that even though today is filled with acrimony, tomorrow may bring some peace and goodwill.

There is also a significant change in the way adolescence is being understood. Most parents dread the onset of adoles-cence, much as they would a serious illness. We expect that it has to be a nightmare—an explosion of negativity, rebellion, and loss. Yet major studies of adolescents and their families have shown something quite different. In fact, most adoles-cents and parents survive the teenage years with their rela-tionships intact and even improved. What's heartening is that, despite the influence of peer groups, adolescents them-selves report that the most important relationship in their lives is still their parents. Equally encouraging is the finding by Douglas Powell, the author of *Teenagers*, that fewer than one percent of all adolescents have severe maladjustments and paralyzing mental disorders. So, for the vast majority of families entering those turbulent years there is certainly rea-son for hope.

In terms of the wider social context—how modern parents end up raising kids without a safety net—there are also changes. Both schools and private industry are beginning to grasp the fact that a majority of parents need help—*lots of it.* Between the family therapy movement and the remarkable impact of twelve-step programs, there is a growing recognition that parents cannot live as isolated individuals, and that without support, children end up in trouble. To this end, the idea of an everyday safety net for families is slowly taking hold.

The split that I mentioned earlier between school and home—which sometimes leads to antagonism between parents and teachers—is beginning to narrow. Family involvement in the school is becoming more popular. Throughout the country, the pioneering work of Dr. James Comer has become a blueprint for school-based family interventions. As a result, a team approach that builds bridges between the world of school and home is gaining ground. In addition, the growing popularity of early-bird drop-off rooms, after-school programs, and the possibility of expanding the school year all offer some relief for working parents trying to provide reliable coverage for their kids. Indeed, over the next decade the whole concept of school will evolve toward school as a learning and nurturing center—for *both* children and parents.

In the private sector, corporations are clearly recognizing that parents need help with all aspects of normal parenting if they are to be productive workers. Many companies are developing "safety net" programs. Some firms, like Prudential, make day care available for the children of employees. American Express actually operates a school on site to allow working parents easier access to kids. Stride-Rite Shoes has tried to approach both ends of the generational continuum by having retired people do child-care work in its company day-care centers. And hundreds of companies now offer workplace seminars on parenting and family issues.

Positive changes have been slow in coming, especially in

providing adequate support for the nation's poor. As T. Berry Brazelton, among others, reminds us, for too long we have ignored the growing numbers of children in poverty. A majority of poor households are run by single mothers who desperately need reliable day care, health services, and housing relief. This tragedy is being kept on the social agenda, in part, by respected child-rearing experts, who are beginning to focus on the wider social context. Hopefully, their impact will be felt in future governmental policy decisions.

All of these efforts, like the many suggestions made in this book, require taking one small step that leads to the next. And small changes can make major differences to people. So, to be a better Parent Protector, Chum and Realist, I urge you to THINK SMALL! Do only what feels appropriate to your judgment and make first moves that are modest—that you can handle and that you trust. Remember: The empathic envelope is made up of *your* values and *your* beliefs. When you do decide to make a change in the way you handle your child, be prepared for your child's or family's reactions, and try not to be disappointed when they press you to keep the same old dance going.

Faith in ourselves and confidence in our instincts are what parents need more of in today's world. Children agree, and their unanimous conclusion can be summed up in one child's heartfelt remark: "I just wish they would have more confidence in themselves as parents."

Self-conscious deference to experts and to child-rearing myths gets in the way of connecting with kids. A little faith in ourselves immediately puts us on the same wavelength with our children, because they need the same basic thing we do: Children need us to be parents who are strong and sure. And if even one or two new options taken from these pages helps you toward that end, helps you connect and hold your child firmly and compassionately, it's a great beginning.

Index